Legal Self-Help

Prepare Your
Own Will

Legal Self Help

Prepare Your Own Will

by Daniel Sitarz
Attorney-at-Law

Nova Publishing Company
Small Business and Consumer Legal Books and Software
Carbondale, Illinois

ISBN 10: 1-892949-14-8   ISBN 13: 978-1-892949-14-1   Book only   price: $19.95
ISBN 10: 1-892949-15-6   ISBN 13: 978-1-892949-15-8   Book w/CD-Rom   price: $29.95
ISBN 10: 1-892949-16-4   ISBN 13: 978-1-892949-16-5   CD-Rom only   price: $12.95

Library of Congress Cataloging-in-Publication Data
        Sitarz, Dan, 1948-
        Prepare Your Own Will: The National Will Kit / Daniel Sitarz -- Rev. and expand. 6th Edition.
        248 pp. (Legal Self-Help Series) Includes index
        1. Wills--United States--Popular Works 2. Wills--United States--Forms 3. Wills--United States--States--Popular Works I. Sitarz, Dan, 1948- II. Title III. Series

        KF755.Z9S49 2006   346.7305'4--dc20   [347.30654]   LC94-1325 (pbk) CIP

        Formerly titled: Prepare Your Last Will and Testament-Without a Lawyer (1st and 2nd Editions)

Nova Publishing Company is dedicated to providing up-to-date and accurate legal information to the public. All Nova publications are periodically revised to contain the latest available legal information.

6th Edition, 1st Printing / June 2005   3rd Edition; 5th Printing / October, 1993
5th Edition, 4th Printing / April 2004   3rd Edition; 4th Printing / January, 1993
5th Edition; 3rd Printing / October, 2002   3rd Edition; 3rd Printing / June, 1992
5th Edition; 2nd Printing / April, 2001   3rd Edition; 2nd Printing / October, 1991
5th Edition; 1st Printing / June, 2000   3rd Edition; 1st Printing / September, 1991
4th Edition; 5th Printing / June, 1999   2nd Edition; 3rd Printing / December, 1990
4th Edition; 4th Printing / February, 1997   2nd Edition; 2nd Printing / April, 1990
4th Edition; 3rd Printing / May, 1996   2nd Edition; 1st Printing / June, 1989
4th Edition; 2nd Printing / January, 1996   1st Edition; 2nd Printing / December, 1988
4th Edition; 1st Printing / April, 1994   1st Edition; 1st Printing / April, 1988

This publication is designed to provide accurate and authoritative information in regard to the subject matter covered. It is sold with the understanding that the publisher and author are not engaged in rendering legal, accounting, or other professional services. If legal advice or other expert assistance is required, the services of a competent professional person should be sought.

—From a Declaration of Principles jointly adopted by a Committee of the American Bar Association and a Committee of Publishers

DISCLAIMER

Because of possible unanticipated changes in governing statutes and case law relating to the application of any information contained in this book, the author, publisher, and any and all persons or entities involved in any way in the preparation, publication, sale, or distribution of this book disclaim all responsibility for the legal effects or consequences of any document prepared or action taken in reliance upon information contained in this book. No representations, either express or implied, are made or given regarding the legal consequences of the use of any information contained in this book. Purchasers and persons intending to use this book for the preparation of any legal documents are advised to check specifically on the current applicable laws in any jurisdiction in which they intend the documents to be effective.

Nova Publishing Company   Distributed by:
Small Business and Consumer Legal Books and Software   National Book Network
1103 West College St.   4501 Forbes Blvd., Suite 200
Carbondale, IL 62901   Lanham, MD 20706
Editorial: (800) 748-1175   Orders: (800) 462-6420 or
free shipping on all internet orders   www.novapublishing.com

Nova Publishing Company Green Business Policies

Nova Publishing Company is committed to preserving ancient forests and natural resources. Our company's policy is to print all of our books on recycled paper, with no less than 30% post-consumer waste de-inked in a chlorine-free process. In addition, all Nova books are printed using soy-based inks. As a result, for the printing of this book, we have saved:

33.8 trees • 9,765 gallons of water • 5,719 kilowatt hours of electricity • 83.7 pounds of pollution

Nova Publishing Company is a member of Green Press Initiative, a nonprofit program dedicated to supporting publishers in their efforts to reduce their use of fiber obtained from endangered forests. For more information, go to www.greenpressinitiative.org. In addition, Nova uses all compact fluorescent lighting; recycles all office paper products, aluminum and plastic beverage containers, and printer cartridges; uses 100% post-consumer fiber, process-chlorine-free, acid-free paper for 95% of in-house paper use; and, when possible, uses electronic equipment that is EPA Energy Star-certified. Finally, all carbon emissions from office energy use are offset by the purchase of wind-energy credits that are used to subsidize the building of wind turbines on the Rosebud Sioux Reservation in South Dakota (see www.nativeenergy.com/coop).

Table of Contents

List of Forms

Property Questionnaire
Beneficiary Questionnaire
Executor Duties Checklist
Executor Information Checklist
Will for Married Person with Children
Will for Single Person with Children
Will for Married Person with No Children
Will for Single Person with No Children
Codicil
Living Will and Directive to Physicians
Revocation of Living Will
Health Care Power of Attorney
Revocation of Health Care Power of Attorney
Children's Identification Clause
Children's Trust Fund Clause
Cremation Arrangements Clause
Debt Forgiveness Clause
Disinheritance Clause
Entire Estate Gift Clause
Executor Clause
Funeral Arrangements Clause
Grandchildren Identification Clause
Guardianship Clause
Identification Clause
Marital Status Clauses
Organ Donation Clause
Residuary Clause
Signature and Witness Clause
Specific Gifts Clause
Survivorship Clause
Title Clause

NOTE: Forms-on-CD for this book are available for purchase at www.novapublishing.com
for $12.95. There is free shipping on all internet orders.

Introduction

This book is intended to serve as a guide and explanation of the process and legal procedure required in preparing a valid will without the aid of an attorney. With the proper information, the average person in today's world can easily understand and apply many areas of law. Preparing your own will is one of these areas. This book and others in Nova's Legal Self Help Series are intended to provide the necessary information to those members of the public who wish to use and understand the law for themselves.

This book is designed to assist its readers in understanding the general aspects of the law as it relates to wills and after-death distribution of property and to assist its readers in the preparation of their own wills. However, the range of personal finances, property, and desires is infinite and one book cannot hope to cover all potential situations or contingencies. In situations involving complex personal or business property holdings, complicated or substantial financial investments, or unusual or highly-complex post-death distribution plans, readers are advised to seek additional competent legal advice. In addition, estate and inheritance tax laws and regulations are among the most complex laws in existence. Consequently, although a general overview of these laws is provided and the vast majority of people are exempt from Federal estate taxes, readers with very large estates (generally, over $1 million) or complex financial resources are encouraged to seek the assistance of a tax professional if they wish to limit or lessen the tax consequences of the transfer of any property using a will.

Regardless of whether or not a lawyer is ultimately retained in certain situations, however, the legal information in this handbook will enable the reader to understand the framework of law in this country as it relates to wills. To try and make that task as easy as possible, technical legal jargon has been eliminated whenever possible and plain English used instead. When it is necessary to use a legal term which may be unfamiliar to most people, it will be shown in *italics* and defined when first used. There is a glossary of most legal terms used in wills at the end of this book for your reference in deciphering your current will if it was prepared by an attorney using outdated technical legal language. Lawyers often caution people that such antiquated language is most important and that, of course, only they, the lawyers, can properly prepare and interpret legal documents using such language. Naturally, plain and easily-understood English is not only perfectly proper for use in all legal documents, but in most cases, leads to far less confusion on the part of later readers.

Chapter 1 of this guide will attempt to explain the usefulness and in many cases the necessity of a valid will for insuring that your property and money are passed on to the loved ones whom you desire. It will also explain the legal effects of having a will and the potential consequences of not having a will. In Chapter 2, guidelines are provided for planning the distribution of your estate. Your *estate* consists of all of your assets, both real estate and personal property. Other estate planning tools, such as trusts and powers of attorneys, are discussed. In addition, the qualifications necessary for having a will are explained and a step-by-step outline of the procedures to follow to prepare your own will using this book are shown. Chapter 3 provides a discussion of what property may be disposed of using a will and provides a detailed Property Questionnaire which will allow you to assemble the necessary property and financial information that you will need in preparing your will. This chapter also includes information on the inheritance and estate tax consequences of the transfer of property at death. Chapter 4 provides information on who may be a *beneficiary* (one who benefits or receives a gift through a will). This chapter also explains the various forms your gifts may take and also provides a thorough Beneficiary Questionnaire for setting out your decisions on who should receive which of your assets. Chapter 5 includes an overview of information relating to the *probate* (court administration) of your estate, information, and a checklist for use by your executor, and a final information sheet for your executor's use in locating your assets and administering your estate.

Fill-in-the-blank will clauses are contained in Chapter 6 for use in preparing your own personally-tailored will. An explanation of each clause and instructions on how to properly fill them in are also provided. The included clauses should be sufficient for most people and most circumstances. In Chapter 7, four pre-assembled wills are provided for use. An actual sample will is shown and its various provisions are explained in Chapter 8. The mechanics of actually preparing your will are set forth in Chapter 9. The legal formalities and requirements for signing your will are contained in Chapter 10. These requirements, although not at all difficult, must be followed precisely to insure that your will is acceptable as a valid legal document. Methods and instructions for safeguarding your will are also contained in this chapter. Chapter 11 contains information regarding when it may be prudent and how to accomplish any changes or alterations to your will at a later date. Chapter 12 provides an explanation and form for your preparation of a living will—a document directing that, if you are diagnosed as terminally ill, you desire that no extraordinary life support measures be instituted to artificially prolong your life. In Chapter 13, instructions are provided for preparing a basic Health Care Power of Attorney form, a document that provides a person of your choosing with the legal authority to issue instructions to your physician in the event that you are unable to communicate.

The Appendix contains a detailed listing of the individual state legal requirements relating to wills and living wills for each of the 50 states and the District of Columbia. Finally, a Glossary of legal terms most often encountered in wills is included.

As with many routine legal tasks, preparation of a will is not as difficult as most people fear. With the proper information before them, most people will be able to prepare a legally-valid will which specifically addresses their individual needs in a matter of a few hours. Read through this manual carefully, follow the step-by-step instructions, and be assured that your wishes will be safely contained in your own will.

Note to computer users: If you are using this book in conjunction with the Forms-on-CD that is available, you need not retype the forms as noted in the instructions in this book. Instead, you need only to fill in the appropriate information on the necessary forms files on your Forms-on-CD and print out the form on your computer's printer. For additional information on completing the Forms-on-CD, please refer to the Readme.doc file that is included on your Forms-on-CD. If you wish to purchase a Forms-on-CD for this book, please see ordering information in the back of this book.

CHAPTER 1
Why Do You Need a Will?

Your entire life has been spent accumulating possessions and wealth for your own comfort and the comfort of your loved ones. It is the purpose of this book to assist you in the difficult task of showing these loved ones your continuing concern for their well-being after you are gone. Through the proper use of a will, you have a once-in-a-lifetime opportunity to personally decide what will happen to your accumulated wealth and possessions when you are gone. It is your entirely personal decision. Indeed, it is your legal privilege to make this decision. No one but you has the power to decide, prior to your death, how and to whom your property should be distributed on your demise. But to do so, you must take the initiative and overcome the understandable difficulty of these decisions. If you do not take the initiative and prepare your own will, on your death an impersonal court will decide who will receive your wealth.

To actually sit down and decide how your property and possessions should be divided amongst your loved ones in the event of your own death is not an easy task. However, it is you alone who knows your wishes. The property and possessions that you own may be land, your home, your personal household furnishings, keepsakes, heirlooms, money, stocks, bonds, or any other type of property. It may be worth thousands of dollars or it may be worth far less. If you are like most people, you want to insure that it is passed on to the persons whom you choose. But again, if you are like most people, you have put off making a will. Nearly 75 percent of Americans are without a valid will.

A *will* is a legal document that, when accepted by the probate court, is proof of an intent to transfer property to the person(s) or organization(s) named in the will upon the death of the maker of the will. The maker of the will is known as the *testator*. A will is effective for the transfer of property that is owned by the testator on the date of his or her death. A will can be changed, modified, or revoked at any time by the testator prior to death.

It is equally important to understand that for a will to be valid, it must generally be prepared, witnessed, and signed according to certain technical legal procedures. Although a will is perfectly valid if it is written in plain English and does not use technical legal language, it *must* be prepared, witnessed, and signed in the manner outlined in this book. This cannot be overemphasized. You cannot take any shortcuts when following the instructions as they relate to the procedures necessary for completing and signing your will. These procedures are not at all difficult and consist generally of carefully typing your will in the manner outlined later, signing it in the manner specified, and having three witnesses and a notary public also sign the document. (Although not a legal requirement, the notarization of your will can aid in its proof in court later, if necessary).

In the past, in many cases it was possible to simply write down your wishes, sign the paper, and be confident that your wishes would be followed upon your death. Unfortunately, this is, in most cases, no longer possible. *Holographic* (or handwritten and unwitnessed) wills are no longer accepted as valid in most jurisdictions. *Nuncupative* (or oral) wills are also not admissible in most probate courts to prove a person's intent to dispose of property on death. For this reason, a valid, typewritten will that is prepared, signed, and witnessed according to formal legal requirements is necessary. This type of will is now essentially the only secure method to ensure the desired disposition of your property, possessions, and money after your death and to assure that your loved ones are taken care of according to your final wishes.

In some cases (for example, those situations involving extremely complicated business or personal financial holdings or the desire to create a complex trust arrangement), it is clearly advisable to consult an attorney for the preparation of your will. However, in most circumstances and for most people, the terms of a will which can provide for the necessary protection are relatively routine and may safely be prepared without the added expense of consulting a lawyer.

Reasons for Having a Will

There are many reasons why it is desirable to have a will. Perhaps most important is to ensure that it is *you* who decides how your estate is distributed upon your death and to be assured that those loved ones whom you wish to share in your bounty actually receive your gifts.

To Avoid Having the State Decide Who Will Receive Your Property

What happens to your property and possessions if you do not have a valid will or if the will that you have is found to be invalid by the probate court because it was not signed or witnessed properly? Law books are filled with many unfortunate cases in which, because of the lack of a formal and valid will, the true desires and wishes of a person as to who should inherit their property have been frustrated. If there is no valid will to use for direction, a probate judge must give a person's property to either the spouse, children, or the closest blood relatives of the deceased person. This result is required even in situations where it is perfectly clear that the deceased person did not, under any circumstances, want those relatives to inherit the property. Although the probate judge is required to interpret a will to best satisfy what appears to be the written intentions of the person who signed it, the judge must first have before him a valid will.

To be valid, the document must, generally, have been signed and witnessed in a formal manner and prepared in such a way as to satisfy certain legal requirements. These requirements are strictly enforced to ensure that the document presented to a probate court is, indeed, the real and valid will of the deceased person whose property is to be divided.

Without such a valid will before him or her, a judge must rely on a legislative scheme that has been devised to provide for an orderly distribution of property in all cases where there is no valid will. This scheme is present as law, in one form or another, in all 50 states and is generally referred to as *intestate distribution*.

The terms of state intestate distribution plans are very complex in most states. In general, a person's spouse is first in line to receive the property when there is no will at death. Most states provide that the spouse and children will either share the entire estate or the surviving spouse will take it all in the hopes that the spouse will share it with the children. Generally, the spouse will receive one-half and the children will receive one-half. In many states, if a person dies without a valid will and is survived by a spouse but not by any children, the spouse will inherit the entire estate and the surviving parents, brothers, sisters, and any other blood relatives of the deceased will be entitled to nothing.

If there is no surviving spouse or children, the blood relatives of the deceased will receive the estate. If there are several persons within the next closest relationship level (for example, parents, brothers, or sisters) who are alive upon the death of the person, then these relatives will receive all of the person's property or share it equally with all the others alive who are in a similar relationship level. Once a level of blood relationship is found in which there is at least one living person, all persons who are more distantly related inherit nothing.

In addition, these legislative distribution plans are set up on the assumption that family members are the only parties that a deceased person would wish to have inherit his or her property. Thus, without a will, it is impossible to leave any gifts to close friends, in-laws, relatives more distant then your closest living relatives, charities, or organizations of any type. If there is no will and no blood relatives are alive, the state confiscates all of a person's property under a legal doctrine entitled *escheat*.

As an example of a typical legislative intestate distribution scheme, the following is a general representative outline of the various levels of distribution that are set up in many states. Keep in mind, however, that this example is only an illustration of the method that states may use and is not intended to be used in determining how your own estate would be divided. Check the listing in the Appendix for your own state's intestate distribution plan for specific details:

- If a spouse and children of the spouse are surviving: $50,000.00 and one-half of balance of the estate will go to the spouse and one-half of balance of the estate will go to the children in equal shares. If one of the children has *predeceased* (died before) the parent and leaves surviving children (grandchildren of the deceased parent), then the grandchildren will split the deceased child's share equally.

- If a spouse and children not born of the spouse are surviving: one-half of balance of the estate will go to the spouse and one-half of balance of the estate will go to the children equally. If one of the children has predeceased the parent and leaves surviving children (grandchildren of the deceased parent), then the grandchildren will split the deceased child's share equally.

- If a spouse is surviving, but no children or parents of the deceased are surviving: All of the estate will go to the spouse.

- If a spouse and one or both parents are surviving, but no children are surviving: $50,000.00 and one-half of balance of the estate will go to the spouse and one-half of balance of the estate will go to the parents equally. If only one parent is surviving, that parent gets the entire one-half share of the estate.

- If there are children of the deceased surviving, but no spouse is surviving: All of the estate goes to the children. If one of the children has predeceased the parent and leaves surviving children (grandchildren of the deceased parent), then the grandchildren will split the deceased child's share equally.

- If one or both parents are surviving, but no spouse or children are surviving: All of the estate will go to the parents equally, or the entire estate will go to the surviving parent.

- If there is no spouse surviving, or no children or parents are surviving: All of the estate will go to brothers and sisters in equal shares. If a brother or sister has predeceased the deceased sibling and has left surviving children, those children will split the deceased brother or sister's share equally.

- If there is no spouse, no children, no parents, and no brothers and sisters or their children surviving: one-half of the estate will go to the maternal grandparents and one-half will go to the paternal grandparents. If the grandparents on either side have predeceased the decedent, their children will split their share.

- If there is no spouse, no children, no parents, no brothers and sisters or their children, and no grandparents or their children surviving: The estate will pass to the surviving members of the closest level of blood relatives: aunts, uncles, nephews, nieces, great-grandparents, great uncles, great aunts, first cousins, great-great grandparents, second cousins, etc.

- If there are no surviving kin: The estate will be claimed by the state under the doctrine of *escheat*.

Many disastrous consequences can result from having your property distributed according to a standardized state plan. Take, for example, a situation in which a person and his or her spouse die from injuries sustained in a single accident, but one spouse survives a few hours longer. If there is no will, the result in this scenario is that the property of the first spouse to die passes to the spouse who survives. A few hours later, upon the death of the surviving spouse, the property automatically passes only to the relatives of the spouse who survived the longest. The relatives of the first spouse to die can inherit nothing at all. This, obviously would not normally be the desired consequence. Under the typical state scheme, luck and chance play a large role in deciding who is to inherit property.

Each state has a complicated and often different method for deciding which particular family members will take property when there is no will. However, the results are often far from the desires of how the person actually wished to have the property distributed. Obviously, under this type of state distribution of your property, the individual circumstances of your family are not taken into consideration at all. Neither are any intentions that you may have had, regardless of how strongly you may have expressed them during your lifetime. The only way to avoid having the state decide who is to receive your property is to have prepared a legally-valid will. If you die without a valid will, the state essentially writes one for you on its own terms.

To Appoint an Executor Who Will Administer Your Property

Another very important reason for having a will is the ability to appoint an executor of your own choice. An *executor* is your personal representative for seeing that your wishes, as contained in your will, are carried out after your death and that your taxes and debts are paid. An executor also collects and inventories all of your property and is in charge of seeing that it is distributed according to your wishes as expressed in your will.

Typically, a spouse, brother, sister, other close family member, or trusted friend is chosen to act as executor. However, your executor can be any responsible adult whom you would feel confident having this duty. The executor can even be a local bank or trust company. In that case, of course, there will be an often substantial fee charged to your estate for the completion of these generally routine duties by the corporate executor. If you choose an individual, he or she should be a resident of your home state. The wills in this book will enable you to appoint your executor and an alternate executor so that in the event your first choice cannot perform, it is still your personal choice as to who will administer your will.

If you do not have a will or do not choose an executor in your will, the probate court judge will appoint someone to administer the distribution of your property. Often it will be a local attorney, court official, or bank officer who may not know you or your beneficiaries at all. Your estate will then be distributed by a stranger who will charge your estate a hefty fee for the collection and distribution of your assets.

By appointing your own executor, you are also able to waive the posting of a bond by your executor and, most often, a family member executor will not accept a fee for serving. This will allow more of your assets to reach your beneficiaries, rather than paying for the expenses of administration of your estate.

To Appoint a Guardian for Your Minor Children

For those with minor children, the appointment of a guardian for any children is another very important item which may be accomplished through the use of a will. A *guardian "of the person,"* as this type of guardian is usually referred to, is responsible for the actual care, custody, and upbringing of a child. If your spouse is alive, he or she would generally be appointed as guardian in any event, with or without a will. However, there is the possibility that you both will be killed in a single accident or catastrophe. Also, if you are a single parent, you will need to designate a choice for guardian. Without a will for direction, a probate judge has little guidance in choosing the person whom you feel would be the best alternative for caring for your children. With a will, however, you can select a guardian for just such an eventuality.

To Appoint a Guardian or Trustee to Administer Property for a Minor Child

You can also have such a guardian administer the property or money that you leave to your children (a *guardian "of the property"*), or you may set up a trust and appoint a trustee to administer your children's inheritance until a time when you feel that they will be able to handle their own affairs. A *trust* consists of assets that are managed and distributed by a *trustee* to benefit one or more *beneficiaries.* Instructions to provide for these alternatives are simply stated in a will, but are more difficult to accomplish without one. If such instruction is not provided for in a will, and a minor child is left money or property by way of the state intestate succession laws, the courts will generally decide who should administer the property. Such court-supervised guardianship of the property or money will automatically end at the child's reaching the legal age of majority in the state (usually 18 years of age). At this age, without a will to direct otherwise, the child will receive full control over the property and/or money. This may not be the most prudent result, as many 18 year-olds are not capable of managing property or large sums of money. With a will, it is easy to arrange for the property or money to be held in trust and used to benefit the child until a later age, perhaps 21, 25, or even 30 years of age.

To Disinherit a Child or Other Relative

Disinheritance of a child or other relative whom you feel is not deserving of your property, or has no need of your property, is also something that can be accomplished only through the use of a will. Although the total disinheritance of a spouse is not possible under the laws of any state, any other relative may, generally, be cut off without a penny from your estate through the use of a will.

To Accomplish Other Results

Many other things may be accomplished only through the use of a will. You can forgive a debt that is owed to you in your will. You can revoke any other previous wills. You can provide instructions for organ donations, the disposition of your body, and burial, although it is generally wise to also leave these instructions with your executor on a separate sheet. Additionally, the proper use of a will normally lessens the expenses of probate, since the disposition of all of your property has been planned in advance, by you.

Even if you have used the various estate planning tools outlined in the next chapter to attempt to have your estate avoid probate, a will is still highly recommended. There may be assets that you have neglected, forgotten about, or will not be uncovered until your death. If you have used a trust, joint property agreements, and other estate planning tools, these unknown or forgotten assets may wind up passing to your heirs as intestate property and causing probate proceedings to be instituted. Through the use of a simple will, you can avoid this possibility.

Although it can be short and simple, a will is an important document that can accomplish many tasks. The proper use of a will can eliminate much confusion for those left behind. Since it provides a clear and legal record of your wishes, it can prevent feuding and squabbles among your family members. Perhaps most importantly, it can make your last wishes come true.

CHAPTER 2

Planning Your Will

A will is the cornerstone of any comprehensive arrangement to plan for the distribution of your property upon your death. In this chapter, the basic qualifications for having a will are outlined. Various other estate planning tools that may be useful in certain situations are also detailed. Finally, an overview of the steps you will take in preparing your own will is presented.

Qualifications for Having a Will

Are you legally qualified to have a will? In general, if you are over 18 years of age and of "sound mind," you will qualify. There are a few states that have different minimum ages, some allowing wills by children as young as 14, and a few requiring the testator to be over 18. For the specific age requirements, check your own state's age requirements in the Appendix.

It is also important to understand that laws of different states may apply to a single will. The laws of the state in which you have your principal residence will be used to decide the validity of the will as to any personal property and real estate located in that state. However, if any real estate outside of your home state is mentioned in the will, then the laws of the state in which that real estate is found will govern the disposition of that particular real estate. Thus, if you own property outside of the state where you live, when you check the Appendix for information concerning specific state laws, be certain to check both your own state's laws and those of the state in which your other property is located.

The requirement to have a "sound mind" refers to the ability to understand the following:

- You are signing a will
- You know who your beneficiaries are
- You understand the nature and extent of your assets

Having a "sound mind" refers only to the moment when you actually *execute* (or sign) the will. A person who is suffering from a mental illness or uses drugs or alcohol, or even a person who is senile may legally sign a will. This is acceptable as long as the will is signed and understood during a period when the person is lucid and has sufficient mental ability to understand the extent of his or her property, who is to receive that property, and that it is a will that is being signed.

The fact that a person has a physical incapacity makes no difference in his or her right to sign a will. Regardless of whether a person is blind, deaf, cannot speak, is very weak physically, or is illiterate; as long as he or she understands what he or she is doing and is signing, the "sound mind" requirement is met.

Related to the requirement that the testator have a "sound mind" at the time of signing the will is the requirement that the will be signed without any undue influence, fraud, or domination by others. In other words, the will must be freely signed and reflect the wishes of the person signing it for it to be legally valid. You do not ever have to sign a will that is not exactly what you desire. Do not let anyone coerce or force you to sign a will that does not accurately reflect your own personal wishes. If you are in a situation of this nature, it is highly recommended that you immediately seek the assistance of a competent lawyer.

Other Estate Planning Tools

The use of a will is, by far, the most popular and widespread legal tool for planning for the distribution of your estate. Your *estate* consists of everything that you own, whether it is real estate or personal property. As explained in Chapter 1, through the use of a will you can accomplish the planned distribution of your estate property and many other goals. However, there may be other objectives in your planning that cannot be accomplished solely through the use of a will. Other estate planning documents may be necessary to achieve all of your goals. There are three basic reasons that other estate planning tools may be useful in certain situations: avoidance of probate, reducing taxes, and healthcare considerations.

Avoiding Probate

First, many people desire to avoid having their property be subject to probate proceedings. Although in some situations, the probate process has been abused, there are valid reasons for allowing your property to be handled through probate. It allows for an examination of the validity of your will. It provides a process by which the improper distribution of your assets is guarded against. Having your property distributed through a probate process also puts a definite limit on the length of time that a creditor can file a claim against your estate.

The drawbacks of probate are that it can delay the distribution of your property while the probate process continues. The probate of an estate can take, generally, from four to 18 months, and sometimes much longer. Additionally, probate costs can be substantial.

Court costs, appraisal fees, lawyer's fees, and accounting bills can all cut deeply into the amount of property and funds that will eventually be distributed to your beneficiaries. However, for small estates (generally, under $100,000.00) most states have simplified probate procedures that can be handled without lawyers and can substantially reduce these costs. The probate process itself is explained in more detail in Chapter 5.

There are various methods for avoiding having property pass to others through the probate process. The four most important are as follows:

Joint Tenancy with Right of Survivorship

Upon one owner's death, any property held as *joint tenants with right of survivorship* passes automatically to the surviving owner without probate or court intervention of any kind. Under the laws of most states, the description of ownership on the deed or other title document must specifically state that the property is being held by the people as "joint tenants with right of survivorship." If not, the property is usually presumed to be held as *tenants-in-common*, which means that each owner owns a certain specific share of the property that they may leave by way of a will or other estate-planning device. Some states have another class of property known as *tenancy-by-the-entirety* which is, essentially, a joint tenancy specifically for spouses. More information on property ownership is provided in Chapter 3.

Living or Revocable Trusts

An increasingly popular estate planning tool, living or revocable trusts can be effectively used to avoid probate. This type of document generally provides that all or most of a person's property be transferred to trust ownership. The owner of the property generally retains full control and management of the trust as *trustee*. In the trust document, beneficiaries are chosen, much the same as in a will. The terms of the trust can actually parallel the terms of a will. The difference is that, upon the death of the creator (*trustor*) of the trust, all of the property that has been transferred to trust ownership passes immediately and automatically to the beneficiaries without any court intervention or supervision.

The owner of the property retains full control over the property until death and the creator of the trust can terminate this type of trust at any time prior to death. However, there are increased paperwork requirements in setting up and operating a trust. The trust itself must be prepared and all of your property ownership (stocks, bonds, bank accounts, real estate deeds, car titles, etc.) actually transferred to the trust. For information regarding the use and preparation of living trusts, please refer to the Nova Publishing Company book *Living Trusts Simplified*, by Dan Sitarz.

Life Insurance

Another common method of passing funds to a person upon death while avoiding probate is through the use of life insurance. By making the premium payments throughout your life, you are accumulating assets for distribution on your death. The life insurance benefits are paid directly to your chosen beneficiaries without probate court intervention. However, life insurance benefits are still considered part of your taxable estate. For more information on insurance, you are advised to consult an insurance professional.

Payable-on-Death Bank Accounts
This type of property ownership consists of a bank account held in trust for a named beneficiary. It may also be referred to as a *Totten* trust or a *Bank* trust account. It is a very simple method for providing that the assets in a bank account are paid immediately to a beneficiary upon your death without the beneficiary having any control over the account during your life, as is the case with a joint bank account. This trust-type bank account allows for the property to be transferred without probate and is very simple to set up. Any type of bank account, whether checking, savings, money market, or even certificates of deposit, may be designated as a payable-on-death account by filling out simple forms at your financial institution.

Reducing Taxes

The second major use for estate planning tools is to attempt to lessen or completely avoid the payment of any taxes on the transfer of property upon death. Upon death, the transfer of property may be subject to federal estate taxes, state estate taxes, and state inheritance taxes. However, much of the taxation of estates (most importantly, federal taxation) does not become a factor unless your estate is valued at over $1 million. Thus, for most people, the need to pursue complicated tax avoidance estate plans is unnecessary. For reference, however, details regarding taxation of estates are provided in Chapter 3. In addition, the Appendix contains information regarding each individual state's laws on gift, inheritance, and estate taxation. The complexity of tax laws and of the methods to avoid taxes through estate planning is beyond the scope of this book. If your estate is over $1 million, it may be wise to seek the assistance of a tax professional.

Healthcare Concerns

The third main purpose of estate planning is a relatively new concern. Recent advances in medical technology have allowed modern medicine, in many cases, to significantly extend the lives of many people. In addition, many people have become aware of the possibility of their lives being continued indefinitely through technological life support procedures. Two legal documents have been developed to deal with these concerns.

Living Will
A living will is a document that can be used to state your desire that extraordinary life support means not be used to artificially prolong your life in the event that you are stricken with a terminal disease or injury. Its use has been recognized in all states in recent years. The Appendix provides information regarding the recognition of liv-

ing wills in each state. For detailed information on preparing a living will, please see Chapter 12.

Health Care Power of Attorney

This relatively new legal document has been developed to allow a person to appoint another person to make health care decisions on one's behalf, in the event that he or she becomes incapacitated or incompetent. Generally, this document will only take effect upon a person becoming unable to manage his or her own affairs. This document may be carefully tailored to fit your needs and concerns and can be used in conjunction with a living will. It can be a valuable tool for dealing with difficult healthcare situations. For instructions and forms for preparing health care power of attorney, please refer to Chapter 13.

If you believe that your situation warrants additional estate planning, please consult an experienced financial planner, tax professional, or attorney. You may, of course, also wish to research and prepare any of the above documents yourself without the aid of an attorney or accountant. There are many estate-planning books available. Check your public or local law library.

Steps in Preparing Your Will

There are several steps that must be followed to properly prepare your will using this book. None of them are very difficult or overly complicated. However, they must be done carefully in order to effectively accomplish what you set out to do: be assured that your property is left to those loved ones whom you choose and that your loved ones are properly cared for after your death.

What follows is a brief outline of the necessary steps which must be followed to prepare a valid will with this book. You will probably refer back to this chapter several times in the course of preparing your own will to be certain that you are on the right track and have not left out any steps.

The following steps are numbered 1 through 10 for your ease in following them:

1. Read through this entire book. You are advised to read carefully through this entire book before you actually begin preparing your own will. By doing this you will gain an overview of the entire process and will have a much better idea of where you are heading before you actually begin the preparation of your will.

2. Fill in the Property Questionnaire contained in Chapter 3 and the Beneficiary Questionnaire in Chapter 4. These questionnaires are designed to compile all of the necessary personal information for your will preparation. Information regarding

your personal and business assets, percentages of ownership of these assets, marital relationship, names and addresses of relatives, and many other items will be gathered together in these questionnaires for your use. As you fill in these questionnaires, you will be making the actual decisions regarding distribution of your assets. In addition, in Chapter 5, you will fill out an Executor Information Checklist which will provide important data for use by your chosen executor.

3. Review your own state's legal requirements as contained in the Appendix. The Appendix contains a concise listing of the laws relating to wills in every state. Although the standard will clauses used in this book will alleviate most of the concerns raised by these legal requirements, there may be certain of your own state's requirements that will affect how you decide to prepare your own will.

4. This book contains two methods by which to prepare a will: (1) by choosing individual will clauses from chapter 6 and assembling you own custom-tailored will or (2) by filling in the blanks of pre-assembled wills contained in Chapter 7. Read through all of the will clauses and preassembled wills and decide which clauses or complete will most clearly fits your needs. This is one of the most important steps in the process and one which must be done very carefully. The various clauses and wills are, for the most part, self-explanatory and you should be able to easily decide which one applies to your situation. However, you are advised to read through each and every clause before you decide on the final choices for your own will.

5. Make a photocopy of all of those portions of Chapter 6 or Chapter 7 which will be included in your own will, including any mandatory clauses noted. These photocopies will be your will preparation worksheets. After you have done this, fill in the appropriate information on the photocopies using your Property and Beneficiary Questionnaires. When your worksheets have been completely filled in, number each included will clause consecutively beginning with #1.

6. Type a clean original of your will as explained in Chapter 9. With your filled-in photocopy worksheet before you, this should be a relatively easy task.

7. Proofread your entire will very carefully to be certain that it is exactly what you want. If there are any typographical errors or if you want to change some provision, no matter how slight, you *must* retype that page of your will. *Do not* make any corrections on the will itself.

8. Assemble your witnesses and notary public and formally sign your will. This is known as the *execution* of your will and must be done very carefully following the details contained in Chapter 10.

9. Make a photocopy of your original signed will and give it to the executor whom you have named in your will. You may also wish to give the executor a copy of the Executor Information List from Chapter 5. Store the original of your will in a safe place as outlined in Chapter 10.

10. Review your will periodically and prepare a new will or *codicil* (a formally-executed change to a will) if necessary, as detailed in Chapter 11.

That's all there is to it. Actually, that may sound like a lot of work and bother, but realize that you would have to follow many of the same steps even if a lawyer were to prepare your will. However, in that case, you would give him or her all of the information and he or she would simply prepare a will in much the same fashion that you will use in this book. The difference, of course, is that you must pay an often exorbitant price to have this done by a lawyer. Additionally, by preparing your will yourself and doing so at your own pace, you are certain to take more care and give more thought to the entire process than if you have someone else prepare it for you.

The following is a quick checklist of the 10 steps noted above:

- ☐ Read this entire book first
- ☐ Fill in the Property and Beneficiary Questionnaires
- ☐ Review your state's legal requirements
- ☐ Choose the appropriate pre-assembled will
- ☐ Make a photocopy rough-draft version of your will and fill it in
- ☐ Type an original of your will
- ☐ Carefully proofread your will
- ☐ Assemble the witnesses and notary public and sign your will
- ☐ Give a copy of your will to your executor and store the original in a safe place
- ☐ Review your will periodically and make any changes in a formal manner

CHAPTER 3

Property Questionnaire

The methods and manners of disposition of your property using a will are discussed in this chapter. Your assets consist of different types of property. They may be personal property, real estate, "community" property, stocks, bonds, cash, heirlooms, or keepsakes. Regardless of the type of property you own, there are certain general rules that must be kept in mind as you prepare your will.

In addition, in this chapter you will prepare an inventory of all of your assets and liabilities. This will allow you to have before you a complete listing of all of the property that you own as you begin to consider which beneficiaries should receive which property.

What Property May You Dispose of with Your Will?

In general, you may dispose of any property that you own at the time of your death. This simple fact, however, contains certain factors which require further explanation. There are forms of property which you may "own," but which may not be transferred by way of a will. In addition, you may own only a percentage or share of certain other property. In such situations, only that share or percentage which you actually own may be left by your will. Finally, there are types of property ownership which are automatically transferred to another party at your death, regardless of the presence of a will.

In the first category of property which *cannot* be transferred by will are properties that have a designated beneficiary outside of the provisions of your will. These types of properties include:

- Life insurance policies
- Retirement plans
- IRAs and KEOGHs
- Pension plans
- Trust bank accounts
- Living trust assets
- Payable-on-death bank accounts
- U.S. Savings Bonds, with payable-on-death beneficiaries

In general, if there is already a valid determination of who will receive the property upon your death (as there is, for example, in the choice of a life insurance beneficiary), you may not alter this choice of beneficiary through the use of your will. If you wish to alter your choice of beneficiary in any of these cases, alter the choice directly with the holder of the particular property (for instance, the life insurance company or bank).

The next category of property that may have certain restrictions regarding its transfer by will is property in which you may only own a certain share or percentage. Examples of this might be a partnership interest in a company or jointly-held property. Using a will, you may only leave that percentage or fraction of the ownership of the property that is actually yours. For business interests, it is generally advisable to pass the interest that you own to a beneficiary intact. The forced sale of the share of a business for estate distribution purposes often results in a lower value being placed on the share. Of course, certain partnership and other business ownership agreements require the sale of a partner's or owner's interest upon death. These buy-out provisions will be contained in any ownership or partnership documents that you may have. Review such documentation carefully to determine both the exact share of your ownership and any post-death arrangements.

The ownership rights and shares of property owned jointly must be considered. This is discussed below under *common-law* property states, although most joint ownership laws also apply in *community property* states as well. Another example of property in which only a certain share is actually able to be transferred by will is a spouse's share of marital property in states that follow community property designation of certain jointly-owned property. The following is a discussion of the basic property law rules in both community property and common-law property states. The rules regarding community property only apply to married persons in those states that follow this type of property designation. If you are single, please disregard this section and use the common-law property states rules below to determine your ownership rights.

Community Property States

Several states, mostly in the Western United States, follow the *community property* type of marital property system. Please refer to the Appendix to see if your state has this type of system. The system itself is derived from ancient Spanish law. It is a relatively simple concept. All property owned by either spouse during a marriage is divided into two types: separate property and community property.

Separate property consists of all property considered owned entirely by one spouse. Separate property, essentially, is all property owned by the spouse prior to the marriage and kept separate during the marriage; and all property received individually by the spouse by gift or inheritance during the marriage. All other property is considered *community property*. In other words, all property acquired during the marriage by either spouse, unless by gift or inheritance, is community property. Community property is considered to be owned in equal shares by each spouse, regardless of whose efforts actually went into acquiring the property. (Major exceptions to this general rule are Social Security and Railroad retirement benefits, which are considered to be separate property by Federal law).

Specifically, separate property generally consists of:

- All property owned by a spouse prior to a marriage (if kept separate)
- All property a spouse receives by gift or inheritance during a marriage (if kept separate)
- All income derived from separate property (if kept separate). In Texas and Idaho, income from separate property is considered community property

Community property generally consists of:

- All property acquired by either spouse during the course of a marriage, unless it is separate property (thus it is community property unless it is acquired by gift or inheritance or is income from separate property)
- All pensions and retirement benefits earned during a marriage (except Social Security and Railroad retirement benefits)
- All employment income of either spouse acquired during the marriage
- All separate property which is mixed or co-mingled with community property during the marriage

Thus, if you are a married resident of a community property state, the property that you may dispose of by will consists of all of your separate property and one-half of your jointly-owned marital community property. The other half of the community property automatically becomes your spouse's sole property upon your death.

Residents of community property states may also own property jointly as tenant-in-common or as joint tenants. These forms of property ownership are discussed below.

Common-Law Property States

Residents of all other states are governed by a *common-law property* system, which was derived from English law. Under this system, there is no rule that gives fifty percent ownership of the property acquired during marriage to each spouse.

In common-law states, the property that you may dispose of with your will consists of all the property held by title in your name, any property that you have earned or purchased with your own money, and any property that you may have been given as a gift or have inherited, either before or during your marriage.

If your name alone is on a title document in these states (for instance, a deed or automobile title), then you own the property solely. If your name and your spouse's name is on the document, you both generally own the property as *tenants-in-common*, unless the title specifically states that your ownership is to be as *joint tenants*, or if your state allows, as a *tenancy-by-the-entireties* (a form of joint tenancy between married persons). There is an important difference between these types of joint ownership: namely, survivorship.

With property owned as tenants-in-common, the percentage or fraction that each tenant-in-common owns is property that may be disposed of under a will. If the property is held as joint tenants or as tenants-by-the entireties, the survivor automatically receives the deceased party's share. Thus, in your will, you may not dispose of any property held in joint tenancy or tenancy-by-the entirety since it already has an automatic legal disposition upon your death. For example: if two persons own a parcel of real estate as equal tenants-in-common, each person may leave a one-half interest in the property to the beneficiary of their choice by their will. By contrast, if the property is owned as joint tenants with right of survivorship, the one-half interest that a person owns will automatically become the surviving owner's property upon death.

In common-law states, you may dispose of any property that has your name on the title in whatever share that the title gives you, unless the title is held specifically as joint tenants or tenants-by-the entireties. You may also dispose of any property that you earned or purchased with your own money, and any property that you have been given as a gift or have inherited. If you are married, however, there is a further restriction on your right to dispose of property by will.

All common-law states protect spouses from total disinheritance by providing a statutory scheme under which a spouse may choose to take a minimum share of the deceased spouse's estate, regardless of what the will states. This effectively prevents any spouse from being entirely disinherited through the use of the common law rules of property: name on the title equals ownership of property.

In most states, the spouse has a right to a one-third share of the deceased spouse's estate, regardless of what the deceased spouse's will states. However, all states are slightly different in how they apply this type of law and some allow a spouse to take up to one-half of the estate. Please check your particular state's laws on this aspect in the Appendix. The effect of these statutory provisions is to make it impossible to disinherit a spouse entirely. If you choose to leave nothing to your spouse under your will or by other means (such as life insurance or joint tenancies), he or she may take it anyway, generally from any property that you tried to leave to others. The details of each state's spousal statutory share are outlined in the Appendix.

Some states also allow a certain *family allowance* or *homestead allowance* to the spouse or children to insure that they are not abruptly cut off from their support by any terms of a will. These allowances are generally of short duration for relatively minor amounts of money and differ greatly from state to state.

Thus, the property that you may dispose of by will is as follows:

- **In all states:** Your share of any of the following property, except property for which a beneficiary has been chosen by the terms of the ownership of the property itself (for example: life insurance or living trusts).

- **In community property states:** All separate property (property that was brought into a marriage, or obtained by gift or inheritance during the marriage) and one-half of the community property (all other property acquired during the marriage by either spouse). If you are single, follow the common-law state rules below.

- **In common-law states:** Your share of all property where your name is on the title document, unless the property is held as joint tenants or tenants-by-the-entireties and your share of all other property that you own, earned, or purchased in your own name. Please check the Appendix for information relating to the spouse's minimum statutory share of an estate in your state.

Federal Estate Taxes and State Inheritance and Estate Taxes

Various taxes may apply to property transfers upon death. In general, there are two main type of taxes: estate taxes and inheritance taxes. An *estate tax* is a government tax on the privilege of being allowed to transfer property to others upon your death. This tax is assessed against the estate itself and is paid out of the estate before the assets are distributed to the beneficiaries. An *inheritance tax* is a tax on property received and is paid by the person who has actually inherited the property. The federal government assesses an estate tax. Various states impose additional estate taxes and inheritance taxes. Additionally, the federal government and a few states apply a gift tax on property transfers during a person's life. Nevada is the only state that does not impose any estate, inheritance, or gift taxes. Basic information regarding each state's tax situation is provided in the Appendix.

With regard to estate taxes, recent changes in the federal Income Tax Code, as it relates to estate taxes, have released an estimated 95 percent of the American public from any federal estate tax liability on their death. The current Internal Revenue Service rules provide for the equivalent of an exemption from all estate tax for the first $1.5 million of a person's assets. If you are married, both you and your spouse are entitled to separate $1.5 million exemptions. The current $1.5 million figure is scheduled to increase in stages over the next few years: $2 million in 2006; and $3.5 million in 2009. In 2010, the estate tax is scheduled to be repealed altogether. In addition, all of the value of a person's estate that is left to a spouse is exempt from any federal estate tax. Even if your particular assets are over this minimum exemption, there are still methods to lessen or eliminate your tax liability. These methods, however, are beyond the scope of this book. Therefore, if your assets (or your joint assets, if married) total over approximately $1.5 million, it is recommended that you consult a tax professional prior to preparing your will.

State estate taxes are, as a rule, also very minimal or even non-existent until the value of your estate is over $1.5 million. Most state's estate tax laws are tied directly to the federal estate tax regulations and thus allow for the same level of exemption equivalent from state estate taxes on death if the estate property totals under $1.5 million. A few states may impose an additional level of estate tax. The details of each state's estate tax situation are outlined in the Appendix.

Less than half of the states impose an inheritance tax on the receipt of property resulting from someone's death. There are generally relatively high exemptions allowed and the inheritance taxes are usually scaled such that spouses, children, and close relatives pay much lower rates than more distant relatives or unrelated persons.

From a planning standpoint, the changes in the federal estate tax have virtually eliminated any consideration of tax consequences from the preparation of a will for most Americans. Other factors, however, will affect the planning of your will.

Property Questionnaire Instructions

Before you begin to actually prepare your own will, you must understand what your assets are, who your beneficiaries are to be, and what your personal desires are as to how those assets should be distributed among your beneficiaries.

Since you may only give away property that you actually own, before you prepare your will it is helpful to gather all of the information regarding your personal financial situation together in one place. The following Property Questionnaire will assist you in that task.

Determining who your dependents are, what their financial circumstances are, what gifts you wish to leave them, and whether you wish to make other persons or organizations beneficiaries under your will are questions that will be answered as you complete the Beneficiary Questionnaire in Chapter 4.

Together, these two questionnaires should provide you with all of the necessary information to make the actual preparation of your will a relatively easy task. In addition, the actual process of filling out these questions will gently force you to think about and make the important decisions that must be made in the planning and preparation of your will.

When you have finished completing this Questionnaire, have it in front of you as you select and fill in your will in Chapters 6 and 7.

It may also be prudent to leave a photocopy of these questionnaires with the original of your will and provide a copy to your executor, in order to provide a readily-accessible inventory of your assets and list of your beneficiaries for use by your executor in managing your estate.

Property Questionnaire

What Are Your Assets?

Cash and Bank Accounts

Individual accounts can be left by will; joint tenancy and payable-on-death accounts cannot.

Checking Account .... $ _____
Bank _____
Account number _____
Name(s) on account _____

Checking Account .... $ _____
Bank _____
Account number _____
Name(s) on account _____

Savings Account .... $ _____
Bank _____
Account number _____
Name(s) on account _____

Savings Account .... $ _____
Bank _____
Account number _____
Name(s) on account _____

Certificate of Deposit .... $ _____
Held by _____
Expiration date _____
Name(s) on account _____

Other Account .... $ _____
Bank _____
Account number _____
Name(s) on account _____

Total Cash and Bank Accounts .... (A) $ _____

Insurance and Annuity Contracts

Life insurance benefits cannot be left by will.

Ordinary Life .... $ _____
Company _____
Policy number _____
Beneficiary _____
Address _____

Ordinary Life .... $ _____
Company _____
Policy number _____
Beneficiary _____
Address _____

Endowment .... $ _____
Company _____
Policy number _____
Beneficiary _____
Address _____

Term Life .... $ _____
Company _____
Policy number _____
Beneficiary _____
Address _____

Term Life .... $ _____
Company _____
Policy number _____
Beneficiary _____
Address _____

Annuity Contract .... $ _____
Company _____
Policy number _____
Beneficiary _____
Address _____

Total Insurance and Annuity Contracts .... (B) $ _____

Accounts and Notes Receivable

Debts payable to you may be left by will.

Accounts Receivable .... $ _____
Due from _____
Address _____

Accounts Receivable .... $ _____
Due from _____
Address _____

Accounts Receivable .... $ _____
Due from _____
Address _____

Notes Receivable .... $ _____
Due from _____
Address _____

Notes Receivable .... $ _____
Due from _____
Address _____

Notes Receivable .... $ _____
Due from _____
Address _____

Other Debts .... $ _____
Due from _____
Address _____

Other Debts .... $ _____
Due from _____
Address _____

Other Debts .... $ _____
Due from _____
Address _____

Other Debts .... $ _____
Due from _____
Address _____

Total Accounts and Notes Receivable .... (C) $ _____

Stocks and Mutual Funds

Ownership of individually-held stock and mutual funds may be left by will.

Company _____
CUSIP or certificate number _____
Number and type of shares _____
Value .... $ _____

Company _____
CUSIP or certificate number _____
Number and type of shares _____
Value .... $ _____

Company _____
CUSIP or certificate number _____
Number and type of shares _____
Value .... $ _____

Company _____
CUSIP or certificate number _____
Number and type of shares _____
Value .... $ _____

Company _____
CUSIP or certificate number _____
Number and type of shares _____
Value .... $ _____

Company _____
CUSIP or certificate number _____
Number and type of shares _____
Value .... $ _____

Company _____
CUSIP or certificate number _____
Number and type of shares _____
Value .... $ _____

Company _____
CUSIP or certificate number _____
Number and type of shares _____
Value .... $ _____

Total Stocks and Mutual Funds .... (D) $ _____

Bonds and Mutual Bond Funds

Ownership of individually-held bonds and mutual bond funds may be left by will.

Company _____
CUSIP or certificate number _____
Number and type of shares _____
Value .... $ _____

Company _____
CUSIP or certificate number _____
Number and type of shares _____
Value .... $ _____

Company _____
CUSIP or certificate number _____
Number and type of shares _____
Value .... $ _____

Company _____
CUSIP or certificate number _____
Number and type of shares _____
Value .... $ _____

Company _____
CUSIP or certificate number _____
Number and type of shares _____
Value .... $ _____

Company _____
CUSIP or certificate number _____
Number and type of shares _____
Value .... $ _____

Company _____
CUSIP or certificate number _____
Number and type of shares _____
Value .... $ _____

Company _____
CUSIP or certificate number _____
Number and type of shares _____
Value .... $ _____

Total Bonds and Mutual Bond Funds .... (E) $ _____

Business Interests

Ownership of business interests may generally be left by will.

Individual Proprietorship
Name _____
Location _____
Type of business _____
Your net value .... $ _____

Individual Proprietorship
Name _____
Location _____
Type of business _____
Your net value .... $ _____

Interest in Partnership
Name _____
Location _____
Type of business _____
Gross value .... $ _____
Percentage interest _____ %
Your net value .... $ _____

Interest in Partnership
Name _____
Location _____
Type of business _____
Gross value .... $ _____
Percentage interest _____ %
Your net value .... $ _____

Closely-held Corporation Interest
Name _____
Location _____
Type of business _____
Gross value .... $ _____
Percentage of shares held _____ %
Your net value .... $ _____

Total Business Interests .... (F) $ _____

Real Estate

Property owned individually or as tenants-in-common may be left by will. Property held in joint tenancy or tenancy-by-the-entirety may not.

Personal Residence
Location _____
Value .... $ _____
How is property held (joint tenants, tenancy-in-common, etc.)? _____
What is your percent? _____ %
Value of your share .... $ _____

Vacation Home
Location _____
Value .... $ _____
How is property held (joint tenants, tenancy-in-common, etc.)? _____
What is your percent? _____ %
Value of your share .... $ _____

Vacant Land
Location _____
Value .... $ _____
How is property held (joint tenants, tenancy-in-common, etc.)? _____
What is your percent? _____ %
Value of your share .... $ _____

Income Property
Location _____
Value .... $ _____
How is property held (joint tenants, tenancy-in-common, etc.)? _____
What is your percent? _____ %
Value of your share .... $ _____

Other Property
Location _____
Value .... $ _____
How is property held (joint tenants, tenancy-in-common, etc.)? _____
What is your percent? _____ %
Value of your share .... $ _____

Total Real Estate .... (G) $ _____

Personal Property

Personal property owned individually or as a tenant-in-common may be left by will.

Car .... $ _____
Description _____

Car .... $ _____
Description _____

Boat .... $ _____
Description _____

Other Vehicle .... $ _____
Description _____

Furniture .... $ _____
Description _____

Furniture .... $ _____
Description _____

Furniture .... $ _____
Description _____

Appliance .... $ _____
Description _____

Jewelry and Furs .... $ _____
Description _____

Music System .... $ _____
Description _____

Artwork .... $ _____
Description _____

Other .... $ _____
Description _____

Other .... $ _____
Description _____

Total Personal Property .... (H) $ _____

Miscellaneous Assets

Royalties .... $ _____
Description _____

Royalties .... $ _____
Description _____

Patents .... $ _____
Description _____

Copyrights .... $ _____
Description _____

Heirlooms .... $ _____
Description _____

Heirlooms .... $ _____
Description _____

Heirlooms .... $ _____
Description _____

Heirlooms .... $ _____
Description _____

Heirlooms .... $ _____
Description _____

Other .... $ _____
Description _____

Other .... $ _____
Description _____

Other .... $ _____
Description _____

Other .... $ _____
Description _____

Other .... $ _____
Description _____

Total Miscellaneous Assets .... (I) $ _____

Employee Benefit and Pension/Profit-sharing Plans

Retirement benefits cannot be left by will.

Company _____
Plan type _____
Net value .... $ _____

Company _____
Plan type _____
Net value .... $ _____

Company _____
Plan type _____
Net value .... $ _____

Company _____
Plan type _____
Net value .... $ _____

Company _____
Plan type _____
Net value .... $ _____

Total Employee Benefit and Pension/Profit-sharing Plans .... (J) $ _____

Total Assets

Insert totals from previous pages.

Cash and Bank Accounts Total .... (A) $ _____
Insurance and Annuity Contracts Total .... (B) $ _____
Accounts and Notes Receivable Total .... (C) $ _____
Stocks and Mutual Funds Total .... (D) $ _____
Bonds and Mutual Fund Bonds Total .... (E) $ _____
Business Interests Total .... (F) $ _____
Real Estate Total .... (G) $ _____
Personal Property Total .... (H) $ _____
Miscellaneous Assets Total .... (I) $ _____
Employee Benefit and Pension/Profit-sharing Plans Total .... (J) $ _____

Total Assets .... (1) $ _____

What Are Your Liabilities?

Notes and Loans Payable

Payable to _____
Address _____
Term _____
Interest rate   _____ %
Amount due .... $ _____

Payable to _____
Address _____
Term _____
Interest rate   _____ %
Amount due .... $ _____

Payable to _____
Address _____
Term _____
Interest rate   _____ %
Amount due .... $ _____

Total Notes and Loans Payable .... (K) $ _____

Accounts Payable

Payable to _____
Address _____
Term _____
Interest rate   _____ %
Amount due .... $ _____

Payable to _____
Address _____
Term _____
Interest rate   _____ %
Amount due .... $ _____

Payable to _____
Address _____
Term _____
Interest rate   _____ %
Amount due .... $ _____

Total Accounts Payable .... (L) $ _____

Mortgages Payable

Property Location _____
Payable to _____
Address _____
Term _____
Interest rate _____ _____ %
Amount due .... $ _____

Property Location _____
Payable to _____
Address _____
Term _____
Interest rate _____ _____ %
Amount due .... $ _____

Property Location _____
Payable to _____
Address _____
Term _____
Interest rate _____ _____ %
Amount due .... $ _____

Property Location _____
Payable to _____
Address _____
Term _____
Interest rate _____ _____ %
Amount due .... $ _____

Total Mortgages Payable .... (M) $ _____

Taxes Payable

Federal Income Taxes .... $ _____
State Income Taxes .... $ _____
Personal Property Taxes .... $ _____
Real Estate Taxes .... $ _____
Payroll Taxes .... $ _____
Other Taxes .... $ _____
Other Taxes .... $ _____
Other Taxes .... $ _____

Total Taxes Payable .... (N) $ _____

Credit Card Accounts Payable

Credit Card Company _____

Credit card account number _____

Address _____

Interest rate _____ %

Amount due .... $ _____

Credit Card Company _____

Credit card account number _____

Address _____

Interest rate _____ %

Amount due .... $ _____

Credit Card Company _____

Credit card account number _____

Address _____

Interest rate _____ %

Amount due .... $ _____

Credit Card Company _____

Credit card account number _____

Address _____

Interest rate _____ %

Amount due .... $ _____

Credit Card Company _____

Credit card account number _____

Address _____

Interest rate _____ %

Amount due .... $ _____

Credit Card Company _____

Credit card account number _____

Address _____

Interest rate _____ %

Amount due .... $ _____

Credit Card Company _____

Credit card account number _____

Address _____

Interest rate _____ %

Amount due .... $ _____

Total Credit Card Accounts Payable .... (O) $ _____

Miscellaneous Liabilities Payable

To Whom Due _____
Address _____
Term _____
Interest rate _____ %
Amount due .... $ _____

To Whom Due _____
Address _____
Term _____
Interest rate _____ %
Amount due .... $ _____

To Whom Due _____
Address _____
Term _____
Interest rate _____ %
Amount due .... $ _____

To Whom Due _____
Address _____
Term _____
Interest rate _____ %
Amount due .... $ _____

To Whom Due _____
Address _____
Term _____
Interest rate _____ %
Amount due .... $ _____

To Whom Due _____
Address _____
Term _____
Interest rate _____ %
Amount due .... $ _____

To Whom Due _____
Address _____
Term _____
Interest rate _____ %
Amount due .... $ _____

Total Miscellaneous Liabilities Payable .... (P) $ _____

Total Liabilities

Insert totals from previous pages.

Notes and Loans Payable Total .... (K) $ _____
Accounts Payable Total .... (L) $ _____
Mortgages Payable Total .... (M) $ _____
Taxes Payable Total .... (N) $ _____
Credit Card Accounts Payable Total .... (O) $ _____
Miscellaneous Liabilities Payable Total .... (P) $ _____

Total Liabilities .... (2) $ _____

Net Worth Of Your Estate

Total Assets .... (1) $ _____
Minus (-) *Total Liabilities* .... (2) $ _____

Equals (=) **Your Total Net Worth** .... $ _____

CHAPTER 4

Beneficiary Questionnaire

In this chapter you will determine both whom you would like your beneficiaries to be and what specific property you will leave each beneficiary in your will. First, there is a brief discussion regarding who may be a beneficiary. Next, there is an explanation of the various methods that you may use to leave gifts to your beneficiaries. Finally, there is a Beneficiary Questionnaire that you will use to actually make the decisions regarding which beneficiaries will receive which property.

Who May Be a Beneficiary?

Any person or organization who receives property under a will is termed a *beneficiary* of that will. Just as there are certain requirements that the person signing the will must meet, there are certain requirements relating to who may receive property under a will. These generally, however, are in the form of negative requirements. Stated in another way, this means that any person or organization may receive property under a will unless they fall into certain narrow categories of disqualification.

Besides these few exceptions noted below, any person or organization you choose may receive property under your will. This includes any family members, the named executor, illegitimate children (if named specifically), corporations, charities (but see below on possible restrictions), creditors, debtors, friends, acquaintances, or even strangers.

The few categories of disqualified beneficiaries are as follows:

- An attorney who drafts the will is generally assumed to have used undue influence if he or she is made a beneficiary
- Many states disqualify any witnesses to the execution of the will. Check the Appendix to see if your state has this restriction. However, to be safe, it is recommended that none of your witnesses be beneficiaries under your will
- A person who murders a testator is universally disqualified from receiving any property under the murdered person's will
- An unincorporated association is typically not allowed to receive property under a will. This particular disqualification stems from the fact that such associations generally have no legal right to hold property

A few states also have restrictions on the right to leave property to charitable organizations and churches. These restrictions are usually in two forms: a time limit prior to death when changes to a will that leave large amounts of money or property to a charitable organization are disallowed and also a percentage limit on the amount of a person's estate that may be left to a charitable organization (often a limit of 50 percent). The reasoning behind this rule is to prevent abuse of a dying person's desire to be forgiven. There have been, in the past, unscrupulous individuals or organizations who have obtained last-minute changes in a will in an attempt to have the bulk of a person's estate left to them or their group. If you intend to leave large sums of money or property to a charitable organization or church, please check the Appendix to see if there are any restrictions of this type in force in your state.

Under this same category as to who may be a beneficiary under your will are several points related to marriage, divorce, and children. First and foremost, you are advised to review your will periodically and make any necessary changes as your marital or family situation may dictate. If you are divorced, married, remarried, or widowed, or adopt or have a child, there may be unforeseen consequences based on the way you have written your will. Each state has differing laws on the effect of marriage and divorce on a person's will. In some states, divorce entirely revokes a will as pertaining to the divorced spouse. In other states, divorce has no effect and your divorced spouse may inherit your estate if you do not change your will. Marriage and the birth of children are also treated somewhat differently by each state. You are advised to review the Appendix as it relates to these aspects of your life and prepare your will accordingly.

Your will should be prepared with regard to how your life is presently arranged. It should, however, always be reviewed and updated each time there is a substantial change in your life.

What Types of Gifts May You Make?

There are various standard terms and phrases that may be employed when making gifts under your will. The wills that are used in this book incorporate these standard terms. Using these standard phrases, you may make a gift of any property that you will own at your death to any beneficiary whom you choose (remembering the few disqualified types of beneficiaries).

A few type of gifts are possible but are not addressed in the wills that may be prepared using this book. Simple shared gifts (for example: I give all my property to my children, Alice, Bill, and Carl, in equal shares) are possible using this book. However, any complex shared gift arrangements will require the assistance of an attorney. In addition, you may impose simple conditions on any gifts in wills prepared using this book. However, complex conditional gifts that impose detailed requirements that the beneficiary must comply with in order to receive the gift are also beyond the scope of this book. Finally, although it is possible to leave any gifts under your will in many types of trusts, a simple trust for leaving gifts to children is the only trust available for wills prepared using this book. If you desire to leave property in trust to an adult or in a complex trust arrangement, you are advised to seek professional advice.

The terms that you use to make any gifts can be any that you desire, as long as the gift is made in a clear and understandable manner. Someone reading the will at a later date, perhaps even a stranger appointed by a court, must be able to determine exactly what property you intended to be a gift and exactly who it is you intended to receive it. If you follow the few rules that follow regarding how to identify your gifts and beneficiaries, your intentions will be clear to whomever may need to interpret your will in the future:

1. Always describe the property in as detailed and clear a manner as possible. For example: do not simply state "my car;" instead state "my 2002 Buick Skylark, Serial #123456789." Describe exactly what it is you wish for each beneficiary to receive. You may make any type of gift that you wish, either a cash gift, a gift of a specific piece of personal property or real estate, or a specific share of your total estate. If you wish to give some of your estate in the form of portions of the total, it is recommended to use fractional portions. For example, if you wish to leave your estate in equal shares to two persons, use "I give one-half of my total estate to ..." for each party.

    In your description of the property, you should be as specific and precise as possible. For land, it is suggested that you use the description exactly as shown on the deed to the property. For personal property, be certain that your description clearly differentiates your gift from any other property.

2. Always describe the beneficiaries in as precise and clear a manner as is possible. For example: do not simply state "my son;" instead state "my son, Robert Edward Smith, of Houston Texas." This is particularly important if the beneficiary is an adopted child.

3. Never provide a gift to a group or class of people without specifically stating their individual names. For example: do not simply state "my sisters;" instead state "my sister Katherine Mary Jones, and my sister Elizabeth Anne Jones, and my sister Annette Josephine Jones."

4. You may put simple conditions on the gift if they are reasonable and not immoral or illegal. For example: you may say "This gift is to be used to purchase daycare equipment for the church nursery;" but you may not say "I give this gift to my sister only if she divorces her deadbeat husband Ralph Edwards."

5. You should always provide for an alternate beneficiary for the purpose of allowing you to designate someone to receive the gift if your first choice to receive the gift dies before you do (or, in the case of a organization chosen as primary beneficiary, is no longer in business). Your choice for alternate beneficiary may be one or more persons or an organization. In addition, you may delete the alternate beneficiary choice and substitute the words "the residue" instead. The result of this change will be that if your primary beneficiary dies before you do, your gift will pass under your residuary clause, which is discussed next.

6. Although not a technical legal requirement, a *residuary clause* should be included in every will in this book. With this clause, you will choose the person, persons, or organization to receive anything not covered by other clauses of your will. Even if you feel that you have given away everything that you own under other clauses of your will, this can be a very important clause.

   If, for any reason, any other gifts under your will are not able to be completed, this clause takes effect. For example, if a beneficiary refuses to accept your gift or the chosen beneficiary has died and no alternate was selected or both the beneficiary and alternate have died, the gift will be returned to your estate and would pass under the "residuary clause." If there is no "residuary clause" included in your will, any property not disposed of under your will is treated as though you did not have a will and could potentially be forfeited to the state.

7. A survivorship clause also should be included in every will. This provides for a period of survival for any beneficiary. For wills prepared using this book, the period is set at 30 days. The practical effect of this is to be certain that your property passes under your will and not that of a beneficiary who dies shortly after receiving your gift.

   Without this clause in your will, it would be possible that property would momentarily pass to a beneficiary under your will. When that person dies (possibly immediately if a result of a common accident or disaster), your property could wind up being left to the person whom your beneficiary designated, rather than to your alternate beneficiary.

8. To disinherit anyone from receiving property under your will, you should specifically name the person to be disinherited, rather than rely upon simply not mentioning them in your will. To disinherit children and grandchildren of deceased children, they must be mentioned specifically. In the case of children born after a will is executed and of spouses of a marriage that takes place after a will is executed, there are differing provisions in many states as to the effect of their not being mentioned in a will. Please also note that although one may choose to leave nothing to a spouse in a will, all states provide rules that allow a spouse the right to a certain share

of the other spouse's property on death Please see the Appendix for information regarding the laws in your particular state. The safest method of disinheritance, however, is to specifically mention anyone to be disinherited. Be sure to clearly identify the person being disinherited by full name. (Also note, in Louisiana, in order to disinherit children or grandchildren, specific and just reasons must be stated in the will). Another legal method to achieve approximately the same result as disinheritance is to leave the person a very small amount (at least $1.00) as a gift in your will. Also, be sure to review your will each time there is a change in your family circumstances. Please see Chapter 11 for a discussion regarding changing your will.

9. Finally, property may be left to your children in trust using the Children's Trust Clause that is included in Chapters 6 or 7. Please refer to the discussion of that clause in that chapter.

If you state your gifts simply, clearly, and accurately, you can be assured that they will be able to be carried out after your death regardless of who may be required to interpret the language in your will.

Beneficiary Questionnaire

Who Will Receive Which of Your Assets?

Spouse

Spouse _____

    Maiden name _____

    Date of marriage _____

    Date of birth _____

    Address _____

    Current income .... $ _____

    Amount, specific items, or share of estate that you desire to leave _____

_____

_____

    Alternate beneficiary _____

Children

Child _____

    Date of birth _____

    Address _____

_____

    Spouse's name (if any) _____

    Amount, specific items, or share of estate that you desire to leave _____

_____

_____

    Alternate beneficiary _____

Child _____

    Date of birth _____

    Address _____

_____

    Spouse's name (if any) _____

    Amount, specific items, or share of estate that you desire to leave _____

_____

_____

    Alternate beneficiary _____

Child _____
    Date of birth _____
    Address _____
    _____
    Spouse's name (if any) _____
    Amount, specific items, or share of estate that you desire to leave _____
    _____
    _____
    Alternate beneficiary _____

Child _____
    Date of birth _____
    Address _____
    _____
    Spouse's name (if any) _____
    Amount, specific items, or share of estate that you desire to leave _____
    _____
    _____
    Alternate beneficiary _____

Child _____
    Date of birth _____
    Address _____
    _____
    Spouse's name (if any) _____
    Amount, specific items, or share of estate that you desire to leave _____
    _____
    _____
    Alternate beneficiary _____

Child _____
    Date of birth _____
    Address _____
    _____
    Spouse's name (if any) _____
    Amount, specific items, or share of estate that you desire to leave _____
    _____
    _____
    Alternate beneficiary _____

Grandchildren

Grandchild _____
    Date of birth _____
    Address _____
    _____
    Spouse's name (if any) _____
    Amount, specific items, or share of estate that you desire to leave _____
    _____
    _____
    Alternate beneficiary _____

Grandchild _____
    Date of birth _____
    Address _____
    _____
    Spouse's name (if any) _____
    Amount, specific items, or share of estate that you desire to leave _____
    _____
    _____
    Alternate beneficiary _____

Grandchild _____
    Date of birth _____
    Address _____
    _____
    Spouse's name (if any) _____
    Amount, specific items, or share of estate that you desire to leave _____
    _____
    _____
    Alternate beneficiary _____

Grandchild _____
    Date of birth _____
    Address _____
    _____
    Spouse's name (if any) _____
    Amount, specific items, or share of estate that you desire to leave _____
    _____
    _____
    Alternate beneficiary _____

Parents

Parent _____
    Date of birth _____
    Address _____
    _____
    Spouse's name (if any) _____
    Amount, specific items, or share of estate that you desire to leave _____
    _____
    _____
    Alternate beneficiary _____

Parent _____
    Date of birth _____
    Address _____
    _____
    Spouse's name (if any) _____
    Amount, specific items, or share of estate that you desire to leave _____
    _____
    _____
    Alternate beneficiary _____

Siblings

Sibling _____
    Date of birth _____
    Address _____
    _____
    Spouse's name (if any) _____
    Amount, specific items, or share of estate that you desire to leave _____
    _____
    _____
    Alternate beneficiary _____

Sibling _____
    Date of birth _____
    Address _____
    _____
    Spouse's name (if any) _____
    Amount, specific items, or share of estate that you desire to leave _____
    _____
    _____
    Alternate beneficiary _____

Sibling _____
    Date of birth _____
    Address _____
    _____
    Spouse's name (if any) _____
    Amount, specific items, or share of estate that you desire to leave _____
    _____
    _____
    Alternate beneficiary _____

Sibling _____
    Date of birth _____
    Address _____
    _____
    Spouse's name (if any) _____
    Amount, specific items, or share of estate that you desire to leave _____
    _____
    _____
    Alternate beneficiary _____

Sibling _____
    Date of birth _____
    Address _____
    _____
    Spouse's name (if any) _____
    Amount, specific items, or share of estate that you desire to leave _____
    _____
    _____
    Alternate beneficiary _____

Sibling _____
    Date of birth _____
    Address _____
    _____
    Spouse's name (if any) _____
    Amount, specific items, or share of estate that you desire to leave _____
    _____
    Alternate beneficiary _____

Other Dependents

Other Dependent _____
    Date of birth _____
    Address _____
    _____
    Spouse's name (if any) _____
    Amount, specific items, or share of estate that you desire to leave _____
    _____
    _____
    Alternate beneficiary _____

Other Dependent _____
    Date of birth _____
    Address _____
    _____
    Spouse's name (if any) _____
    Amount, specific items, or share of estate that you desire to leave _____
    _____
    _____
    Alternate beneficiary _____

Other Dependent _____
    Date of birth _____
    Address _____
    _____
    Spouse's name (if any) _____
    Amount, specific items, or share of estate that you desire to leave _____
    _____
    _____
    Alternate beneficiary _____

Other Dependent _____
    Date of birth _____
    Address _____
    _____
    Spouse's name (if any) _____
    Amount, specific items, or share of estate that you desire to leave _____
    _____
    _____
    Alternate beneficiary _____

Are There Any Other Relatives, Friends, Or Organizations to Whom You Wish to Leave Gifts?

Name _____
    Relationship _____
    Address _____

    _____
    Spouse's name (if any) _____
    Amount, specific items, or share of estate that you desire to leave _____

    _____
    _____
    Alternate beneficiary _____

Name _____
    Relationship _____
    Address _____

    _____
    Spouse's name (if any) _____
    Amount, specific items, or share of estate that you desire to leave _____

    _____
    _____
    Alternate beneficiary _____

Name _____
    Relationship _____
    Address _____

    _____
    Spouse's name (if any) _____
    Amount, specific items, or share of estate that you desire to leave _____

    _____
    _____
    Alternate beneficiary _____

Name _____
    Relationship _____
    Address _____

    _____
    Spouse's name (if any) _____
    Amount, specific items, or share of estate that you desire to leave _____

    _____
    _____
    Alternate beneficiary _____

Name _____

    Relationship _____

    Address _____

    _____

    Spouse's name (if any) _____

    Amount, specific items, or share of estate that you desire to leave _____

    _____

    _____

    Alternate beneficiary _____

Name _____

    Relationship _____

    Address _____

    _____

    Spouse's name (if any) _____

    Amount, specific items, or share of estate that you desire to leave _____

    _____

    _____

    Alternate beneficiary _____

Name _____

    Relationship _____

    Address _____

    _____

    Spouse's name (if any) _____

    Amount, specific items, or share of estate that you desire to leave _____

    _____

    _____

    Alternate beneficiary _____

Name _____

    Relationship _____

    Address _____

    _____

    Spouse's name (if any) _____

    Amount, specific items, or share of estate that you desire to leave _____

    _____

    Alternate beneficiary _____

Are There Any Persons Whom You Wish to Specifically Leave out of Your Will?

Name _____
    Relationship _____
    Address _____
    _____
    Spouse's name (if any) _____
    Reason for disinheritance _____
    _____
    _____

Name _____
    Relationship _____
    Address _____
    _____
    Spouse's name (if any) _____
    Reason for disinheritance _____
    _____
    _____

Name _____
    Relationship _____
    Address _____
    _____
    Spouse's name (if any) _____
    Reason for disinheritance _____
    _____
    _____

Name _____
    Relationship _____
    Address _____
    _____
    Spouse's name (if any) _____
    Reason for disinheritance _____
    _____
    _____

CHAPTER 5

Information for the Executor

In this chapter, various information relating to the executor of your will and the probate process is provided. Before actually planning your will, an overview of how the legal system operates after a person's death may be useful to keep in mind. The system of court administration of the estates of deceased parties is generally entitled *probate*. How to avoid the probate court was the subject of one of the first self-help law books to challenge the legal establishment's monopoly on law. Probate, however, despite what many lawyers would have you believe, is not all that mysterious a matter.

Overview of a Typical Probate Proceeding

Upon a person's death, in most states there is a general sequence of events which takes place. First, the executor appointed in the will (who, hopefully, has been notified of her or his duties in advance) locates the will and files it with the proper authority. If necessary, the executor arranges for the funeral and burial. If the estate is complicated or very large, it may be prudent to hire a lawyer to handle the probate proceeding. Upon presenting the will to the probate court, the will is *proved*, which means that it is determined whether or not the document presented is actually the deceased's will. This may be done in most states with a *self-proving affidavit* that is prepared and notarized at the time your will is signed (see Chapters 6 and 7). The wills in this book are designed to be self-proving when completed and signed as indicated.

Upon proof that the will is valid, the executor is officially given legal authority to gather together all of the estate's property. This authority for the executor to administer the estate is generally referred to as *letters testamentary*. The probate court also officially appoints any trustees and also the parties who are designated as guardians of any minor children.

If no executor was chosen in the will, or if the one chosen cannot serve, the probate court will appoint one. The order of preference for appointment is commonly as follows: surviving spouse, next of kin, and then a person having an interest in the estate or claims against the estate.

If the will is shown to be invalid, or if there is no will, the same sequence of events generally is followed. However, in this case, the party appointed to administer the estate is usually titled an *administrator* of the estate rather than an executor. The court orders granting authority to an administrator are generally referred to as *letters of administration*.

After the executor or administrator is given authority, he or she handles the collection of assets, management of the estate, and payment of any debts and taxes until such time as all creditors' claims have been satisfied and other business of the estate completed. An inventory of all of the assets is typically the first official act of an executor. Creditors, by the way, only have a certain time period in which to make a claim against an estate. The same holds true for any *contests* (challenging the validity) of the will. Contesting a will is a fairly rare occurrence and is most difficult if the will was properly prepared and signed by a competent, sane adult.

The executor generally will also be empowered under state law to provide an allowance for the surviving spouse and children until such time as all affairs of the deceased person are completed and the estate is closed.

Upon completion of all business and payment of all outstanding charges against the estate, an accounting and inventory of the estate's assets are then presented to the probate court by the executor. At this time, if everything appears to be in order, the executor is generally empowered to distribute all of the remaining property to the persons or organizations named in the will and probate is officially closed. The entire probate process generally takes from four to 18 months to complete. The distribution of your property and money is usually handled solely by the executor (possibly with a lawyer's help to be certain that all legal requirements are fulfilled). Normally, this is done without further court approval of the disbursement.

Choosing an Executor

Your choice of who should be your executor is a personal decision. A spouse, sibling, or other trusted party is usually chosen to act as executor, although a bank officer, accountant, or attorney can also be chosen. The person chosen should be someone you trust and whom you feel can handle or at least efficiently delegate the complicated tasks of making an inventory of all of your property and distributing it to your chosen beneficiaries. The person chosen should be a resident of the state in which you currently reside. In addition, all states require that executors be competent, of legal age (generally, over 18) and a citizen of the United States. Although it is possible, it is generally not wise to appoint two or more persons as co-executors. It is preferable to appoint your first choice as primary executor and the other person as alternate executor.

In your will, you will grant the executor broad powers to manage your estate and will also provide that he or she is not required to post a bond in order to be appointed to serve as executor. This provision can save your estate considerable money, depending upon the estate's size. The fees for executor bonds are based upon the size of the estate and can amount to hundreds of dollars for every year that your estate is being managed. By waiving this bond requirement, these potential bond fees can be eliminated and the money saved can be passed on to your beneficiaries.

You should discuss your choice with the person chosen to be certain that he or she will be willing to act as executor. In addition, it is wise to provide your executor, in advance, with a copy of the will, a copy of any organ-donation desires, a copy of your Property and Beneficiary Questionnaires, and a copy of the information contained in this chapter.

Executor Duties Checklist Instructions

Provided on the following pages is a checklist of items that your executor may have to deal with after your death. Although this list is extensive, there may be other personal tasks that are not included. Scanning this list can give you an idea of the scope and range of the executor's duties. You can provide invaluable assistance to your executor by being aware of his or her duties and providing the executor with information to help him or her. This checklist is divided into immediate and first-month time periods. These time periods are approximations and many of the duties may be required to be performed either before or after the exact time specified. Also included in the checklist are the financial duties. These duties cannot be delegated. Following this list, a section is provided for listing such information for your executor.

Executor Duties Checklist

Immediate Executor Duties

- ❏ Contact mortuary or funeral home regarding services

- ❏ Contact cemetery regarding burial or cremation

- ❏ Contact local newspaper with obituary information

- ❏ Contact relatives and close friends

- ❏ Contact employer and business associates

- ❏ Contact lawyer and accountant

- ❏ Arrange for pallbearers

- ❏ Contact guardians or trustees named in will

- ❏ Arrange for immediate care of decedent's children

- ❏ Arrange for living expenses for decedent's spouse

- ❏ Contact veterans' organizations

Executor Duties within First Month

- ☐ Contact life insurance agent and report death

- ☐ Contact general insurance agent

- ☐ Contact medical and health insurance companies

- ☐ Contact Medicare

- ☐ Contact union regarding pensions and death benefits

- ☐ Contact employer regarding pensions and death benefits

- ☐ Contact military regarding pensions and death benefits

- ☐ Contact Social Security Administration

- ☐ Obtain death certificates from attending physician

- ☐ Contact IRA or KEOGH account trustees

- ☐ Contact county recorder

- ☐ Contact post office

- ☐ Contact Department of Motor Vehicles

- ☐ Arrange for management of business or real estate holdings

- ☐ Review all of decedent's records and legal documents

- ☐ Contact gas, telephone, cable, electric, trash, and water companies

- ☐ Contact newspaper and magazine subscription departments

- ☐ Contact credit card companies

Executor Financial Duties

These cannot be delegated.

- ☐ Begin inventory of assets

- ☐ Arrange for appraisal of assets

- ☐ Begin collection of assets

- ☐ Contact banks, savings and loans, and credit unions

- ☐ Contact mortgage companies

- ☐ Contact stockbroker and investment counselor

- ☐ Open bank accounts for estate

- ☐ Open decedent's safe deposit box

- ☐ File the will with probate court

- ☐ Inventory all estate assets

- ☐ Collect all monies and property due to decedent

- ☐ Pay all taxes due and file all necessary tax returns

- ☐ Provide notice to all creditors of time limit for claims

- ☐ Pay all debts and expenses of decedent, including funeral expenses

- ☐ Arrange for sale of estate assets, if necessary

- ☐ Distribute all remaining assets according to will

- ☐ Submit final accounting and receipts to probate court

- ☐ Close estate books and affairs

Executor Information Checklist Instructions

The following listing will provide your executor with valuable information that will make performing his or her difficult task much easier. Included in this questionnaire is information relating to the location of your records, any funeral or burial arrangements that you have made, lists of important persons, businesses, or organizations whom the executor will need to contact after your death, and information that will assist your executor in preparing any obituary listing. It may be very difficult to confront your own mortality and the need for this information. Please take the time to provide this valuable record of information for your executor. After your death, he or she may be under tremendous emotional stress and this information will help him or her perform the executor's necessary duties with the least difficulty. You will probably wish to give this information list and a copy of your will to the person whom you have chosen as your executor.

Executor Information Checklist

Location of Records

Original of will _____

Original of codicil _____

Trust documents _____

Safe deposit box and key _____

Bankbook and savings passbook _____

Treasury bills and certificates of deposit _____

_____

Social Security records _____

Real estate deeds and mortgage documents _____

Veteran's information _____

Stock certificates and bonds _____

_____

Promissory notes and loan documents _____

_____

Business records _____

Partnership records _____

Corporation records _____

Automobile titles _____

Income tax records _____

Credit card records _____

Birth certificate _____

Warranties _____

_____

Other important papers _____

_____

_____

_____

_____

_____

_____

_____

Funeral or Cremation Arrangements

Name of mortuary, funeral home, or crematorium _____

_____

Name of person contacted _____
Phone _____
Address _____

_____

Arrangements made _____

_____
_____
_____
_____
_____
_____
_____

Name of cemetery _____
Name of person contacted _____
Phone _____
Address _____

_____

Arrangements made _____

_____
_____
_____
_____
_____
_____

Location of memorial or church service _____

_____

Name of person contacted _____
Phone _____
Address _____

_____

Arrangements made _____

_____
_____
_____
_____
_____
_____
_____

Persons, Businesses, and Organizations to Contact

Clergy _____
Address _____
City, State, Zip _____
Phone _____

Lawyer _____
Address _____
City, State, Zip _____
Phone _____

Accountant _____
Address _____
City, State, Zip _____
Phone _____

IRA or Keogh account trustee _____
Address _____
City, State, Zip _____
Phone _____

Stockbroker _____
Address _____
City, State, Zip _____
Phone _____

Investment counselor _____
Address _____
City, State, Zip _____
Phone _____

Life insurance agent _____
Address _____
City, State, Zip _____
Phone _____

General insurance agent _____
Address _____
City, State, Zip _____
Phone _____

Medical insurance agent _____
Address _____
City, State, Zip _____
Phone _____

Health insurance agent _____
Address _____
City, State, Zip _____
Phone _____

Physician _____
Address _____
City, State, Zip _____
Phone _____

Dentist _____
Address _____
City, State, Zip _____
Phone _____

Employer _____
Address _____
City, State, Zip _____
Phone _____

Employer _____
Address _____
City, State, Zip _____
Phone _____

Business associate _____
Address _____
City, State, Zip _____
Phone _____

Business associate _____
Address _____
City, State, Zip _____
Phone _____

Union representative _____
Address _____
City, State, Zip _____
Phone _____

Guardian named in will _____
Address _____
City, State, Zip _____
Phone _____

Guardian named in will _____
Address _____
City, State, Zip _____
Phone _____

Trustee named in will _____
Address _____
City, State, Zip _____
Phone _____

Trustee named in will _____
Address _____
City, State, Zip _____
Phone _____

Military unit _____
Address _____
City, State, Zip _____
Phone _____

Veteran's organization _____
Address _____
City, State, Zip _____
Phone _____

Bank, savings and loan, or credit union _____
Address _____
City, State, Zip _____
Phone _____

Bank, savings and loan, or credit union _____
Address _____
City, State, Zip _____
Phone _____

Mortgage company _____
Address _____
City, State, Zip _____
Phone _____

Utility _____
Address _____
City, State, Zip _____
Phone _____

Utility _____
Address _____
City, State, Zip _____
Phone _____

Utility _____
Address _____
City, State, Zip _____
Phone _____

Utility _____
Address _____
City, State, Zip _____
Phone _____

Newspaper _____
Address _____
City, State, Zip _____
Phone _____

Magazine _____
Address _____
City, State, Zip _____
Phone _____

Credit card company _____
Address _____
City, State, Zip _____
Phone _____

Credit card company _____
Address _____
City, State, Zip _____
Phone _____

Credit card company _____
Address _____
City, State, Zip _____
Phone _____

Relatives to Contact

Relative name _____
Address _____
City, State, Zip _____
Phone _____

Relative name _____
Address _____
City, State, Zip _____
Phone _____

Relative name _____
Address _____
City, State, Zip _____
Phone _____

Relative name _____
Address _____
City, State, Zip _____
Phone _____

Relative name _____
Address _____
City, State, Zip _____
Phone _____

Relative name _____
Address _____
City, State, Zip _____
Phone _____

Relative name _____
Address _____
City, State, Zip _____
Phone _____

Relative name _____
Address _____
City, State, Zip _____
Phone _____

Friends to Contact

Friend name _____
Address _____
City, State, Zip _____
Phone _____

Friend name _____
Address _____
City, State, Zip _____
Phone _____

Friend name _____
Address _____
City, State, Zip _____
Phone _____

Friend name _____
Address _____
City, State, Zip _____
Phone _____

Friend name _____
Address _____
City, State, Zip _____
Phone _____

Friend name _____
Address _____
City, State, Zip _____
Phone _____

Friend name _____
Address _____
City, State, Zip _____
Phone _____

Friend name _____
Address _____
City, State, Zip
Phone _____

Newspaper Obituary Information

Newspaper _____

Address _____

City, State, Zip _____

Phone _____

Newspaper _____

Address _____

City, State, Zip _____

Phone _____

Newspaper _____

Address _____

City, State, Zip _____

Phone _____

Name _____

Date of birth _____

Place of birth _____

Current residence _____

_____

Former residence _____

_____

_____

Occupation _____

_____

Education _____

_____

Military service _____

_____

Club, union, civic, or fraternal organizations _____

_____

Special achievements _____

_____

_____

_____

_____

_____

_____

Survivors _____

_____

_____

_____

_____

_____

_____

Date of death _____

Place of service _____

Date of service _____

Time of service _____

Memorial contribution preference _____

_____

_____

_____

_____

CHAPTER 6

Will Clauses

This chapter contains a listing of all of the necessary will clauses which you will need to complete your own will. Although not every possible contingency is covered by these clauses, most choices for dispositions under your will should be covered by the clauses shown in this chapter. By following the instruction in this chapter, you will be shown how to custom-tailor a will to exactly fit your own individual circumstances. These same clauses have been assembled into basic wills for use in certain specific personal situations in Chapter 7. Please read that chapter to determine if one of the pre-assembled wills would be appropriate in your circumstances.

Using the clauses in this Chapter you will be able to prepare a will in which you may:

- ❏ Make specific gifts of cash, real estate, or personal property to anyone
- ❏ Make specific gifts of to anyone
- ❏ Make specific gifts of certain shares of your estate
- ❏ Disinherit anyone from receiving anything from your estate
- ❏ Make a gift of the rest (*residue*) of your assets to anyone
- ❏ Choose an executor to administer your estate
- ❏ Choose a guardian for any minor children
- ❏ Set up a trust and choose a trustee for children's gifts
- ❏ Declare your intention to be an organ donor
- ❏ Declare your choice for funeral/cremation arrangements

Instructions

1. Carefully read through this entire chapter. Then, select those clauses you desire to use in your will and make a photo-copy of each clause you have chosen. These photo-copies will serve as your worksheets. You may, if you wish, simply use this book as a worksheet and fill-in the information directly onto the pages of this book (unless you are borrowing this book from a library!) Please note that there are certain clauses which are mandatory for all wills and you must include these clauses in your own will. These mandatory clauses are clearly marked.

2. In choosing your own individual clauses, simply follow the directions and instructions which are given immediately prior to each specific clause and fill in the appropriate blanks as indicated. As you are choosing and preparing your specific will clauses, it is suggested that you have before you the completed Property and Beneficiary Questionnaires from Chapters 3 and 4. The information which you compiled for those Questionnaires will be your guide for preparing your will, both in terms of being certain that you have disposed of all of your assets and in terms of being certain that you have left gifts to all those persons or organizations that you wished to.

3. When you have completed your selection of clauses and filled in all of the appropriate information, read through them carefully to be sure that you have filled in the blanks exactly to your wishes. Then starting at the beginning of your will clauses, cross out all of the words and phrases that do not apply in your situation. .

4. Finally, when you are satisfied that you have filled in the information on your worksheet will correctly, read through the sample will contained in Chapter 8 to see how a completed will is arranged. Following that, turn to Chapter 9 for instructions on typing and preparing your will for signature.

Will Clauses

Title Clause

Mandatory: This clause must be included in all wills.

① Fill in the name blank with your full legal name. If you have been known under more than one name, use your principle name.

Last Will and Testament of ① _____

Identification Clause

Mandatory: This clause must be included in all wills.

① full legal name
② full address including county, state and zip code

> I, ① _____, whose address is ② _____, declare
>
> that this is my Last Will and Testament and I revoke all previous wills.

Marital Status Clause (unmarried and no children).

Mandatory: This clause is required if you are not married and have no children.

> I have never been married and I have no children.

Marital Status Clause (currently married)

Mandatory: This clause is required if you are currently married.

① full legal name of spouse.

> I am married to ① _____.

Marital Status Clause (previously married)

Mandatory: This clause is required if you were previously married.

① full legal name of previous spouse
② date marriage ended including year
③ how marriage ended - divorce, death or annulment

> I was previously married to ① _____. That marriage ended ,
>
> on ② _____ by ③ _____.

Children Identification Clause

Mandatory: This clause is required if you have any living children. Repeat the information for every child.

① number of living children

② name, address and date of birth of each living child

I have ① _____child(ren) living.

Their names, addresses, and dates of birth is as follows: ② _____

Grandchildren Identification Clause

Mandatory: This clause is required if you have any living grandchildren. Repeat the information for every grandchild.

① number of living grandchildren

② name, address and date of birth of each living grandchild

I have ① _____grandchild(ren) living.

Their names, addresses, and dates of birth is as follows: ② _____

Entire Estate Gift Clause

Optional: Use this clause if you are leaving all of your property to one person or organization. Many people choose to leave their entire estate to their spouse or some other individual. Where you are asked in the clause to state the beneficiary's relationship, simply state their kinship, (for example: my wife), their status as a friend or co-worker, or the status as an organization (for example: my church or my alma mater). If you use this clause, do not use any other clause which leaves a gift to another person or organization. However, you should still use the residuary clause which is explained later. If you desire to leave portions of your estate to more than one person or organization, do not use this particular clause. Rather, use one or more of the "Specific Gift" clauses that follow.

You should always name an alternate beneficiary. The choice of alternate beneficiary is for the purpose of allowing you to designate someone to receive the gift if your first choice to receive the gift dies before you do (or, in the case of a organization chosen as primary beneficiary, is no longer in business), or refuses the gift. In this or any of the other gift clauses, your choice for alternate beneficiary may be one or more persons or an organization. It is recommended to always specifically name your beneficiary(s), rather than using a description only, such as "my children". In addition, you may delete the alternate beneficiary choice and substitute the words "the residue" instead. The result of this change will be that if your primary beneficiary dies before you do, your gift to pass under your residuary clause, which is discussed later in this chapter.

Be sure to clearly identify the beneficiary and alternate beneficiary by full name. You can also name joint beneficiaries, such as several children, if you choose. The space provided for an identification of the relationship of the beneficiary can be simply a descriptive phrase like "my wife", or "my brother-in-law", or "my best friend". It does not mean that the beneficiary must be related to you personally.

① full name of beneficiary
② relationship of beneficiary
③ name of alternate beneficiary
④ relationship of alternate beneficiary

I give my entire estate to ① _____ , my ② _____ ,
or if not surviving to ③ _____ , my ④ _____ .

Specific Gifts Clause

Optional: Use the following line and the paragraphs that follow as one entire clause. Number the whole clause consecutively. Use as many of the "I give . . ." paragraphs as is necessary to complete your chosen gifts. In these paragraphs, you may make any type of gift that you wish, either a cash gift, a gift of a specific piece of personal property or real estate, or a specific share of your total estate. If you wish to give some of your estate in the form of portions of the total, it is recommended to use fractional portions. For example, if you wish to leave your estate in equal shares to two persons, use "I give one-half of my total estate to . . . " for each party.

In your description of the property, you should be as specific and precise as possible. For land, it is suggested that you use the description exactly as shown on the deed to the property. For personal property, be certain that your description clearly differentiates your gift from any other property. For example: "I give my blue velvet coat which was a gift from my brother John to . . . ". Use serial numbers, colors, or any other descriptive words to clearly indicate the exact nature of the gift. For cash gifts, specifically indicate the amount of the gift. For gifts of securities, state the amount of shares and the name of the company. You may add simple conditions to the gifts that you make, if you desire. For example: You may state "I give $1,000 to the Centerville Church for use in purchasing a new roof for the church". Complex conditions, however, are not possible in this clause, and immoral or illegal conditions are not acceptable.

Be sure to clearly identify the beneficiary and alternate beneficiary by full name. You can also name joint beneficiaries, such as several children, if you choose. The space provided for an identification of the relationship of the beneficiary can be simply a descriptive phrase like "my wife", or "my brother-in-law", or "my best friend". It does not mean that the beneficiary must be related to you personally.

The choice of alternate beneficiary is for the purpose of allowing you to designate someone to receive the gift if your first choice to receive the gift dies before you do (or, in the case of a organization chosen as primary beneficiary, is no longer in business). In this or any of the other gift clauses, your choice for alternate beneficiary may be one or more persons or an organization. It is recommended to always specifically name your beneficiary(s), rather than using a description only, such as "my children". In addition, you may delete the alternate beneficiary choice and substitute the words "the residue" instead. The result of this change will be that if your primary beneficiary dies before you do, your gift to pass under your residuary clause, which is discussed later in this chapter.

Space is provided for one individual specific gift. If additional gifts are desired, simply photocopy an additional page or repeat as many times as needed.

① complete description of property
② name of beneficiary
③ relationship of beneficiary
④ name of alternate beneficiary
⑤ relationship of alternate beneficiary

I make the following gifts:

I give ① _____

to ② _____ ,

who is my ③ _____ ,

or if not surviving, then to ④ _____ ,

who is my ⑤ _____ .

Residuary Clause

Mandatory: Although not a technical legal requirement, it is strongly recommended that this clause be included in every will. It should be numbered consecutively. With it, you will choose the person, persons, or organization to receive anything not covered by other clauses of your will. Even if you feel that you have given away everything that you own under other clauses of your will, this can be a very important clause. If, for any reason, any other gifts under your will are not able to completed, this clause takes effect. For example, if a beneficiary refuses to accept your gift or the chosen beneficiary has died and no alternate was selected or both the beneficiary and alternate has died, the gift is put back into your estate and would pass under the residuary clause. If there is no residuary clause included in your will, any property not disposed of under your will is treated as though you did not have a will and could potentially be forfeited to the state. To avoid this, it is strongly recommended that you make this clause mandatory in your will.

In addition, you may use this clause to give all of your estate (except your specific gifts) to one or more persons. For example: you make specific gifts of $1,000 to a sister and a car to a friend. By then naming your spouse as the residuary clause beneficiary, you will have gifted everything in your estate to your spouse except the $1,000 and the car. You could then name your children, in equal shares, as the alternate residuary beneficiaries. In this manner, if your spouse were to die first, your children would then equally share your entire estate except the $1,000 and the car.

Be sure to clearly identify the beneficiary and alternate beneficiary by full name. You can also name joint beneficiaries, such as several children, if you choose. The space provided for an identification of the relationship of the beneficiary can be simply a descriptive phrase like "my wife", or "my brother-in-law", or "my best friend". It does not mean that the beneficiary must be related to you personally.

① name of beneficiary
② relationship of beneficiary
③ name of alternate beneficiary
④ relationship of alternate beneficiary

I give all the rest of my property, whether real or personal, wherever

located to ① _____ , who is my ② _____ ,

or if not surviving to ③ _____ , who is my ④ _____ .

Debt Forgiveness Clause

Optional: You may use this clause to forgive any debts owed to you personally. You should provide a clear description of the amount and nature of the debt being forgiven. You should also be certain to provide the full name and address of the debtor.

Be aware, however, that if you are married and the debt is owed to you and your spouse jointly, you may not legally be able to forgive the debt. On joint debts which you may wish to forgive, you are advised to consult an attorney.

① description of debt
② full name of debtor
③ address of debtor

I fully forgive the following debt(s) which are owed to me:

① _____

② _____

③ _____

Survivorship Clause

Mandatory: This clause should be included in every will. Number it consecutively. This clause provides for two possibilities. First, it provides for a required period of survival for any beneficiary to receive a gift under your will. The practical effect of this is to be certain that your property passes under your will and not that of a beneficiary who dies shortly after receiving your gift. The second portion of this clause provides for a determination of how your property should pass in the eventuality that both you and a beneficiary (most likely your spouse) should die in a manner that makes it impossible to determine who died first.

Without this clause in your will it would be possible that property would momentarily pass to a beneficiary under your will. When that person dies (possibly immediately if a result of a common accident or disaster) your property could wind up being left to the person whom your beneficiary designated, rather than to your alternate beneficiary.

If you and your spouse are both preparing wills, it is a good idea to be certain that each of your wills contains identical survivorship clauses. If you are each others primary beneficiary, it is also wise to attempt to coordinate who your alternate beneficiaries may be in the event of a simultaneous death.

> All Beneficiaries named in this will must survive me by thirty days to receive any gift under this will. If any beneficiary and I should die simultaneously, I shall be conclusively presumed to have survived that beneficiary for the purposes of this will.

Disinheritance Clause

Optional: Use this clause to specifically disinherit anyone from receiving property under your will. It is much safer to specifically name the person to be disinherited than to rely upon simply not mentioning them in your will. To disinherit children and grandchildren of deceased children, they must be mentioned specifically. In the case of children born after a will is executed and of spouses of a marriage which takes place after a will is executed, there are differing provisions in many states as to the effect of their not being mentioned in a will. Please also note that although one may choose to leave nothing to a spouse, in all states spouses have a right to a certain share of the other's property on death. Please see the Appendix for information regarding the laws in your particular state. (Also note: To disinherit children or grandchildren in Louisiana, just reasons must be stated in the will). Be sure to clearly identify the person being disinherited by full name. The space provided for an identification of the relationship of the executor can be simply a descriptive phrase like "my son", or "my brother". If you do not wish to name anyone specifically, you may use the second clause as a general disinheritance clause. Do not use both clauses.

① relationship of person being disinherited
② full name of person being disinherited

Disinheritance Clause #1

> I specifically disinherit my ① _____, ② _____, and any other person not specifically named in the will.

Disinheritance Clause #2

> I intentionally disinherit any person not specifically named in this will.

Executor Clause

Mandatory: This clause must be included in every will. With this clause, you will make your choice of *executor*, the person who will administer and distribute your estate and an alternate choice if your first choice is unable to serve. A spouse, sibling, or other trusted party is usually chosen to act as executor. The person chosen should be a resident of the state in which you currently reside. Please refer back to Chapter 5 for more information regarding executors.

Note that you allow your executor to seek independent administration of your estate. Where allowed by state law, this enables your executor to manage your estate with minimal court supervision and can save your estate extensive court costs and legal fees. Additionally, you grant the executor broad powers to manage your estate and also provide that he or she not be required to post a bond in order to be appointed to serve as executor.

Be sure to clearly identify the executor and alternate executor by full name. The space provided for an identification of the relationship of the executor can be simply a descriptive phrase like "my wife", or "my brother-in-law", or "my best friend". It does not mean that the executor must be related to you personally.

① full name of executor
② relationship to executor
③ address of executor
④ full name of alternate executor
⑤ relationship to alternate executor
⑥ address of alternate executor

I appoint ① _____, my ② _____, whose

address is ③ _____, as Executor, to serve without bond.

If not surviving or otherwise unable to serve, I appoint ④ _____,

my ⑤ _____, whose address is ⑥ _____,

as Alternate Executor, also to serve without bond.

In addition to any powers, authority, and discretion granted by law, I

grant such Executor or Alternate Executor any and all powers necessary

to perform any acts, in his and her sole discretion and without court

approval, for the management and distribution of my estate, including

independent administration of my estate.

Guardianship Clause

Optional: With this clause you may designate your choice as to whom you wish to care for any of your minor children after you are gone. If you are married, your spouse is generally appointed by the probate or family court, regardless of your designation in a will. However, even if you are married, it is a good idea to choose your spouse as first choice and then provide a second choice. This will cover the contingency in which both you and your spouse die in a single accident. Your choice should obviously be a trusted person whom you feel would provide the best care for your children in your absence. Be aware, however, that the court is guided, but not bound, by this particular choice in your will. In most situations, however, a parent's choice as to who should be their child's guardian is almost universally followed by the courts. Be sure to clearly identify the guardian and alternate guardian by full name. The space provided for an identification of the relationship of the guardian can be simply a descriptive phrase like "my wife", or "my brother-in-law", or "my best friend". Additionally, you grant the guardian broad power to care for and manage your children's property and also provide that the appointed guardian not be required to post a bond in order to be appointed.

① full name of guardian
② relationship to guardian
③ address of guardian
④ full name of alternate guardian
⑤ relationship to alternate guardian
⑥ address of alternate guardian.

If a Guardian is needed for any of my minor child(ren), I appoint

① _____ , my ② _____ , whose address is

③ _____ as Guardian of the person(s) and property of

my minor child(ren), to serve without bond. If not surviving or unable to

serve, I appoint ④ _____ my ⑤ _____ , whose

address is ⑥ _____ as Alternate Guardian, also to serve

without bond. In addition to any powers, authority, and discretion granted

by law, I grant such Guardian or Alternate Guardian any and all powers

necessary to perform any acts, in his and her sole discretion and without

court approval, for the management and distribution of the property of

my minor child(ren) and for their care.

Children's Trust Fund Clause

Optional: It is with this clause that you may set up a Trust Fund for any gifts you have made to your minor children. You also may delay the time when they will actually have unrestricted control over your gift. It is not recommended, however, to attempt to delay receipt of control beyond the age of 30. If you have left assets to more than one child, this clause provides that separate individual trusts be set up for each child.

The choice for trustee under a children's trust should generally be the same person as you have chosen to be the children's guardian. This is not, however, a requirement. The choice of trustee is generally a spouse if alive, with the alternate being a trusted friend or family member. Be sure to clearly identify the trustee and alternate trustee by full name. The space provided for an identification of the relationship of the trustee can be simply a descriptive phrase like "my wife", or "my brother-in-law", or "my best friend". It does not mean that the trustee must be related to you personally.

The terms of the trust provide that the trustee may distribute any or all of the income or principal to the children as he or she deems necessary to provide for their health, support, and education. The trust will terminate when either the specific age is reached, all of the money is spent prior to that age, or the child dies prematurely. Upon termination, any remaining trust funds will be distributed to the child (beneficiary), if surviving; if not surviving, to the heirs of the beneficiary (if any), or to the residue of your estate. Additionally, you grant the trustee broad power to manage the trust and also provide that he or she not be required to post a bond in order to be appointed.

① age child must be to be subject to trust
② age child must be to end the trust
③ full name of trustee
④ relationship to trustee
⑤ address of trustee
⑥ full name of alternate trustee
⑦ relationship to alternate trustee
⑧ address of alternate trustee

If any of my children are under ① _____ years old at the time of my death, I direct that any property that I give them under this will be held in an individual trust for each child, under the following terms, until each shall reach ② _____ years old:

A. I appoint ③ _____, my ④ _____, whose address is ⑤_____, as trustee of any and all required trusts, to serve without bond. If not surviving or otherwise unable to serve, then I appoint ⑥_____, my ⑦_____, whose address is ⑧ _____, address is as Alternate Trustee, also to serve without bond. In addition to all powers, authority, and discretion granted by law, I grant such trustee or alternate trustee full power to perform any act, in his or her sole discretion and without court approval, to distribute and manage the assets of any such trust.

B. In the trustee's sole discretion, the trustee may distribute any or all of the principal, income, or both as deemed necessary for the beneficiary's health, support, welfare, and education. Any income not distributed shall be added to the trust principal.

C. Any such trust shall terminate when the beneficiary reaches the required age, when the beneficiary dies prior to reaching the required age, or when all trust funds have been distributed. Upon termination, any remaining undistributed principal and income shall pass to the beneficiary; or if not surviving, to the beneficiary's heirs; or if none to the residue of my estate.

Organ Donation Clause

Optional: Use this clause to provide for any use of your body after death. You may, if you so desire, limit your donation to certain parts, for example, your eyes. If so desired, simply delete "any of my body parts and/or organs" and insert your chosen donation. A copy of your will or instructions regarding this donation should be given to your spouse and/or executor.

I declare that, pursuant to the Uniform Anatomical Gift Act, I donate any of my body parts and/or organs to any medical institution willing to accept them, and I direct my executor to carry out such donation.

Funeral and Burial Arrangements Clause

Optional: Use this clause to make known your wishes as to funeral and burial arrangements. Since it may be difficult to obtain your will quickly in an emergency, it is also a good idea to leave information regarding these desires with your executor, your spouse, or a close friend or relative.

① name of funeral home/service
② address of funeral home
③ name of cemetery
④ address of cemetery

Funeral arrangements have been made with ① _____ ,

ocated at ② _____ , for the burial at ③ _____ ,

located in ④ _____ , and I direct my Executor to carry out

such arrangements.

Cremation Arrangements Clause

Optional: Use this clause to make known your wishes as to any cremation arrangements. It is also a good idea to leave information regarding these desires with your spouse or a close friend or relative, in as much as it may be difficult to obtain your will quickly in an emergency.

① name of crematorium
② address of crematorium

Cremation arrangements have been made with ① _____ ,

located at ② _____ and I direct my Executor to carry out

such arrangements.

Signature, Witness and Notary Clauses

Mandatory: All of the following remaining portions of your will are mandatory and must be included in your will. You will fill in the number of pages and the appropriate dates where indicated after you have properly typed or had your will typed. At the bottom of each page, you should also type the following line:

Page _____ of _____ pages   Testator's initials _____

DO NOT SIGN YOUR WILL OR HAVE YOUR WITNESSES SIGN YOUR WILL UNTIL YOU HAVE READ CHAPTER 10 REGARDING SIGNING YOUR WILL. The Notary Public will complete the Notary Acknowledgement section after the signing.

I publish and sign this Last Will and Testament, consisting of_____

typewritten pages, on_____, and declare that I do so

freely, for the purposes expressed, under no constraint or undue influence,

and that I am of sound mind and of legal age.

_____

Signature of Testator

_____

Printed name of Testator

We, the undersigned, being first sworn on oath and under penalty of

perjury, state that:

On_____, in the presence of all of us, the

above-named Testator published and signed this Last Will and Testament,

and then at Testator's request, and in Testator's presence, and in each

other's presence, we all signed below as witnesses, and we declare, that

to the best of our knowledge, the Testator signed this instrument freely,

under no constraint or undue influence, and is of sound mind and

legal age.

_____   _____
Signature of Witness   Signature of Witness
_____   _____
Printed name of Witness   Printed name of Witness
_____   _____
Address of Witness   Address of Witness

_____
Signature of Witness
_____
Printed name of Witness
_____
Address of Witness

Page _____ of _____ pages   Testator's initials _____

Notary Acknowledgement

State of _____

County of _____

On _____, _____, the testator, and

_____, _____, and

_____, the witnesses, personally came before me

and, being duly sworn, did state that they are the persons described in the

above document and that they signed the above document in my presence,

as a free and voluntary act for the purposes stated.

_____

Signature of Notary Public

Notary Public, In and for the County of _____

State of _____

My commission expires: _____   Notary Seal

Page _____ of _____ pages   Testator's initials _____

CHAPTER 7

Pre-Assembled Wills

In this chapter are contained four separate wills that have been prepared for the purpose of allowing persons whose situations fall into certain standard formats to prepare their wills quickly and easily on pre-assembled forms. Generally, the wills are for a single person with or without children and for a married person with or without children. Please read the description prior to each will to be certain that the will you choose is appropriate for your particular situation. Please note that each of the wills in this book is intended to be a *self-proving* will. This means that the signatures of the witnesses and the testator will be verified by a notary public and thus, the witnesses' testimony will not be needed in probate court at a later date in order to authenticate their signatures.

Instructions

These pre-assembled will forms are intended to be used as simplified worksheets for preparing your own personal will. The forms should be filled-in by hand and then re-typed according to the following instructions and the instructions contained in Chapter 9. These pre-assembled wills are not intended to be filled-in and used "as is" as an original will. Such use would most likely result in an invalid will. The forms *must* be retyped. (*Note*: if you are using a version of this book that came with Forms-on-CD, please follow the instructions on the CD's "readme.doc" file.) Be certain to carefully follow all of the instructions for use of these forms. They are not difficult to fill out, but must be prepared properly to be legally valid. In order to prepare any of the wills in this chapter, you should follow these simple steps:

1. Carefully read through all of the clauses in the blank pre-assembled will to determine if the clauses provided are suitable in your situation. Choose the will that is most appropriate. Make a photocopy to use as a worksheet of the will that you select. If you wish, you may use this book itself as a worksheet (unless it is a library book!).

2. Using your Property and Beneficiary Questionnaires, fill in the appropriate information where necessary on these forms.

3. After you have filled in all of the appropriate information, carefully reread your entire will. Be certain that it contains all of the correct information that you desire.

Then, starting at the beginning of the will, cross out all of the words and phrases in the pre-assembled will that do not apply in your situation.

4. When you have completed all of your will clauses, look over the sample will in the next chapter to see how a completed will should look. Then, turn to Chapter 9 for instructions on the typing and the final preparation of your will.

As you fill in the information for each clause, keep in mind the following instructions:

Title Clause: The title clause is mandatory for all wills and must be included. Fill in the name blank with your full legal name. If you have been known by more than one name, use your principal name.

Identification Clause: The identification clause is mandatory and must be included in all wills. In the first blank, include any other names that you are known by. Do this by adding the phrase: "also known as" after your principal full name. For example:

John James Smith, also known as Jimmy John Smith.

In the spaces provided for your residence, use the location of your principal residence; that is, the place where you currently live permanently.

Marital Status Clause: Each of the pre-assembled wills in this chapter is either for a married or single person. Select the proper will and if you are married, fill in the appropriate information. If you have previously been married, please add and complete the following sentence:

I was previously married to [_name of your former spouse_], and that marriage ended by [_select either death, divorce, or annulment_].

Identification of Children Clause: This clause will only be present in the pre-assembled wills that relate to children. In this clause, you should specifically identify all of your children, indicating their full names, current addresses, and dates of birth. Cross out those spaces that are not used.

Identification of Grandchildren Clause: This clause will only be used in the pre-assembled wills that relate to grandchildren. If you do not have grandchildren, cross out this entire clause. If you do have grandchildren, you should specifically identify all of your grandchildren in this clause, indicating their full names, current addresses, and dates of birth. Cross out those spaces that are not used.

Specific Gifts Clause: For making specific gifts, use as many of the "I give …" paragraphs as is necessary to complete your chosen gifts. In these paragraphs, you may make any type of gift that you wish; either a cash gift, a gift of a specific piece of personal property or real estate, or a specific share of your total estate. If you wish to give some of your estate in the form of portions of the total, it is recommended to use fractional portions. For example, if you wish to leave your estate in equal shares to two persons, use "I give one-half of my total estate to…" for each party. Although none of the wills in this chapter contain a specific clause that states that you give one person your entire estate, you may make such a gift using this clause by simply stating:

"I give my entire estate to…."

Be sure that you do not attempt to give any other gifts. However, you should still include the residuary clause in your will, which is explained on the next page.

In your description of the property, you should be as specific and precise as possible. For land, it is suggested that you use the description exactly as shown on the deed to the property. For personal property, be certain that your description clearly differentiates your gift from any other property. For example: "I give my blue velvet coat which was a gift from my brother John to…." Use serial numbers, colors, or any other descriptive words to clearly indicate the exact nature of the gift. For cash gifts, specifically indicate the amount of the gift. For gifts of securities, state the amount of shares and the name of the company. You may add simple conditions to the gifts that you make, if you desire. For example, you may state "I give $1,000.00 to the Centerville Church for use in purchasing a new roof for the church." Complex conditions, however, are not possible in this clause, and immoral or illegal conditions are not acceptable.

Be sure to clearly identify the beneficiary and alternate beneficiary by full name. You can also name joint beneficiaries, such as several children, if you choose. The space provided for an identification of the relationship of the beneficiary can simply be a descriptive phrase like "my wife," "my brother-in-law," or "my best friend." It does not mean that the beneficiary must be related to you personally.

The choice of alternate beneficiary is for the purpose of allowing you to designate someone to receive the gift if your first choice to receive the gift dies before you do (or, in the case of a organization chosen as primary beneficiary, is no longer in business). In this or any of the other gift clauses, your choice for alternate beneficiary may be one or more persons or an organization. It is recommended to always specifically name your beneficiary(ies), rather than using a description only, such as "my children." In addition, you may delete the alternate beneficiary choice and substitute the words "the residue" instead. The result of this change will be that if your primary beneficiary dies before you do, your gift will pass under your residuary clause, which is discussed below. If additional gifts are desired, simply photocopy an additional page to use as a worksheet.

Residuary Clause: Although not a technical legal requirement, it is strongly recommended that you include the residuary clause in every will. With this clause, you will choose the person(s) or organization(s) to receive anything not covered by other clauses of your will. Even if you feel that you have given away everything that you own under other clauses of your will, this can be a very important clause.

If, for any reason, any other gifts under your will are not able to be completed, this clause goes into effect. For example, if a beneficiary refuses to accept your gift, the chosen beneficiary has died and no alternate was selected, or both the beneficiary and alternate has died, the gift is put back into your estate and would *pass under* (be distributed under the terms of) the residuary clause. If there is no residuary clause included in your will, any property not disposed of under your will is treated as though you did not have a will and could potentially be forfeited to the state. To avoid this, it is strongly recommended that you make this clause mandatory in your will.

In addition, you may use this clause to give all of your estate (except your specific gifts) to one or more persons. For example: you make specific gifts of $1,000.00 to a sister and a car to a friend. By then naming your spouse as the residuary clause beneficiary, you will have gifted everything in your estate to your spouse—except the $1,000.00 and the car. You could then name your children, in equal shares, as the alternate residuary beneficiaries. In this manner, if your spouse were to die first, your children would then equally share your entire estate—except the $1,000.00 and the car.

Be sure to clearly identify the beneficiary by full name. The space provided for an identification of the relationship of the beneficiary can simply be a descriptive phrase like "my wife," "my brother-in-law," or "my best friend." It does not mean that the beneficiary must be related to you personally.

Survivorship Clause: This clause is included in every will. This clause provides for two possibilities. First, it provides for a required period of survival for any beneficiary, in order to receive a gift under your will. The practical effect of this is to be certain that your property passes under your will and not under that of a beneficiary who dies shortly after receiving your gift. The second portion of this clause provides for a determination of how your property should pass in the eventuality that both you and a beneficiary (most likely your spouse) should die in a manner that makes it impossible to determine who died first.

Without this clause in your will, it would be possible that property could momentarily pass to a beneficiary under your will. When that person dies (possibly immediately if a result of a common accident or disaster), your property could wind up being left to the person whom your beneficiary designated, rather than to your alternate beneficiary.

If you and your spouse are both preparing wills, it is a good idea to be certain that each of your wills contains identical survivorship clauses. If you are each other's primary beneficiary, it is also wise to attempt to coordinate who your alternate beneficiaries may be in the event of simultaneous deaths.

Executor Clause: The executor clause must be included in every will. With this clause, you will make your choice of executor, the person who will administer and distribute your estate, and an alternate choice if your first choice is unable to serve. A spouse, sibling, or other trusted party is usually chosen to act as executor. The person chosen should be a resident of the state in which you currently reside. Please refer to Chapter 5 for more information on executors.

Note that you allow your executor to seek independent administration of your estate. Where allowed by state law, this enables your executor to manage your estate with minimal court supervision and can save your estate extensive court costs and legal fees. Additionally, you grant the executor broad powers to manage your estate and also provide that he or she not be required to post a bond in order to be appointed to serve as executor.

Be sure to clearly identify the executor and alternate executor by full name. The space provided for an identification of the relationship of the executor can simply be a descriptive phrase like "my wife," "my brother-in-law," or "my best friend." It does not mean that the executor must be related to you personally.

Child Guardianship Clause: This clause will only be present in the pre-assembled wills that relate to children. With this clause you may designate your choice as to whom you wish to care for any of your minor children after you are gone. If none of your children are minors, you may delete this clause.

Who you choose to be the guardian of your children is an important matter. If you are married, your spouse is generally appointed by the probate or family court, regardless of your designation in a will. However, even if you are married, it is a good idea to choose your spouse as first choice and then provide a second choice. This will cover the contingency in which both you and your spouse die in a single accident.

Your choice should obviously be a trusted person whom you feel would provide the best care for your children in your absence. Be aware, however, that the court is guided, but not bound, by this particular choice in your will. The court's decision in appointing a child's guardian is based upon what would be in the best interests of the child. In most situations, however, a parent's choice as to who should be their child's guardian is almost universally followed by the courts. Additionally, you grant the guardian broad power to care for and manage your children's property and also provide that the appointed guardian not be required to post a bond in order to be appointed.

Be sure to clearly identify the guardian and alternate guardian by full name. The space provided for an identification of the relationship of the guardian can simply be a descriptive phrase like "my wife," "my brother-in-law," or "my best friend." It does not mean that the guardian must be related to you personally.

Children's Trust Fund Clause: This clause will only be present in the pre-assembled wills that relate to children. It is with this clause that you may set up a trust fund for any gifts you have made to your minor children. You also may delay the time when they will actually have unrestricted control over your gift. It is not recommended, however, to attempt to delay receipt of control beyond the age of 30. If you have left assets to more than one child, this clause provides that individual trusts be set up for each child. If none of your children are minors, you may delete this clause.

The choice for trustee under a children's trust should generally be the same person whom you have chosen to be the children's guardian. This is not, however, a requirement. The choice of trustee is generally a spouse if alive, with the alternate being a trusted friend or family member. Be sure to clearly identify the trustee and alternate trustee by full name. The space provided for an identification of the relationship of the trustee can simply be a descriptive phrase like "my wife," "my brother-in-law," or "my best friend." It does not mean that the trustee must be related to you personally.

The terms of the trust provide that the trustee may distribute any or all of the income or principal to the children as he or she deems necessary to provide for the children's health, support, and education. The trust will terminate when either the specific age is reached, all of the money is spent prior to that age, or the child dies prematurely. Upon termination, any remaining trust funds will be distributed to the child (beneficiary) if surviving; if not surviving, to the heirs of the beneficiary (if any); or if there are no heirs of the beneficiary, to the residue of your estate. Additionally, you grant the trustee broad power to manage the trust and also provide that he or she not be required to post a bond in order to be appointed.

Organ Donation Clause: The use of this clause is optional. If you choose not to use this clause, you may delete it from your will. Use this clause to provide for any use of your body after death. You may, if you so desire, limit your donation to certain parts; for example, your eyes. If so desired, simply delete "any of my body parts and/or organs" from the following provision and insert your chosen donation. A copy of your will or instructions regarding this donation should be kept in a place that is readily-accessible by your executor and spouse.

Funeral Arrangements Clause: The use of this clause is optional. If you choose not to use this clause, you may delete it from your will. Use this clause to make known your wishes as to funeral and burial arrangements. Since it may be difficult to obtain your will quickly in an emergency, it is also a good idea to leave information regarding these desires with your executor, your spouse, a close friend, or a relative.

Signature, Witness, and Notary Clauses: The signature lines and final paragraph of this clause must be included in your will. You will fill in the number of pages and the appropriate dates where indicated after you have properly typed your will or had it typed. The use of the notary acknowledgment, although not a strict legal necessity, is strongly recommended. This allows the will to become "self-proving" and the witnesses need not be called upon to testify in court at a later date (after your death) that they, indeed, signed the will as witnesses. Although a few states have not enacted legislation to allow for the use of this type of sworn and acknowledged testimony to be used in court, the current trend is to allow for its use in probate courts. This saves time, money, and trouble in having your will admitted to probate when necessary.

The actual signing of the will by both you and your witnesses will be explained in Chapter 10. Do *not* sign your will until you carefully follow the instructions contained in that chapter.

Instructions for Will for Married Person with Children (Using Children's Trust)

This will is appropriate for use by a married person with one or more children. There are also provisions in this will for use if the parent has minor children and desires to place the property and assets that may be left to the children into a trust fund. In addition, this will allows a parent to choose a person to act as guardian for any minor children. In most cases, a married person may desire to choose the other spouse as both trustee and guardian for any of their children, although this is not a legal requirement. If the parent has no minor children, the will clauses relating to the children's trust and to guardianship of the children may be deleted. Each spouse/parent must prepare his or her own will. Do not attempt to prepare a joint will for both you and your spouse together.

This will contains the following standard clauses:

- Title Clause
- Identification Clause
- Marital Status Clause
- Children Identification Clause
- Grandchildren Identification Clause
- Specific Gifts Clause
- Residuary Clause
- Survivorship Clause
- Executor Clause
- Guardianship Clause
- Children's Trust Fund Clause
- Organ Donation Clause
- Funeral Arrangements Clause
- Signature and Witness Clause

Fill in each of the appropriate blanks in this will using the information that you included in your Property and Beneficiary Questionnaires. Cross out any information that is not appropriate to your situation. The necessary information to be filled-in is noted below and should be written into the place where the corresponding number appears in the following will form.

①　Full name of testator

②　Full name of testator (and any other names that you are known by)

③　Full address of testator

④　Spouse's full name (give information on previous marriage, if necessary [see page 102])

⑤ Number of children
⑥ Child's name (repeat for each child)
⑦ Child's address (repeat for each child)
⑧ Child's date of birth (repeat for each child)

⑨ Number of grandchildren (if applicable)
⑩ Grandchild's name (repeat for each grandchild)
⑪ Grandchild's address (repeat for each grandchild)
⑫ Grandchild's date of birth (repeat for each grandchild)

⑬ Complete description of specific gift (repeat for each specific gift)
⑭ Full name of beneficiary (repeat for each specific gift)
⑮ Relationship of beneficiary to testator (repeat for each specific gift)
⑯ Full name of alternate beneficiary (repeat for each specific gift)
⑰ Relationship of alternate beneficiary to testator (repeat for each specific gift)

⑱ Full name of residual beneficiary
⑲ Relationship of residual beneficiary to testator
⑳ Full name of alternate residual beneficiary
㉑ Relationship of alternate residual beneficiary to testator

㉒ Full name of executor
㉓ Relationship of executor to testator
㉔ Full address of executor
㉕ Full name of alternate executor
㉖ Relationship of alternate executor to testator
㉗ Full address of alternate executor

㉘ Full name of guardian of children
㉙ Relationship of guardian of children to testator
㉚ Full address of guardian of children
㉛ Full name of alternate guardian of children
㉜ Relationship of alternate guardian of children to testator
㉝ Full address of alternate guardian of children

㉞ Children's age to be subject to children's trust
㉟ Children's age for end of children's trust (21, 25, or 30 years old or older)
㊱ Full name of trustee of children's trust
㊲ Relationship of trustee of children's trust to testator
㊳ Full address of trustee of children's trust
㊴ Full name of alternate trustee of children's trust
㊵ Relationship of alternate trustee of children's trust to testator
㊶ Full address of alternate trustee of children's trust

ⓐ   Name of funeral home
ⓐ   Address of funeral home
ⓐ   Name of cemetery
ⓐ   Address of cemetery

Number of total pages of will (fill in when will is typed or printed)
Date of signing of will (DO NOT FILL IN YET)
Signature of testator (DO NOT FILL IN YET)
Printed name of testator (DO NOT FILL IN YET)
Date of witnessing of will (DO NOT FILL IN YET)
Signature of witness (repeat for each witness) [DO NOT FILL IN YET]
Printed name of witness (repeat for each witness) [DO NOT FILL IN YET]
Address of witness (repeat for each witness) [DO NOT FILL IN YET]

ⓐ   Notary Acknowledgment (to be filled in by Notary Public)

Will for Married Person with Children (Using Children's Trust)

Last Will and Testament of ①

I, ② ,
whose address is ③ ,
declare that this is my Last Will and Testament and I revoke all previous wills.

I am married to ④ .

I have ⑤ child(ren) living. His/Her/Their name(s), address(es), and date(s) of birth is/are as follows:
⑥
⑦
⑧

⑥
⑦
⑧

⑥
⑦
⑧

I have ⑨ grandchild(ren) living. His/Her/Their name(s), address(es), and date(s) of birth is/are as follows:
⑩
⑪
⑫

⑩
⑪
⑫

⑩
⑪
⑫

Page ___ of ___ pages

Testator's initials _____

I make the following specific gifts:

I give ⑬ ,
to ⑭ ,
my ⑮ ,
or if not surviving, then to ⑯ ,
my ⑰ .

I give ⑬ ,
to ⑭ ,
my ⑮ ,
or if not surviving, then to ⑯ ,
my ⑰ .

I give ⑬ ,
to ⑭ ,
my ⑮ ,
or if not surviving, then to ⑯ ,
my ⑰ .

I give ⑬ ,
to ⑭ ,
my ⑮ ,
or if not surviving, then to ⑯ ,
my ⑰ .

I give ⑬ ,
to ⑭ ,
my ⑮ ,
or if not surviving, then to ⑯ ,
my ⑰ .

I give ⑬ ,
to ⑭ ,
my ⑮ ,
or if not surviving, then to ⑯ ,
my ⑰ .

I give ⑬ ,
to ⑭ ,
my ⑮ ,
or if not surviving, then to ⑯ ,
my ⑰ .

Page ___ of ___ pages   Testator's initials _____

I give all the rest of my property, whether real or personal, wherever located,
to ⑱ ,
my ⑲ ,
or if not surviving, to ⑳ ,
my ㉑ .

All beneficiaries named in this will must survive me by thirty (30) days to receive any gift under this will. If any beneficiary and I should die simultaneously, I shall be conclusively presumed to have survived that beneficiary for purposes of this will.

I appoint ㉒ ,
my ㉓ ,
of ㉔ ,
as Executor, to serve without bond. If not surviving or otherwise unable to serve,
I appoint ㉕ ,
my ㉖ ,
of ㉗ ,
as Alternate Executor, also to serve without bond. In addition to any powers, authority, and discretion granted by law, I grant such Executor or Alternate Executor any and all powers to perform any acts, in his/her sole discretion and without court approval, for the management and distribution of my estate, including independent administration of my estate.

If a Guardian is needed for any of my minor child(ren),
I appoint ㉘ ,
my ㉙ ,
of ㉚ ,
as Guardian of the person and property of any of my minor child(ren), to serve without bond. If not surviving, or unable to serve,
I appoint ㉛ ,
my ㉜ ,
of ㉝ ,
as alternate Guardian, also to serve without bond. In addition to any powers, authority, and discretion granted by law, I grant such Guardian or Alternate Guardian any and all powers to perform any acts, in his/her sole discretion and without court approval, for the management and distribution of the property of any of my minor child(ren).

If any of my child(ren) are under ㉞ years of age, upon my death, I direct that any property that I give each child under this will be held in an individual trust for each child(ren), under the following terms, until each shall reach ㉟ years of age.

Page ___ of ___ pages   Testator's initials _____

In addition, I appoint �36 ,
my �37 ,
of �38 ,
as trustee of any and all required trusts, to serve without bond. If not surviving, or otherwise unable to serve, then I appoint �39 ,
my �40 ,
of �41 ,
as alternate Trustee, also to serve without bond. In addition to all powers, authority, and discretion granted by law, I grant such trustee or alternate trustee full power to perform any act, in his/her sole discretion and without court approval, to distribute and manage the assets of any such trust.

In the trustee's sole discretion, the trustee may distribute any or all of the principal, income, or both, of any such trust as deemed necessary for the beneficiary's health, support, welfare, and education. Any income not distributed shall be added to the trust principal.

Any such trust shall terminate when the beneficiary reaches the required age, when the beneficiary dies prior to reaching the required age, or when all trust funds have been distributed. Upon termination, any remaining undistributed principal and income shall pass to the beneficiary; or if not surviving, to the beneficiary's heirs; or if none, to the residue of my estate.

I also declare that, pursuant to the Uniform Anatomical Gift Act, I donate any of my body parts and/or organs to any medical institution willing to accept and use them, and I direct my executor to carry out such donation.

Funeral arrangements have been made with the �42 ,
of �43 ,
for burial at �44 ,
located in �45 ,
and I direct my Executor to carry out such arrangements.

I publish and sign this Last Will and Testament, consisting of _____ typewritten pages, on _____ , and declare that I do so freely, for the purposes expressed, under no constraint or undue influence, and that I am of sound mind and of legal age.

_____   _____
Signature of Testator   Printed Name of Testator

We, the undersigned, being first sworn on oath and under penalty of perjury, state that:

On _____ , in the presence of all of us, the above-named Testator published and signed this Last Will and Testament, and then at Testator's request, and in Testator's presence, and in each other's presence, we all signed below as witnesses, and we declare that, to the best of our knowledge, the Testator signed this instrument freely, under no constraint or undue influence, and is of sound mind and legal age.

_____   _____
Signature of Witness   Signature of Witness

_____   _____
Printed Name of Witness   Printed Name of Witness

_____   _____
Address of Witness   Address of Witness

_____
Signature of Witness

_____
Printed Name of Witness

_____
Address of Witness

㊻ Notary Acknowledgment

State of _____
County of _____

On _____ , _____ the testator, and
_____ , _____ , and
_____ , the witnesses, personally came before me and, being duly sworn, did state that they are the persons described in the above document and that they signed the above document in my presence as a free and voluntary act for the purposes stated.

_____
Signature of Notary Public

Notary Public, In and for the County of _____
State of _____

My commission expires: _____   Notary Seal

Page ___ of ___ pages   Testator's initials _____

Instructions for Will for Single Person with Children
(Using Children's Trust)

This will is appropriate for use by a single person with one or more children. There are also provisions in this will for use if the parent has minor children and desires to place the property and assets that may be left to the children into a trust fund. In addition, this will allows a parent to choose a person to act as guardian for any minor children. In most cases, a parent may desire to choose the other parent as both trustee and guardian for any of their children, although this is not a legal requirement and may not be the best solution if the parents are divorced. If the parent has no minor children, the will clauses relating to the children's trust and to guardianship of the children may be deleted.

This will contains the following standard clauses:

- Title Clause
- Identification Clause
- Marital Status Clause
- Children Identification Clause
- Grandchildren Identification Clause
- Specific Gifts Clause
- Residuary Clause
- Survivorship Clause
- Executor Clause
- Guardianship Clause
- Children's Trust Fund Clause
- Organ Donation Clause
- Funeral Arrangements Clause
- Signature and Witness Clause

Fill in each of the appropriate blanks in this will using the information that you included in your Property and Beneficiary Questionnaires. Cross out any information that is not appropriate to your situation. The necessary information to be filled-in is noted below and should be written into the place where the corresponding number appears in the following will form.

① Full name of testator
② Full name of testator (and any other names that you are known by)
③ Full address of testator

(Give information on previous marriage, if necessary [see page 102])

④ Number of children
⑤ Child's name (repeat for each child)
⑥ Child's address (repeat for each child)
⑦ Child's date of birth (repeat for each child)

⑧ Number of grandchildren (if applicable)
⑨ Grandchild's name (repeat for each grandchild)
⑩ Grandchild's address (repeat for each grandchild)
⑪ Grandchild's date of birth (repeat for each grandchild)

⑫ Complete description of specific gift (repeat for each specific gift)
⑬ Full name of beneficiary (repeat for each specific gift)
⑭ Relationship of beneficiary to testator (repeat for each specific gift)
⑮ Full name of alternate beneficiary (repeat for each specific gift)
⑯ Relationship of alternate beneficiary to testator (repeat for each specific gift)

⑰ Full name of residual beneficiary
⑱ Relationship of residual beneficiary to testator
⑲ Full name of alternate residual beneficiary
⑳ Relationship of alternate residual beneficiary to testator

㉑ Full name of executor
㉒ Relationship of executor to testator
㉓ Full address of executor
㉔ Full name of alternate executor
㉕ Relationship of alternate executor to testator
㉖ Full address of alternate executor

㉗ Full name of guardian of children
㉘ Relationship of guardian of children to testator
㉙ Full address of guardian of children
㉚ Full name of alternate guardian of children
㉛ Relationship of alternate guardian of children to testator
㉜ Full address of alternate guardian of children

㉝ Children's age to be subject to children's trust
㉞ Children's age for end of children's trust (21, 25, or 30 years old or older)
㉟ Full name of trustee of children's trust
㊱ Relationship of trustee of children's trust to testator
㊲ Full address of trustee of children's trust
㊳ Full name of alternate trustee of children's trust
㊴ Relationship of alternate trustee of children's trust to testator
㊵ Full address of alternate trustee of children's trust

④① Name of funeral home
④② Address of funeral home
④③ Name of cemetery
④④ Address of cemetery

Number of total pages of will (fill in when will is typed or printed)
Date of signing of will (DO NOT FILL IN YET)
Signature of testator (DO NOT FILL IN YET)
Printed name of testator (DO NOT FILL IN YET)
Date of witnessing of will (DO NOT FILL IN YET)
Signature of witness (repeat for each witness) [DO NOT FILL IN YET]
Printed name of witness (repeat for each witness) [DO NOT FILL IN YET]
Address of witness (repeat for each witness) [DO NOT FILL IN YET]

④⑤ Notary Acknowledgment (to be filled in by Notary Public)

Will for Single Person with Children (Using Children's Trust)

Last Will and Testament of ①

I, ② ,
whose address is ③ ,
declare that this is my Last Will and Testament and I revoke all previous wills.

I am not currently married.

I have ④ child(ren) living. His/Her/Their name(s), address(es), and date(s) of birth is/are as follows:

⑤
⑥
⑦

⑤
⑥
⑦

⑤
⑥
⑦

I have ⑧ grandchild(ren) living. His/Her/Their name(s), address(es), and date(s) of birth is/are as follows:

⑨
⑩
⑪

⑨
⑩
⑪

⑨
⑩
⑪

Page ___ of ___ pages   Testator's initials _____

119

I make the following specific gifts:

I give ⑫ ,
to ⑬ ,
my ⑭ ,
or if not surviving, then to ⑮ ,
my ⑯ .

I give ⑫ ,
to ⑬ ,
my ⑭ ,
or if not surviving, then to ⑮ ,
my ⑯ .

I give ⑫ ,
to ⑬ ,
my ⑭ ,
or if not surviving, then to ⑮ ,
my ⑯ .

I give ⑫ ,
to ⑬ ,
my ⑭ ,
or if not surviving, then to ⑮ ,
my ⑯ .

I give ⑫ ,
to ⑬ ,
my ⑭ ,
or if not surviving, then to ⑮ ,
my ⑯ .

I give ⑫ ,
to ⑬ ,
my ⑭ ,
or if not surviving, then to ⑮ ,
my ⑯ .

I give ⑫ ,
to ⑬ ,
my ⑭ ,
or if not surviving, then to ⑮ ,
my ⑯ .

Page ___ of ___ pages

I give all the rest of my property, whether real or personal, wherever located,
to ⑰ ,
my ⑱ ,
or if not surviving, to ⑲ ,
my ⑳ .

All beneficiaries named in this will must survive me by thirty (30) days to receive any gift under this will. If any beneficiary and I should die simultaneously, I shall be conclusively presumed to have survived that beneficiary for purposes of this will.

I appoint ㉑ ,
my ㉒ ,
of ㉓ ,
as Executor, to serve without bond. If not surviving or otherwise unable to serve,
I appoint ㉔ ,
my ㉕ ,
of ㉖ ,
as Alternate Executor, also to serve without bond. In addition to any powers, authority, and discretion granted by law, I grant such Executor or Alternate Executor any and all powers to perform any acts, in his or her sole discretion and without court approval, for the management and distribution of my estate, including independent administration of my estate.

If a Guardian is needed for any of my minor child(ren),
I appoint ㉗ ,
my ㉘ ,
of ㉙ ,
as Guardian of the person and property of any of my minor child(ren), to serve without bond. If not surviving, or unable to serve,
I appoint ㉚ ,
my ㉛ ,
of ㉜ ,
as alternate Guardian, also to serve without bond. In addition to any powers, authority, and discretion granted by law, I grant such Guardian or Alternate Guardian any and all powers to perform any acts, in his/her sole discretion and without court approval, for the management and distribution of the property of any of my minor child(ren).

If any of my child(ren) are under ㉝ years of age, upon my death, I direct that any property that I give each child under this will be held in an individual trust for each child(ren), under the following terms, until each shall reach ㉞ years of age.

Page ___ of ___ pages   Testator's initials _____

In addition, I appoint ㉟ ,
my ㊱ ,
of ㊲ ,
as trustee of any and all required trusts, to serve without bond. If not surviving, or otherwise unable to serve, then I appoint ㊳ ,
my ㊴ ,
of ㊵ ,
as alternate Trustee, also to serve without bond. In addition to all powers, authority, and discretion granted by law, I grant such trustee or alternate trustee full power to perform any act, in his/her sole discretion and without court approval, to distribute and manage the assets of any such trust.

In the trustee's sole discretion, the trustee may distribute any or all of the principal, income, or both, of any such trust as deemed necessary for the beneficiary's health, support, welfare, and education. Any income not distributed shall be added to the trust principal.

Any such trust shall terminate when the beneficiary reaches the required age, when the beneficiary dies prior to reaching the required age, or when all trust funds have been distributed. Upon termination, any remaining undistributed principal and income shall pass to the beneficiary; or if not surviving, to the beneficiary's heirs; or if none, to the residue of my estate.

I also declare that, pursuant to the Uniform Anatomical Gift Act, I donate any of my body parts and/or organs to any medical institution willing to accept and use them, and I direct my executor to carry out such donation.

Funeral arrangements have been made with the ㊶ ,
of ㊷ ,
for burial at ㊸ ,
located in ㊹ ,
and I direct my Executor to carry out such arrangements.

I publish and sign this Last Will and Testament, consisting of _____ typewritten pages, on _____ , and declare that I do so freely, for the purposes expressed, under no constraint or undue influence, and that I am of sound mind and of legal age.

_____   _____
Signature of Testator   Printed Name of Testator

We, the undersigned, being first sworn on oath and under penalty of perjury, state that:

On _____ , in the presence of all of us, the above-named Testator published and signed this Last Will and Testament, and then at Testator's request, and in Testator's presence, and in each other's presence, we all signed below as witnesses, and we declare that, to the best of our knowledge, the Testator signed this instrument freely, under no constraint or undue influence, and is of sound mind and legal age.

_____
Signature of Witness

_____
Printed Name of Witness

_____
Address of Witness

_____
Signature of Witness

_____
Printed Name of Witness

_____
Address of Witness

_____
Signature of Witness

_____
Printed Name of Witness

_____
Address of Witness

㊺ Notary Acknowledgment

State of _____
County of _____

On _____ , _____ the testator, and
_____ , _____ , and
_____ , the witnesses, personally came before me and, being duly sworn, did state that they are the persons described in the above document and that they signed the above document in my presence as a free and voluntary act for the purposes stated.

_____
Signature of Notary Public

Notary Public, In and for the County of _____
State of _____

My commission expires: _____

Page ___ of ___ pages

Notary Seal

Testator's initials _____

Instructions for Will for Married Person with No Children

This will is appropriate for use by a married person with no children or grandchildren. Each spouse must prepare his or her own will. Do not attempt to prepare a joint will for both you and your spouse together.

This will contains the following standard clauses:

- Title Clause
- Identification Clause
- Marital Status Clause
- Specific Gifts Clause
- Residuary Clause
- Survivorship Clause
- Executor Clause
- Organ Donation Clause
- Funeral Arrangements Clause
- Signature and Witness Clause

Fill in each of the appropriate blanks in this will using the information that you included in your Property and Beneficiary Questionnaires. Cross out any information that is not appropriate to your situation. The necessary information to be filled-in is noted below and should be written into the place where the corresponding number appears in the following will form.

① Full name of testator
② Full name of testator (and any other names that you are known by)
③ Full address of testator

④ Spouse's full name (give information on previous marriage, if necessary [see page 102])

⑤ Complete description of specific gift (repeat for each specific gift)
⑥ Full name of beneficiary (repeat for each specific gift)
⑦ Relationship of beneficiary to testator (repeat for each specific gift)
⑧ Full name of alternate beneficiary (repeat for each specific gift)
⑨ Relationship of alternate beneficiary to testator (repeat for each specific gift)

⑩ Full name of residual beneficiary
⑪ Relationship of residual beneficiary to testator
⑫ Full name of alternate residual beneficiary
⑬ Relationship of alternate residual beneficiary to testator

⑭ Full name of executor
⑮ Relationship of executor to testator
⑯ Full address of executor
⑰ Full name of alternate executor
⑱ Relationship of alternate executor to testator
⑲ Full address of alternate executor

⑳ Name of funeral home
㉑ Address of funeral home
㉒ Name of cemetery
㉓ Address of cemetery

Number of total pages of will (fill in when will is typed or printed)
Date of signing of will (DO NOT FILL IN YET)
Signature of testator (DO NOT FILL IN YET)
Printed name of testator (DO NOT FILL IN YET)
Date of witnessing of will (DO NOT FILL IN YET)
Signature of witness (repeat for each witness) [DO NOT FILL IN YET]
Printed name of witness (repeat for each witness) [DO NOT FILL IN YET]
Address of witness (repeat for each witness) [DO NOT FILL IN YET]

㉔ Notary Acknowledgment (to be filled in by Notary Public)

Will for Married Person with No Children

Last Will and Testament of ①

I, ② ,
whose address is ③ ,
declare that this is my Last Will and Testament and I revoke all previous wills.

I am married to ④ .

I have no children or grandchildren living.

I make the following specific gifts:

I give ⑤ ,
to ⑥ ,
my ⑦ ,
or if not surviving, then to ⑧ ,
my ⑨ .

I give ⑤ ,
to ⑥ ,
my ⑦ ,
or if not surviving, then to ⑧ ,
my ⑨ .

I give ⑤ ,
to ⑥ ,
my ⑦ ,
or if not surviving, then to ⑧ ,
my ⑨ .

I give ⑤ ,
to ⑥ ,
my ⑦ ,
or if not surviving, then to ⑧ ,
my ⑨ .

Page ___ of ___ pages   Testator's initials _____

I give ⑤ ,
to ⑥ ,
my ⑦ ,
or if not surviving, then to ⑧ ,
my ⑨ .

I give ⑤ ,
to ⑥ ,
my ⑦ ,
or if not surviving, then to ⑧ ,
my ⑨ .

I give ⑤ ,
to ⑥ ,
my ⑦ ,
or if not surviving, then to ⑧ ,
my ⑨ .

I give ⑤ ,
to ⑥ ,
my ⑦ ,
or if not surviving, then to ⑧ ,
my ⑨ .

I give ⑤ ,
to ⑥ ,
my ⑦ ,
or if not surviving, then to ⑧ ,
my ⑨ .

I give ⑤ ,
to ⑥ ,
my ⑦ ,
or if not surviving, then to ⑧ ,
my ⑨ .

I give ⑤ ,
to ⑥ ,
my ⑦ ,
or if not surviving, then to ⑧ ,
my ⑨ .

Page ____ of ____ pages   Testator's initials _____

I give all the rest of my property, whether real or personal, wherever located,
to ⑩ ,
my ⑪ ,
or if not surviving, to ⑫ ,
my ⑬ .

All beneficiaries named in this will must survive me by thirty (30) days to receive any gift under this will. If any beneficiary and I should die simultaneously, I shall be conclusively presumed to have survived that beneficiary for purposes of this will.

I appoint ⑭ ,
my ⑮ ,
of ⑯ ,
as Executor, to serve without bond. If not surviving or otherwise unable to serve,
I appoint ⑰ ,
my ⑱ ,
of ⑲ ,
as Alternate Executor, also to serve without bond. In addition to any powers, authority, and discretion granted by law, I grant such Executor or Alternate Executor any and all powers to perform any acts, in his/her sole discretion and without court approval, for the management and distribution of my estate, including independent administration of my estate.

I also declare that, pursuant to the Uniform Anatomical Gift Act, I donate any of my body parts and/or organs to any medical institution willing to accept and use them, and I direct my executor to carry out such donation.

Funeral arrangements have been made with the ⑳ ,
of ㉑ ,
for burial at ㉒ ,
located in ㉓ ,
and I direct my Executor to carry out such arrangements.

I publish and sign this Last Will and Testament, consisting of _____ typewritten pages,
on _____ , and declare that I do so freely, for the purposes expressed, under no constraint or undue influence, and that I am of sound mind and of legal age.

_____   _____
Signature of Testator   Printed Name of Testator

Page ___ of ___ pages   Testator's initials _____

We, the undersigned, being first sworn on oath and under penalty of perjury, state that:

On _____ , in the presence of all of us, the above-named Testator published and signed this Last Will and Testament, and then at Testator's request, and in Testator's presence, and in each other's presence, we all signed below as witnesses, and we declare that, to the best of our knowledge, the Testator signed this instrument freely, under no constraint or undue influence, and is of sound mind and legal age.

_____
Signature of Witness

_____
Printed Name of Witness

_____
Address of Witness

_____
Signature of Witness

_____
Printed Name of Witness

_____
Signature of Witness

_____
Printed Name of Witness

_____
Address of Witness

_____
Address of Witness

㉔ Notary Acknowledgment

State of _____
County of _____

On _____ , _____ the testator, and
_____ , _____ , and
_____ , the witnesses, personally came before me and, being duly sworn, did state that they are the persons described in the above document and that they signed the above document in my presence as a free and voluntary act for the purposes stated.

_____
Signature of Notary Public

Notary Public, In and for the County of _____
State of _____

My commission expires: _____   Notary Seal

Page ___ of ___ pages   Testator's initials _____

Instructions for Will for Single Person with No Children

This will is appropriate for use by a single person with no children or grandchildren. This will contains the following standard clauses:

- Title Clause
- Identification Clause
- Marital Status Clause
- Specific Gifts Clause
- Residuary Clause
- Survivorship Clause
- Executor Clause
- Organ Donation Clause
- Funeral Arrangements Clause
- Signature and Witness Clause

Fill in each of the appropriate blanks in this will using the information that you included in your Property and Beneficiary Questionnaires. Cross out any information that is not appropriate to your situation. The necessary information to be filled-in is noted below and should be written into the place where the corresponding number appears in the following will form.

① Full name of testator
② Full name of testator (and any other names that you are known by)
③ Full address of testator

(Give information on previous marriage, if necessary [see page 102])

④ Complete description of specific gift (repeat for each specific gift)
⑤ Full name of beneficiary (repeat for each specific gift)
⑥ Relationship of beneficiary to testator (repeat for each specific gift)
⑦ Full name of alternate beneficiary (repeat for each specific gift)
⑧ Relationship of alternate beneficiary to testator (repeat for each specific gift)

⑨ Full name of residual beneficiary
⑩ Relationship of residual beneficiary to testator
⑪ Full name of alternate residual beneficiary
⑫ Relationship of alternate residual beneficiary to testator

⑬ Full name of executor
⑭ Relationship of executor to testator
⑮ Full address of executor

⑯ Full name of alternate executor
⑰ Relationship of alternate executor to testator
⑱ Full address of alternate executor

⑲ Name of funeral home
⑳ Address of funeral home
㉑ Name of cemetery
㉒ Address of cemetery

Number of total pages of will (fill in when will is typed or printed)
Date of signing of will (DO NOT FILL IN YET)
Signature of testator (DO NOT FILL IN YET)
Printed name of testator (DO NOT FILL IN YET)
Date of witnessing of will (DO NOT FILL IN YET)
Signature of witness (repeat for each witness) [DO NOT FILL IN YET]
Printed name of witness (repeat for each witness) [DO NOT FILL IN YET]
Address of witness (repeat for each witness) [DO NOT FILL IN YET]

㉓ Notary Acknowledgment (to be filled in by Notary Public)

Will for Single Person with No Children

Last Will and Testament of ①

I, ② ,
whose address is ③ ,
declare that this is my Last Will and Testament and I revoke all previous wills.

I am not currently married.

I have no children or grandchildren living.

I make the following specific gifts:

I give ④ ,
to ⑤ ,
my ⑥ ,
or if not surviving, then to ⑦ ,
my ⑧ .

I give ④ ,
to ⑤ ,
my ⑥ ,
or if not surviving, then to ⑦ ,
my ⑧ .

I give ④ ,
to ⑤ ,
my ⑥ ,
or if not surviving, then to ⑦ ,
my ⑧ .

I give ④ ,
to ⑤ ,
my ⑥ ,
or if not surviving, then to ⑦ ,
my ⑧ .

Page ___ of ___ pages   Testator's initials _____

I give ④ ,
to ⑤ ,
my ⑥ ,
or if not surviving, then to ⑦ ,
my ⑧ .

I give ④ ,
to ⑤ ,
my ⑥ ,
or if not surviving, then to ⑦ ,
my ⑧ .

I give ④ ,
to ⑤ ,
my ⑥ ,
or if not surviving, then to ⑦ ,
my ⑧ .

I give ④ ,
to ⑤ ,
my ⑥ ,
or if not surviving, then to ⑦ ,
my ⑧ .

I give ④ ,
to ⑤ ,
my ⑥ ,
or if not surviving, then to ⑦ ,
my ⑧ .

I give ④ ,
to ⑤ ,
my ⑥ ,
or if not surviving, then to ⑦ ,
my ⑧ .

I give ④ ,
to ⑤ ,
my ⑥ ,
or if not surviving, then to ⑦ ,
my ⑧ .

Page ___ of ___ pages

Testator's initials _____

I give all the rest of my property, whether real or personal, wherever located,
to ⑨ ,
my ⑩ ,
or if not surviving, to ⑪ ,
my ⑫ .

All beneficiaries named in this will must survive me by thirty (30) days to receive any gift under this will. If any beneficiary and I should die simultaneously, I shall be conclusively presumed to have survived that beneficiary for purposes of this will.

I appoint ⑬ ,
my ⑭ ,
of ⑮ ,
as Executor, to serve without bond. If not surviving or otherwise unable to serve,
I appoint ⑯ ,
my ⑰ ,
of ⑱ ,
as Alternate Executor, also to serve without bond. In addition to any powers, authority, and discretion granted by law, I grant such Executor or Alternate Executor any and all powers to perform any acts, in his/her sole discretion and without court approval, for the management and distribution of my estate, including independent administration of my estate.

I also declare that, pursuant to the Uniform Anatomical Gift Act, I donate any of my body parts and/or organs to any medical institution willing to accept and use them, and I direct my executor to carry out such donation.

Funeral arrangements have been made with the ⑲ ,
of ⑳ ,
for burial at ㉑ ,
located in ㉒ ,
and I direct my Executor to carry out such arrangements.

I publish and sign this Last Will and Testament, consisting of _____ typewritten pages,
on _____ , and declare that I do so freely, for the purposes expressed, under no constraint or undue influence, and that I am of sound mind and of legal age.

_____   _____
Signature of Testator   Printed Name of Testator

Page ___ of ___ pages   Testator's initials _____

We, the undersigned, being first sworn on oath and under penalty of perjury, state that:

On _____ , in the presence of all of us, the above-named Testator published and signed this Last Will and Testament, and then at Testator's request, and in Testator's presence, and in each other's presence, we all signed below as witnesses, and we declare that, to the best of our knowledge, the Testator signed this instrument freely, under no constraint or undue influence, and is of sound mind and legal age.

_____
Signature of Witness

_____
Printed Name of Witness

_____
Address of Witness

_____
Signature of Witness

_____
Printed Name of Witness

_____
Address of Witness

_____
Signature of Witness

_____
Printed Name of Witness

_____
Address of Witness

㉓ Notary Acknowledgment

State of _____
County of _____

On _____ , _____ the testator, and
_____ , _____ , and
_____ , the witnesses, personally came before me and, being duly sworn, did state that they are the persons described in the above document and that they signed the above document in my presence as a free and voluntary act for the purposes stated.

_____
Signature of Notary Public

Notary Public, In and for the County of _____
State of _____

My commission expires: _____

Page ___ of ___ pages

Notary Seal

Testator's initials _____

CHAPTER 8

Sample Will

In this chapter, a complete sample will is presented. It was prepared based on the will for a married person with children contained in Chapter 6. By reviewing this sample will, you will be able to see what a completed will should look like and how the various parts are put together.

In this sample will, a Mrs. Mary Smith is the fictional testator. Mrs. Smith is married to Mr. John Smith, and they have two minor children who live with them. In her will, Mrs. Smith wishes to accomplish the following:

- Leave her oval diamond necklace to a friend
- Leave her brown mink coat to her mother
- Leave $10,000.00 to each of her children, to be held in trust until they are 21 years old
- Leave all the rest of her estate to her husband
- Appoint her husband to act as:
  - Executor of the will
  - Guardian of the children
  - Trustee of the children's trust
- Declare her intention to be an organ donor
- Designate her intentions for funeral arrangements

By filling in the appropriate blanks in the pre-assembled will, the fictional Mrs. Mary Smith is able to easily and quickly prepare a will that accomplishes all of her desires. She may rest assured that, by having properly prepared and signed a Last Will and Testament, her wishes will be carried out upon her death. It would be advisable for Mrs. Smith's husband to also prepare a will that includes similar provisions for survivorship and reciprocal provisions for guardianship and trust funds.

Last Will and Testament of Mary Ellen Smith

I, Mary Ellen Smith, whose address is 16 Main Street, Centerville, IL, declare that this is my Last Will and Testament and I revoke all previous wills.

I am married to John Alan Smith. I was previously married to Robert David Jones. That marriage ended on April 12, 1998, by divorce.

I have two [2] children living. Their names, addresses, and dates of birth are as follows:

Name	Address	Date of Birth
Alice Mary Smith	16 Main Street, Centerville, IL	April 21, 2000
James John Smith	16 Main Street, Centerville, IL	October 26, 2001

I have no grandchildren living.

I make the following specific gifts:

I give my Tiffany Oval Diamond and Gold necklace to Susie Mitchell, my good friend, or if not surviving, then to the residue of my estate.

I give my Brown Mink Coat, which was a gift from my husband, John, to Mrs. Mary Stuart, my mother, or if not surviving, then to John Alan Smith, my husband.

I give Ten Thousand Dollars cash [$10,000.00] to Alice Mary Smith, my daughter, or if not surviving, then to the residue of my estate.

I give Ten Thousand Dollars cash [$10,000.00] to James John Smith, my son, or if not surviving, then to the residue of my estate.

I give all the rest of my property, whether real or personal, wherever located, to John Alan Smith, my husband, or if not surviving, to Alice Mary Smith and James John Smith, my children, in equal shares.

All beneficiaries named in this will must survive me by thirty [30] days to receive any gift under this will. If any beneficiary and I should die simultaneously, I shall be conclusively presumed to have survived that beneficiary for purposes of this will.

I appoint John Alan Smith, my husband, of 16 Main Street, Centerville, IL, as Executor, to serve without bond. If not surviving or otherwise unable to serve, I appoint Harold Stuart, my brother, of 2676 State Street, Middleton, IA, as Alternate Executor, also to serve without bond. In addition to any powers, authority, and discretion granted by law, I grant such Executor or Alternate Executor any and all powers to perform any acts, in his sole discretion and without court approval, for the management and distribution of my estate, including independent administration of my estate.

If a Guardian is needed for any of my minor children, I appoint John Alan Smith, my husband, of 16 Main Street, Centerville, IL, as Guardian of the person and property of my minor children, to serve without bond. If not surviving or unable to serve, I appoint Harold Stuart, my brother, of 2676 State Street, Middleton, IA, as alternate Guardian, also to serve without bond. In addition to any powers, authority, and discretion granted by law, I grant such Guardian or Alternate Guardian any and all powers to perform any acts, in his sole discretion and without court approval, for the management and distribution of the property of any of my minor children.

If any of my children are under 21 years of age, upon my death, I direct that any property that I give them under this will be held in an individual trust for each child, under the following terms, until each shall reach 21 years of age.

In addition, I appoint John Alan Smith, my husband, of 16 Main Street, Centerville, IL, as trustee of any and all required trusts, to serve without bond. If not surviving, or otherwise unable to serve, then I appoint Harold Stuart, my brother, of 2676 State Street, Middleton, IA, as alternate Trustee, also to serve without bond. In addition to all powers, authority, and discretion granted by law, I grant such trustee or alternate trustee full power to perform any act, in his sole discretion and without court approval, to distribute and manage the assets of any such trust.

In the trustee's sole discretion, the trustee may distribute any or all of the principal, income, or both, of any such trust as deemed necessary for the beneficiary's health, support, welfare, and education. Any income not distributed shall be added to the trust principal.

Any such trust shall terminate when the beneficiary reaches the required age, when the beneficiary dies prior to reaching the required age, or when all trust funds have been distributed. Upon termination, any remaining undistributed principal and income shall pass to the beneficiary; or if not surviving, to the beneficiary's heirs; or if none, to the residue of my estate.

Testator's initials _MS_

I also declare that, pursuant to the Uniform Anatomical Gift Act, I donate any of my body parts and/or organs to any medical institution willing to accept and use them, and I direct my executor to carry out such donation.

Funeral arrangements have been made with the Centerville Funeral Parlor, of Centerville, IL, for burial at Shady Hill Cemetery, located in Centerville, IL, and I direct my Executor to carry out such arrangements.

I publish and sign this Last Will and Testament, consisting of four [4] typewritten pages, on June 10, 2005, and declare that I do so freely, for the purposes expressed, under no constraint or undue influence, and that I am of sound mind and of legal age.

Mary Ellen Smith
Signature of Testator

Mary Ellen Smith
Printed Name of Testator

We, the undersigned, being first sworn on oath and under penalty of perjury, state that:

On June 10, 2005, in the presence of all of us, the above-named Testator published and signed this Last Will and Testament, and then at Testator's request, and in Testator's presence, and in each other's presence, we all signed below as witnesses, and we declare that, to the best of our knowledge, the Testator signed this instrument freely, under no constraint or undue influence, and is of sound mind and legal age.

Joan Andrews
Signature of Witness

Christopher Williams
Signature of Witness

Joan Andrews
Printed Name of Witness

Christopher Williams
Printed Name of Witness

12 Main Street, Centerville, IL
Address of Witness

1212 State Street, Centerville, IL
Address of Witness

Sandra Wright
Signature of Witness

Sandra Wright
Printed Name of Witness

64 Meadow Lane, Windsor, IL
Address of Witness

Notary Acknowledgment

State of Illinois
County of Washington

On June 10, 2005, Mary Ellen Smith, the testator, and Joan Andrews, Christopher Williams, and Sandra Wright, the witnesses, personally came before me and, being duly sworn, did state that they are the persons described in the above document and that they signed the above document in my presence as a free and voluntary act for the purposes stated.

Robert Merlin
Signature of Notary Public

Notary Public, In and for the County of Washington
State of Illinois

My commission expires: June 28, 2007

```
Notary Seal
```

Testator's initials *MS*

CHAPTER 9

Preparing Your Will

As you have noted in the sample will in the previous chapter, there is nothing very complicated about the arrangement of your will. This chapter will explain how to put your own will together, properly type it or have it typed, and have it readied for your signature. Using your Property and Beneficiary Questionnaires as guides, you should already have selected and filled in the necessary information on the appropriate will clauses from Chapter 6 or on one of the pre-assembled wills from Chapter 7.

Below are instructions for preparing the final version of your will. As you go about preparing your will, take your time and be very careful to proofread the original will before you sign it, to be certain that it states your desires exactly.

Instructions for Preparing Your Will

1. You should have before you a completed and filled-in photocopy worksheet of the will that you have chosen. On the photocopy worksheet version of your will, cross out all extraneous material that is not to become a part of your will. Then, carefully reread the entire worksheet version of your will to be certain that it is exactly as you wish.

2. After making any necessary changes, type or have typed the entire will on good quality 8-½" x 11" typing paper. (Note: if you are using the Forms-on-CD that accompanies some editions of this book, follow the instructions that are included on the Readme document included on the CD).

3. After you have completed typing your will, fill in the total number of pages in the Signature paragraph. At the bottom of each page, also fill in the page number and the total number of pages. Do not yet sign your will, fill in the date, or initial the spaces on each page.

4. Again, very carefully proofread your entire will. Be certain that there are no errors. If there are any errors, retype the particular page containing the error. *Do not* attempt to correct any errors with type-correcting fluid or tape, or with erasures of any kind. *Do not* cross-out or add anything to the typewritten words using a pen or pencil. Your will, when completed properly, should look similar to the sample

will contained in the previous chapter, except that the signature, initial, and date spaces should be blank.

5. When you have a perfect original of your will, with no corrections and no additions, staple all of the pages together in the upper left-hand corner. You are now ready to prepare for the *execution* (signing) of your will. Please turn to Chapter 10 for instruction on signing your will.

CHAPTER 10
Signing Your Will

After you have had your will typed successfully in the proper form, you are ready to sign it. *Do not* sign your will until you have read this chapter and have all of the necessary witnesses and Notary Public present. The legal requirements listed in this chapter regarding the proper execution (signing) of your will are extremely important and must not be deviated from in any manner in order for your will to be legally valid. These requirements are not at all difficult to follow, but they must be followed precisely. These formal requirements are what transform your will from a mere piece of paper outlining your wishes to a legal document that grants the power to dispose of your property under court order after your death.

The reasons for the formality of these requirements are twofold: first, by requiring a ceremonial-type signing of the document, it is hoped that the testator is made fully aware of the importance of what he or she is doing; and second, by requiring a formal signing witnessed by other adults, it is hoped that any instances of forgery, fraud, and coercion will be avoided, or at least minimized. Again, these legal formalities must be observed strictly. *Do not* deviate from these instructions in any way. The formal execution or signing of your will makes it legally valid and failure to properly sign your will renders it invalid.

Instructions for Signing Your Will

To properly execute your will, follow these few simple steps:

1. Select three (3) witnesses who will be available to assist you in witnessing your will. These persons may be any adults who are not mentioned in the will either as a beneficiary, executor, trustee, or guardian. The witnesses can be friends, neighbors, co-workers, or even strangers. However, it is prudent to choose persons who have been stable members of your community, since they may be called upon to testify in court someday.

2. Arrange for all of your witnesses to meet you at the office or home of a local Notary Public. Many banks, real estate offices, and government offices have notary services and most will be glad to assist you. (The Notary Public may *not* be one of the required three (3) witnesses.)

3. In front of all of the witnesses and the Notary Public, the following should take place in the order shown:

   (a) You should state: "This is my Last Will and Testament, which I am about to sign. I ask that each of you witness my signature." There is no requirement that the witnesses know any of the terms of your will or that they read any of your will. All that is necessary is that they hear you state that it is your will, that you request them to be witnesses, that they observe you sign your will, and that they also sign the will as witnesses in each other's presence.

   (b) You will then sign your will in ink, using a pen, at the end of the will in the place indicated, exactly as your name is typewritten on your will. You should also sign your initials on the bottom of each page of your will at this time.

   (c) After you have signed, pass your will to the first witness, who should sign in the place indicated and fill in his or her address.

   (d) After the first witness has signed, have the will passed to the second witness, who should also sign in the place indicated and fill in his or her address.

   (e) After the second witness has signed, have the will passed to the third and final witness, who also signs in the place indicated and fills in his or her address. Throughout this ceremony, you and all of the witnesses must remain together. It is easier if you are all seated around a table or desk.

   (f) For the final step, the Notary Public completes the notary acknowledgment section of the will and signs in the space indicated. When this step is completed, your will is a valid legal document and you can be assured that your wishes will be carried out upon the presentation of your will to a probate court upon your death.

Safeguarding Your Will

Please note that you should *never* under any circumstances sign a duplicate of your will. Once your will has been properly executed following the steps above, you may make photocopies of it. It is a good idea to label any of these photocopies as "COPIES."

Having completed your will according to the instructions above, it is now time to place your will in a safe place. Many people keep their important papers in a safe deposit box at a local bank. Although this is an acceptable place for storing a will, be advised that there are certain drawbacks. Your will should be in a place that is readily accessible at a moment's notice to your executor. Often there are certain unavoidable delays in gaining access to a safe deposit box in an emergency situation. If you are married, and your safe deposit box is jointly held, many of these delays can be avoided. However, even in this situation, some states prevent immediate access to the safe deposit box of a deceased married person. If you decide to keep the original will in your safe deposit box, it is a good idea to keep a copy of your will clearly marked "COPY" at home in a safe but easily-located place, with a note as to where the original will can be found.

If in the future you should decide to make any changes to your will, make certain that your executor is informed of the changes and that the changes are kept with the original will. For more information regarding changing your will, please refer to the next chapter.

CHAPTER 11
Changing Your Will

In this chapter, instructions will be given on when and how to change your will and how to *revoke* (cancel) your will. It is most important to follow these instructions carefully should you desire to make *any* changes to your will. Failure to follow these instructions and an attempt to change your will by such methods as crossing out a name or penciling in an addition could have the disastrous effect of voiding portions of, or even perhaps, your entire will. Again, these instructions are not difficult to follow, but are very important to insure that your will remains legally valid.

If you desire to totally revoke your will, there are two acceptable methods:

- Signing a new will that expressly states that you revoke all prior wills. All wills prepared using this book contain such a provision.

- Completely destroying, burning, or mutilating your will while it is in your possession, if you actually intend that there be a revocation of your will.

Regarding any potential changes that you may wish to make in your will at a later date, you should periodically review the provisions of your will, keeping in mind the following items as they relate to your present situation:

- Have there been any substantial changes in your personal wealth?
- Have there been any changes in your ownership of any property mentioned in your will?
- Have any of the beneficiaries named in your will died or fallen into your disfavor?
- Are any of the persons whom you named as executor, guardian, or trustee in your will no longer willing or able to serve?
- Have you changed the state of your residence?
- Have you been married since the date of your will?
- Have you been divorced since the date of your will?
- Have you had any children since the date of your will?
- Have you adopted any children since the date of your will?
- Do you simply wish to make any corrections, deletions, or additions to any provisions in your will?

If any of these matters apply, you will need to change your will accordingly. Although it is possible to completely rewrite your will to take account of any of these changes, an easier method is to prepare and formally execute a *codicil*, or a written change to a will. Please bear in mind that all of the formalities surrounding the signing of your original will must again be followed for any such changes contained in a codicil to your will in order to be valid.

Never attempt to change any portions of your will by any other method. For example, *do not* attempt to add provisions in the margin of your will, either by typing or writing them in. *Do not* attempt to cross-out any portions of your will. These are not acceptable methods for the alteration of a will and could subject your will to a court battle to determine its subsequent validity.

Instructions for Changing Your Will

Following are standard clauses for changing provisions of your will and a general form for a codicil. Insert such changes as are necessary where indicated on the form. Prepare the codicil the same way as you prepared your original will using the following simple list of instructions:

1. Make a photocopy of the codicil form. Using the photocopy as a worksheet, fill in the appropriate information for each chosen clause. For the main clause indicating the changes to your will, use one or more of the following phrases. If you wish to change a particular sentence in your will, you should first revoke the original sentence and then add the new sentence. If you merely wish to add new material to the will or revoke a portion of the will, use one of the phrases below:

   I revoke the following sentence of my will:

   or,

   I add the following sentence to my will:

2. Carefully reread your entire codicil to be certain that it is exactly as you wish.

3. After making any necessary changes, type or have typed the entire codicil on good quality 8 ½" x 11" typing paper.

4. After you have completed typing your codicil or having it typed, fill in the total number of pages in the Signature paragraph. *Do not* yet sign your codicil or fill in the date in any of the spaces indicated.

5. Again, proofread your entire codicil very carefully. Be certain that there are no errors. If there are any errors, retype that particular page. *Do not* attempt to correct any errors with type-correcting fluid or tape, or with erasures of any kind. *Do not* cross-out any words and *do not* add anything to the typewritten words using a pen or pencil.

6. When you have a perfect original of your codicil, with no corrections and no additions, staple all of the pages together in the upper left-hand corner. You are now ready to prepare for the *execution* (signing) of your codicil. For signing your codicil, please follow the same instructions that are provided in Chapter 9 for signing your will, substituting the statement:

This is my Codicil to my Last Will and Testament that I am about to sign.

As you fill in the information for each clause, keep in mind the following instructions:

Title Clause: The title clause is mandatory for all codicils and must be included. Fill in the name blank with your full legal name. If you have been known by more than one name, use your principal name. Be sure to use the exact same name as you used in the will that you are changing.

Identification Clause: The identification clause is mandatory and must be included in all codicils. In the first blank, include any other names that you are known by. Do this by adding the phrase: "also known as" after your principal full name. For example:

John James Smith, also known as Jimmy John Smith.

In the spaces provided for your residence, use the location of your principal residence; that is, the place where you currently live permanently. Please note the exact date when you signed your current will.

Addition to Will Clause: Use of this clause is optional. Use if you wish to add additional provisions to your will. In the space provided, simply fill in whatever provisions you desired to be added. For example:

I add the following sentence to the [_name of clause_] clause of my will:

Revocation of Paragraph of Will Clause: This clause is optional. Use in those situations where you desire to delete a clause from your original will. Simply indicate which clause it is that you wish to revoke in the space indicated:

I revoke the following clause of my will:

Correction of Will Clause: Use is optional. Use this clause for those situations where you wish to retain a particular clause in your will, but desire to change a portion of it (for example, substitution of the name of a different beneficiary). Where indicated in this clause, type the correct information that you wish to have become part of your will:

I change the [_name of clause_] clause of my will to read as follows:

Signature, Witness and Notary Clause: This clause is mandatory. You will fill in the number of pages and the appropriate dates where indicated after you have properly typed your codicil or had it typed. The use of the notary acknowledgment, although not a strict legal necessity, is strongly recommended. This allows the codicil to become "self-proving" and the witnesses need not be called upon to testify in court at a later date (after your death) that they, indeed, signed the codicil as witnesses. Although a few states have not enacted legislation to allow for the use of this type of sworn and acknowledged testimony to be used in court, the current trend is to allow for their use in probate courts. This saves time, money, and trouble in having your codicil admitted to probate when necessary.

You will sign your codicil in exactly the same manner as you sign your original will. The actual signing of the codicil by both you and your witnesses is explained in Chapter 9. Do *not* sign your codicil until you carefully follow the instructions contained in that chapter.

Fill in each of the appropriate blanks. Cross out any information that is not appropriate to your situation. The needed information to be filled in is noted below and should be written into the following codicil form in the place where the corresponding number appears.

1. Full name of testator
2. Full name of testator (and any other names that you are known by)
3. Full address of testator
4. Date of original will
5. Insert description of changes to original will
6. Date of signing of codicil (DO NOT FILL IN YET)
   Number of total pages of codicil (fill in when codicil is typed or printed)
   Date of signing of codicil (DO NOT FILL IN YET)
   Signature of testator (DO NOT FILL IN YET)
   Printed name of testator (DO NOT FILL IN YET)
   Date of witnessing of codicil (DO NOT FILL IN YET)
   Signature of witness (repeat for each witness) [DO NOT FILL IN YET]
   Printed name of witness (repeat for each witness) [DO NOT FILL IN YET]
   Address of witness (repeat for each witness) [DO NOT FILL IN YET]

Codicil

Codicil to the Last Will and Testament of

① _____

I, ② _____, whose address is ③_____,

declare that this is a codicil to my Last Will and Testament dated ④ _____.

I make the following changes to my Last Will and Testament: ⑤

Page ___ of ___ pages

Testator's initials _____

On this date, _____, I republish my Last Will and Testament as modiified by this Codicial, consisting of _____typewritten pages, and I declare that I do so freely, for the purposes expressed, under no constraint or undue influence, and that I am of sound mind and legal age.

_____
Signature of Testator

_____
Printed name of Testator

We, the undersigned, being first sworn on oath and under penalty of perjury, state that:

On ⑥ _____, in the presence of all of us, the above-named Testator published and signed this Codicil,.and then at at Testator's request, and in Testator's presence, and in each other's presence, we all signed below as witnesses, and we declare, that to the best of our knowledge, the Testator signed this instrument freely, under no constraint or undue influence, and is of sound mind and legal age.

_____   _____
Signature of Witness   Signature of Witness
_____   _____
Printed name of Witness   Printed name of Witness
_____   _____
Address of Witness   Address of Witness

_____
Signature of Witness
_____
Printed name of Witness
_____
Address of Witness

Page _____ of _____ pages   Testator's initials _____

Notary Acknowledgement

State of _____

County of _____

On _____, _____, the testator, and

_____, _____, and

_____, the witnesses, personally came before me

and, being duly sworn, did state that they are the persons described in the

above document and that they signed the above document in my presence,

as a free and voluntary act for the purposes stated.

_____

Signature of Notary Public

Notary Public, In and for the County of _____

State of _____

My commission expires: _____   Notary Seal

Page _____ of _____ pages   Testator's initials _____

CHAPTER 12
Preparing a Living Will

In this chapter, you will be given instructions on how to prepare a living will. A living will is a relatively new legal document which has been made necessary by the advent of recent technological advances in the field of medicine which can allow for the continued existence of a person on advanced "life support" systems long after any normal semblance of "life", as many people consider it, has ceased.

The inherent problem which is raised by this type of extraordinary medical "life support" is that the person whose life is being artificially continued by such means may not wish to be kept alive beyond what they may consider to be the proper time for their life to end. However, since a person in such condition has no method of communicating their wishes to the medical or legal authorities in charge, a living will was developed which allows one to make these important decisions in advance of the situation.

As more and more advances are made in the medical field in terms of the ability to prevent "clinical" death, the difficult situations envisioned by a living will are destined to occur more often. The legal acceptance of a living will is now the law in all states.

Although this living will does not address all possible contingencies regarding terminally ill patients, it does provide a written declaration for the individual to make known his or her decisions on life-prolonging procedures.

A living will declares your wishes not to be kept alive by artificial or mechanical means if you are suffering from a terminal condition and your death would be imminent without the use of such artificial means. It provides a legally-binding written set of instructions regarding your wishes about this important matter.

In order to qualify for the use of a living will, you must meet the following criteria:

> • You must be at least 19 years of age (although some states allow you to be 18, check the Appendix for information on your state);

> • You must be of "sound mind" and able to comprehend the nature of your action in signing such a document.

You should also read through this statement concerning the importance of the decisions that you make in a Living Will (This notice is also part of the Living Will itself):

Notice to the Adult Signing this Document:

This is an important legal document. This document directs the medical treatment you are to receive in the event you are unable to participate in your own medical decisions and you are in a terminal condition. This document may state what kind of treatment you want or do not want to receive. This document can control whether you live or die. Prepare this document carefully. If you use this form, read it completely.

You may want to seek professional help to make sure the form does what you intend and is completed without mistakes. This document will remain valid and in effect until and unless you revoke it. Review this document periodically to make sure it continues to reflect your wishes. You may amend or revoke this document at any time by notifying your physician and other health-care providers. You should give copies of this document to your physician and your family. This form is entirely optional. If you choose to use this form, please note that the form provides signature lines for you, the three witnesses whom you have selected and a notary public.

Instructions for Preparing and Signing a Living Will

If you desire that your life not be prolonged artificially when there is no reasonable chance for recovery and death is imminent, please follow the instructions below for completion of your living will. The entire following form is mandatory. It has been adapted to be valid in all states. Courts, health care professionals, members of your family, and physicians will be guided by this expression of your desires concerning life support. Please consult the Appendix for further information regarding recognition of living wills in your state.

1. Make a photo-copy of the entire living will form from this chapter. Using the photo-copy as a worksheet, please fill in the correct information in the appropriate blanks.

2. On clean, white, 8 1/2 X 11" paper, have typed or type yourself the entire living will exactly as shown with your information added. Carefully re-read this original living will to be certain that it exactly expresses your desires on this very important matter. When you have a clean, clear original typed version, staple all of the pages

together in the upper left-hand corner. Do not yet sign this document or fill in the date. If you are using Forms-on-CD, follow the instructions which are included on the ReadMe document that accompanied the CD

3. You should now assemble two witnesses and a Notary Public to witness your signature. As noted on the document itself, these witnesses should have no connection with you from a health care or beneficiary standpoint. Specifically, the witnesses must:

    • Be at least 19 years of age.

    • Not be related to you in any manner: by blood, marriage, or adoption.

    • Not be your attending physician, or a patient or employee of your attending physician; or a patient, physician, or employee of the health care facility in which you may be a patient. However, please see below.

    • Not be entitled to any portion of your estate on your death under any laws of intestate succession, nor under your will or any codicil.

    • Have no claim against any portion of your estate on your death.

    • Not be directly financially responsible for your medical care.

    • Not have signed the living will for you, even at your direction

    • Not be paid a fee for acting as a witness.

    In addition, please note that a few states have laws in effect regarding witnesses when the declarant is a patient in a nursing home, boarding facility, hospital, or skilled or intermediate health care facility. In those situation, it is advisable to have a patient ombudsman, patient advocate, or the director of the health care facility to act as the third witness to the signing of a living will. Please check the Appendix for your state's requirements. ***Note: If your state requires and additional witness, a Living Will form for three witnesses is provided with the Forms-on-CD. If you do not have a computer, you will need to retype the form in the book with additional lines for a third witness***.

4. In front of all of the witnesses and in front of the Notary Public, the following should take place in the order shown:

    • You should state: "This is my living will which I am about to sign. I ask that each of you witness my signature." There is no requirement that the witnesses know any of the terms of your living will or that they read any of your living will. All that is necessary is that they hear you state that it is your living will, that you request them to be witnesses, that they observe you sign your living will and that they also sign the living will as witnesses in each other's presence.

• You will then sign your living will at the end, exactly as your name is type-written on your living will, where indicated, in ink using a pen.

• After you have signed, pass your living will to the first witness, who should sign where indicated and fill in his or her address.

• After the first witness has signed, have the living will passed to the second witness, who should also sign where indicated.

• After the second witness has signed, have the living will passed to the third and final witness, who also signs where indicated and fills in his or her address. Throughout this ceremony, you and all of the witnesses must remain together.

The final step is for the Notary Public to sign in the space indicated. When this step is completed, your living will is a valid legal document. Have several copies made and, if appropriate, deliver a copy to your attending physician to have placed in your medical records file. You may also desire to give a copy to the person you have chosen as the executor of your will, a copy to your clergy, and a copy to your spouse or other trusted relative.

Living Will Declaration and Directive to Physicians of

_____

Notice to Adult Signing This Document: This is an important legal document. This document directs the medical treatment you are to receive in the event you are unable to participate in your own medical decisions and you are in a terminal condition. This document may state what kind of treatment you want or do not want to receive. This document can control whether you live or die. Prepare this document carefully. If you use this form, read it completely. You may want to seek professional help to make sure the form does what you intend and is completed without mistakes. This document will remain valid and in effect until and unless you revoke it. Review this document periodically to make sure it continues to reflect your wishes. You may amend or revoke this document at any time by notifying your physician and other health-care providers. You should give copies of this document to your physician and your family. This form is entirely optional. If you choose to use this form, please note that the form provides signature lines for you, the two witnesses whom you have selected and a notary public.

I, _____ , being of sound mind, willfully and voluntarily make known my desire that my life not be artificially prolonged under the circumstances set forth below, and, pursuant to any and all applicable laws in the State of _____ , I declare that:

1.   If at any time I should have an incurable injury, disease, or illness which has been certified as a terminal condition by my attending physician and one additional physician, both of whom have personally examined me, and such physicians have determined that there can be no recovery from such condition and my death is imminent, and where the application of life prolonging procedures would serve only to artificially prolong the dying process, then:

I direct that such procedures be withheld or withdrawn, and that I be permitted to die naturally with only the administration of medication, the administration of nutrition and/or hydration, or the performance of any medical procedure deemed necessary to provide me with comfort, care, or to alleviate pain.

2.   If at any time I should have been diagnosed as being in a persistent vegetative state which has been certified as incurable by my attending physician and one additional physician, both of whom have personally examined me, and such physicians have determined that there can be no recovery from such condition, and where the application of life prolonging procedures would serve only to artificially prolong the dying process, then:

I direct that such procedures be withheld or withdrawn, and that I be permitted to die naturally with only the administration of medication, the administration of nutrition and/or hydration, or the performance of any medical procedure deemed necessary to provide me with comfort, care, or to alleviate pain.

3.　　In the absence of my ability to give directions regarding my treatment in the above situations, including directions regarding the use of such life prolonging procedures, then:

It is my intention that this declaration shall be honored by my family, my physician, and any court of law, as the final expression of my legal right to refuse medical and surgical treatment. I declare that I fully accept the consequences for such refusal.

4.　　If I have any additional directions, I will state them here:

5.　　If I have also signed a Health Care Power of Attorney, Appointment of Health Care Agent, or Health Care Proxy, I direct the person who I have appointed with such instrument to follow the directions that I have made in this document.

6.　　If I am diagnosed as pregnant, this document shall have no force and effect during my pregnancy.

7.　　I understand the full importance of this declaration, and I am emotionally and mentally competent to make this declaration and Living Will. I also understand that I may revoke this document at any time.

I publish and sign this Living Will and Directive to Physicians, consisting of _____ typewritten pages, on _____, 20_____ , and declare that I do so freely, for the purposes expressed, under no constraint or undue influence, and that I am of sound mind and of legal age.

_____
Declarant's Signature

_____
Printed Name of Declarant

On _____, 20_____ , in the presence of all of us, the above-named Declarant published and signed this Living Will and Directive to Physicians, and then at the Declarant's request, and in the Declarant's presence, and in each other's presence, we all signed below as witnesses, and we each declare, under penalty of perjury, that, to the best of our knowledge:

1.   The Declarant is personally known to me and, to the best of my knowledge, the Declarant signed this instrument freely, under no constraint or undue influence, and is of sound mind and memory and legal age, and fully aware of the possible consequences of this action.

2.   I am at least 19 years of age and I am not related to the Declarant in any manner: by blood, marriage, or adoption.

3.   I am not the Declarant's attending physician, or a patient or employee of the Declarant's attending physician; or a patient, physician, or employee of the health care facility in which the Declarant is a patient, unless such person is required or allowed to witness the execution of this document by the laws of the state in which this document is executed.

4.   I am not entitled to any portion of the Declarant's estate on the Declarant's death under the laws of intestate succession of any state or country, nor under the Last Will and Testament of the Declarant or any Codicil to such Last Will and Testament.

5.   I have no claim against any portion of the Declarant's estate on the Declarant's death.

6.   I am not directly financially responsible for the Declarant's medical care.

7.   I did not sign the Declarant's signature for the Declarant or on the direction of the Declarant, nor have I been paid any fee for acting as a witness to the execution of this document.

---------------------------   ---------------------------
Signature of Witness   Signature of Witness

---------------------------   ---------------------------
Printed name of Witness   Printed name of Witness

---------------------------   ---------------------------
Address of Witness   Address of Witness

_____
Signature of Witness

_____
Printed name of Witness

_____
Address of Witness

County of _____
State of _____

On _____ , 20_____ , before me personally appeared _____ , the Declarant, and _____ , the first witness, _____ , the second witness, _____ , the third witness, and, being first sworn on oath and under penalty of perjury, state that, in the presence of all the witnesses, the Declarant published and signed the above Living Will Declaration and Directive to Physicians, and then, at Declarant's request, and in the presence of the Declarant and of each other, each of the witnesses signed as witnesses, and stated that, to the best of their knowledge, the Declarant signed said Living Will Declaration and Directive to Physicians freely, under no constraint or undue influence, and is of sound mind and memory and legal age and fully aware of the potential consequences of this action. The witnesses further state that this affidavit is made at the direction of and in the presence of the Declarant.

_____
Signature of Notary Public

_____
Printed name of Notary Public

Notary Public,
In and for the County of _____
State of _____
My commission expires: _____

Revoking Your Living Will

All states which have recognized living wills have provided methods for the easy revocation of them. Since they provide authority for medical personnel to withhold life-support technology which will likely result in death to the patient, great care must be taken to insure that a change of mind by the patient is heeded.

If revocation of your living will is an important issue, please consult your state's law directly. The name of your particular state's law relating to living wills is provided in the Appendix of this book.

For the revocation of a living will, any one of the following methods of revocation is generally acceptable:

• Physical destruction of the living will, such as tearing, burning, or mutilating the document.

• A written revocation of the living will by you or by a person acting at your direction. A form for this is provided at the end of this chapter. You may use two witnesses on this form, although most states do not require the use of witnesses for the written revocation of a living will to be valid.

• An oral revocation in the presence of a witness who signs and dates a writing confirming a revocation. This oral declaration may take any manner. Most states allow for a person to revoke such a document by any indication (even non-verbal) of the intent to revoke a living will, regardless of their physical or mental condition.

To use the Revocation of Living Will form provided on the next page, simply fill in the appropriate information, retype the form, and sign it. In addition, your two witnesses may sign it at the same time.

Revocation of Living Will

I, _____ , am the Declarant and maker of a Living Will and Directive to Physicians, dated _____ , 20_____ .

By this written revocation, I hereby entirely revoke such Living Will and Directive to Physicians and intend that it no longer have any force or effect whatsoever.

Dated _____ , 20_____ .

_____
Declarant's Signature

_____
Printed Name of Declarant

_____
Signature of Witness

_____
Printed name of Witness

_____
Address of Witness

_____
Signature of Witness

_____
Printed name of Witness

_____
Address of Witness

CHAPTER 13
Preparing a Health Care Power of Attorney

A power of attorney form is a document which is used to allow one person to give authority to another person to act on their behalf. The person signing the power of attorney grants legal authority to another to "stand in their shoes" and act legally for them. The person who receives the power of attorney is called an *attorney-in-fact*. This title and the power of attorney form does not mean that the person receiving the power has to be a lawyer.

Power of attorney forms are useful documents for many occasions. They can be used to authorize someone else to sign certain documents if you can not be present when the signatures are necessary. Traditionally, property matters were the type of actions handled with powers of attorney. Increasingly, however, people are using a specific type of power of attorney to authorize other persons to make health care decisions on their behalf in the event of a disability which makes the person unable to communicate their wishes to doctors or other health care providers. This broad type of power of attorney is called a *health care power of attorney*. It is different from *durable power of attorney*, which gives another person the authority to sign legal papers, transact business, buy or sell property, etc. but is intended to remain in effect even if a person becomes disabled or incompetent. A durable power of attorney does not confer authority on another person to make health care decisions on someone else's behalf. Only a health care power of attorney can do that.

Nearly all states have passed legislation that specifically authorizes health care powers of attorney or some similar legal document. In some states, they are called Appointment of Health Care Agent; in others, they are referred to as a Health Care Proxy. The form included in this book is officially titled Health Care Power of Attorney and Appointment of Health Care Agent and Proxy, and is designed to be legally valid in all states.

The Health Care Power of Attorney included in this chapter and instructions for their use are intended to be used to confer a very powerful authority to another person. In some cases, this may actually mean that you are giving that other person the power of life or death over you. This is not a power that should be conferred lightly. Very serious thought should be given to both who you appoint as your health care attorney-in-fact (the person you authorize to act on your behalf) and to any specific directions that you may want to give to that person regarding health care decisions.

Following is the notice that is included in the document regarding the use of a Health Care Power of Attorney. It clearly explains the importance of caution in the use of this form and is applicable to all states. Please read it carefully before you sign your health care power of attorney.

Notice to Adult Signing this Document: This is an important legal document. Before executing this document, you should know these facts:

This document gives the person you designate (the attorney in fact) the power to make MOST health care decisions for you if you lose the capacity to make informed health care decisions for yourself. This power is effective only when your attending physician determines that you have lost the capacity to make informed health care decisions for yourself and, notwithstanding this document, as long as you have the capacity to make informed health care decisions for yourself, you retain the right to make all medical and other health care decisions for yourself.

You may include specific limitations in this document on the authority of the attorney in fact to make health care decisions for you. Subject to any specific limitations you include in this document, if your attending physician determines that you have lost the capacity to make an informed decision on a health care matter, the attorney in fact GENERALLY will be authorized by this document to make health care decisions for you to the same extent as you could make those decisions yourself, if you had the capacity to do so.

The authority of the attorney in fact to make health care decisions for you GENERALLY will include the authority to give informed consent, to refuse to give informed consent, or to withdraw informed consent to any care, treatment, service, or procedure to maintain, diagnose, or treat a physical or mental condition.

Additionally, when exercising authority to make health care decisions for you, the attorney in fact will have to act consistently with your desires or, if your desires are unknown, to act in your best interest. You may express your desires to the attorney in fact by including them in this document or by making them known to the attorney in fact in another manner.

When acting pursuant to this document, the attorney in fact GENERALLY will have the same rights that you have to receive information about proposed health care, to review health care records, and to consent to the disclosure of health care records. You can limit that right in this document if you so choose.

Generally, you may designate any competent adult as the attorney in fact under this document. You have the right to revoke the designation of the attorney in fact and the right to revoke this entire document at any time and in any manner. Any such revocation generally will be effective when you express your intention to make the revocation. However, if you made your attending physician aware of this document, any such revocation will be effective only when you communicate it to your attending physician, or when a witness to the revocation or other health care personnel to whom the revocation is communicated by such a witness communicate it to your attending physician. If you execute this document and create a valid Health Care Power of Attorney with it, this will revoke any prior, valid power of attorney for health care that you created, unless you indicate otherwise in this document. This document is not valid as a Health Care Power of Attorney unless it is acknowledged before a notary public or is signed by at least two adult witnesses who are present when you sign or acknowledge your signature. No person who is related to you by blood, marriage, or adoption may be a witness. The attorney in fact, your attending physician, and the administrator of any nursing home in which you are receiving care also are ineligible to be witnesses. If there is anything in this document that you do not understand, you should ask a lawyer to explain it to you.

To complete your Health Care Power of Attorney, the names and addresses of the person granting the power and of the person receiving the power should be filled in. If you have any specific instructions, you should include them also. Both persons should sign the document. The signature of the person granting the power should be notarized.

Please note also that if you desire that your appointed health care representative have the authority to order your doctors to withhold food, water, pain medicine and other items for your comfort, you must sign your name above the boldface statement to this effect in the middle of the document. As an example, that statement is included below:

THE FOLLOWING INSTRUCTIONS (IN BOLDFACE TYPE) ONLY APPLY IF I HAVE SIGNED MY NAME IN THIS SPACE: _____

However, if at any time I should have been diagnosed as being in a persistent vegetative state which has been certified as incurable by my attending physician and one additional physician, both of whom have personally examined me, and such physicians have determined that there can be no recovery from such condition, I also direct that my health care representative have sole authority to order the withholding of any aid, including the administration of nutrition, hydration, and any other medical procedure deemed necessary to provide me with comfort, care, or to alleviate pain.

Health Care Power of Attorney and
Appointment of Health Care Agent and Proxy

Notice to Adult Signing this Document: This is an important legal document. Before executing this document, you should know these facts:

This document gives the person you designate (the attorney in fact) the power to make MOST health care decisions for you if you lose the capacity to make informed health care decisions for yourself. This power is effective only when your attending physician determines that you have lost the capacity to make informed health care decisions for yourself and, notwithstanding this document, as long as you have the capacity to make informed health care decisions for yourself, you retain the right to make all medical and other health care decisions for yourself.

You may include specific limitations in this document on the authority of the attorney in fact to make health care decisions for you. Subject to any specific limitations you include in this document, if your attending physician determines that you have lost the capacity to make an informed decision on a health care matter, the attorney in fact GENERALLY will be authorized by this document to make health care decisions for you to the same extent as you could make those decisions yourself, if you had the capacity to do so.

The authority of the attorney in fact to make health care decisions for you GENERALLY will include the authority to give informed consent, to refuse to give informed consent, or to withdraw informed consent to any care, treatment, service, or procedure to maintain, diagnose, or treat a physical or mental condition.

Additionally, when exercising authority to make health care decisions for you, the attorney in fact will have to act consistently with your desires or, if your desires are unknown, to act in your best interest. You may express your desires to the attorney in fact by including them in this document or by making them known to the attorney in fact in another manner.

When acting pursuant to this document, the attorney in fact GENERALLY will have the same rights that you have to receive information about proposed health care, to review health care records, and to consent to the disclosure of health care records. You can limit that right in this document if you so choose.

GENERALLY, you may designate any competent adult as the attorney in fact under this document. You have the right to revoke the designation of the attorney in fact and the right to revoke this entire document at any time and in any manner. Any such revocation generally will be effective when you express your intention

to make the revocation. However, if you made your attending physician aware of this document, any such revocation will be effective only when you communicate it to your attending physician, or when a witness to the revocation or other health care personnel to whom the revocation is communicated by such a witness communicate it to your attending physician. If you execute this document and create a valid Health Care Power of Attorney with it, this will revoke any prior, valid power of attorney for health care that you created, unless you indicate otherwise in this document. This document is not valid as a Health Care Power of Attorney unless it is acknowledged before a notary public or is signed by at least two adult witnesses who are present when you sign or acknowledge your signature. No person who is related to you by blood, marriage, or adoption may be a witness. The attorney in fact, your attending physician, and the administrator of any nursing home in which you are receiving care also are ineligible to be witnesses. If there is anything in this document that you do not understand, you should ask a lawyer to explain it to you.

I, _____ , residing at _____ , City of _____ , State of _____ , appoint the following person as my attorney-in-fact for health care decisions, my health care agent, and confer upon this person my health care proxy. This person shall hereafter referred to as my "health care representative":

_____ , residing at _____ , City of _____ , State of _____ .

I grant my health care representative the maximum power under law to perform any acts on my behalf regarding health care matters that I could do personally under the laws of the State of _____ , including specifically the power to make any health decisions on my behalf, upon the terms and conditions set forth below. My health care representative accepts this appointment and agrees to act in my best interest as he or she considers advisable. This health care power of attorney and appointment of health care agent and proxy may be revoked by me at any time and is automatically revoked on my death. However, this power of attorney shall not be affected by my present or future disability or incapacity.

This health care power of attorney and appointment of health care agent and proxy has the following terms and conditions:

1.   If I have signed a Living Will or Directive to Physicians, and it is still in effect, I direct that my health care representative abide by the directions that I have set out in that document.

2.   If at any time I should have an incurable injury, disease, or illness which has been certified as a terminal condition by my attending physician and one additional physician, both of whom have personally examined me, and such physicians have determined that there can be no recovery from such condition and my death is imminent, and where the application of life prolonging procedures would serve only to artificially prolong the dying process, then:

I direct my health care representative to assure that such procedures be withheld or withdrawn, and that I be permitted to die naturally with only the administration of medication, the administration of nutrition and/or hydration, or the performance of any medical procedure deemed necessary to provide me with comfort, care, or to alleviate pain.

3.   If at any time I should have been diagnosed as being in a persistent vegetative state which has been certified as incurable by my attending physician and one additional physician, both of whom have personally examined me, and such physicians have determined that there can be no recovery from such condition, and where the application of life prolonging procedures would serve only to artificially prolong the dying process, then

I direct that my health care representative assure that such procedures be withheld or withdrawn, and that I be permitted to die naturally with only the administration of medication, the administration of nutrition and/or hydration, or the performance of any medical procedure deemed necessary to provide me with comfort, care, or to alleviate pain.

THE FOLLOWING INSTRUCTIONS (IN BOLDFACE TYPE) ONLY APPLY IF I HAVE SIGNED MY NAME IN THIS SPACE: _____

However, if at any time I should have been diagnosed as being in a persistent vegetative state which has been certified as incurable by my attending physician and one additional physician, both of whom have personally examined me, and such physicians have determined that there can be no recovery from such condition, I also direct that my health care representative have sole authority to order the withholding of any aid, including the administration of nutrition, hydration, and any other medical procedure deemed necessary to provide me with comfort, care, or to alleviate pain.

4.   If I am able to communicate in any manner, including even blinking my eyes, I direct that my health care representative try and discuss with me the specifics of any proposed health care decision.

5.   If I have any further terms or conditions, I state them here:

I have discussed my health care wishes with the person whom I have herein appointed as my health care representative, I am fully satisfied that the person who I have herein appointed as my health care representative will know my wishes with respect to my health care and I have full faith and confidence in their good judgement.

I further direct that my health care representative shall have full authority to do the following, should I lack the capacity to make such a decision myself, provided however, that this listing shall in no way limit the full authority that I give my health care representative to make health care decisions on my behalf:

    a. to give informed consent to any health care procedure;

    b. to sign any documents necessary to carry out or withhold any health care procedures on my behalf, including any waivers or releases of liabilities required by any health care provider;

    c. to give or withhold consent for any health care or treatment;

    d. to revoke or change any consent previously given or implied by law for any health care treatment;

    e. to arrange for or authorize my placement or removal from any health care facility or institution;

    f. to require that any procedures be discontinued, including the withholding of any medical treatment and/or aid, including the administration of nutrition, hydration, and any other medical procedure deemed necessary to provide me with comfort, care, or to alleviate pain, subject to the conditions earlier provided in this document.

    g. to authorize the administration of pain-relieving drugs, even if they may shorten my life.

I desire that my wishes with respect to all health care matters be carried out through the authority that I have herein provided to my health care representative, despite any contrary wishes, beliefs, or opinions of any members of my family, relatives, or friends.

I have read the Notice that precedes this document. I understand the full importance of this appointment, and I am emotionally and mentally competent to make this appointment of health care representative.

Dated _____ , 20_____

_____
Signature of person granting health care power of attorney and appointing health care representative

State of _____
County of _____

On _____ , 20_____ , _____ came before me personally and, under oath, stated that he/she is the person described in the above document and he/she signed the above document in my presence.

_____
Notary Signature

Notary Public
In and for the County of _____
State of _____
My commission expires: _____

I accept my appointment as health care attorney-in-fact and health care representative.

_____
Signature of person granted health care power of attorney and appointed as health care representative

Instructions for Revocation of Health Care Power of Attorney

On the following page, there is included a Revocation of Health Care Power of Attorney. You have the right at any time to revoke your Health Care Power of Attorney. Remember, however, that should you become disabled or incapacitated and unable to communicate your wishes to anyone, you may be unable to communicate your desire to revoke your Health Care Power of Attorney. In any event, if you choose to revoke your health care power of attorney, a copy of this revocation should be provided to the person to whom the power was originally given. Copies should also be given to any party that may have had dealings with the attorney-in-fact before the revocation and to any party with whom the attorney-in-fact may be expected to attempt to deal with after the revocation, for example, your family physician.

This form should be filled out and signed by the person revoking the Health Care Power of Attorney. It should also be notarized.

Revocation of Health Care Power of Attorney

I, _____ , residing at _____ , City of _____ , State of _____ , revoke the Health Care Power of Attorney dated _____ , 20_____ , which was granted to _____ , residing at _____ , City of _____ , State of _____ , to act as my attorney-in-fact for health care decisions and I revoke any appointment of the above person as my health care agent, health care representative, or health care proxy.

Dated _____ , 20___

_____
Signature of person revoking power of attorney

State of _____
County of _____

On _____ , 20_____ , _____ came before me personally and, under oath, stated that he/she is the person described in the above document and he/she signed the above document in my presence.

_____
Notary Signature

Notary Public
In and for the County of _____
State of _____
My commission expires: _____

Appendix: State Laws Relating to Wills & Living Wills

This book is part of Nova Publishing Company's *Legal Self-Help Series*. This Appendix contains a summary of the laws relating to wills and living wills for all states and the District of Columbia (Washington D.C.). It has been compiled directly from the most recently-available statutes and has been abridged for clarity and succinctness. It is recommended that you review the listing that pertains to your home state and any state in which you own real estate before you complete your will. The will clauses used in this book are generally designed to overcome and eliminate most potential legal problems raised by any of these individual state laws. There may be, however, some information that will directly affect the manner in which you decide to prepare your will.

As you review your state's particular laws, keep in mind that your will is going to be interpreted under the laws of the state where you resided at the time of your death. Your personal property will be also distributed according to the laws of the state in which you were a resident at the time of your death. Your real estate, however, will be distributed under the laws of the state in which it is located, regardless of where you were a resident.

Every effort has been made to ensure that the information contained in this Appendix is as complete and up-to-date as possible. However, state laws are subject to constant change. While most laws relating to wills are relatively stable, it is advisable to check your particular state statutes to be certain there have been no major modifications since this book was prepared, especially for those legal points that are particularly important in your situation.

To simplify this process as much as possible, the exact name of the statute and the chapter or section number of where the information can be found is noted after each section of information. Any of these official statute books should be available at any public library or on the internet. A librarian will be glad to assist you in locating the correct book and in finding the appropriate pages.

The correct terminology for each state is used in these listings. However, some states use certain language interchangeably. In those states, the most commonly-used language is stated. Although it has been simplified to some extent, you will find that the language in the Appendix is somewhat more complicated than the language used in the rest of this book. This is due to the fact that much of the language in the Appendix has been taken directly from the laws and statutes of each state, and most legislators are lawyers. We apologize for this. We feel, however, that, as a reference, the technical details of the laws should be provided. Use the Glossary located at the end of this book to translate this language.

The state-by-state listings following in this Appendix contain the following information for each state:

State Website: This listing provides the internet website address of the location of the state's statutes. The addresses were current at the time of this book's publication; however, like most websites, the page addresses are subject to change. If an expired state webpage is not automatically redirected to a new site, laws can be searched at http://www.findlaw.com

State Law Description: This is the title where most of the relevant state laws on wills, living wills and probate are contained.

Court with Probate Jurisdiction: This listing provides the name of the particular court in each state that has exclusive jurisdiction over probate and will-related legal matters.

Minimum Age for Disposing of Property by Will: This listing details the minimum age for having a legally-valid will. For most states, this age is 18, but there are a few states that have differing laws.

Required Number of Witnesses for Wills: For most states, the *minimum* number of required witnesses is two. Be advised, however, that it is recommended to use at least three witnesses for your will.

Can Witnesses Be Beneficiaries?: Under this listing is information regarding whether witnesses to the signing of the will can be beneficiaries under the will. Again, be advised that to be safe, your witnesses should *not* be beneficiaries.

Are There Provisions for Self-Proving Wills?: This listing details whether there are specific state law provisions for self-proving wills. All wills (except Louisiana) provided in this book are designed to be self-proving when completed as indicated.

Are Holographic Wills Permitted?: Under this listing, the name of any relevant state law regarding living wills is shown.

How Does Divorce Affect the Will?: The effect of divorce on the will under state law is shown in this listing. State law varies widely on this point and in some states a divorce may automatically revoke your entire will. It is highly recommended that you review and update your will if you are ever divorced.

How Does Marriage Affect the Will?: This listing provides the state law on the effect of marriage on the will. Again, state law provides various provisions and marriage may have the drastic effect of entirely revoking your will. It is, therefore, recommended that you review and update your will if you are ever married.

Who Must Be Mentioned in the Will?: Under this listing is shown which parties must be specifically mentioned in the will. Certain parties must be mentioned in your will or they may be entitled to an intestate share of your estate regardless of your will. Most states provide this protection for children born after a will is made and for new spouses from a marriage that takes place after a will is prepared. However, it is recommended that you review and change your will if you adopt or have any new children, are married, or if any of your named beneficiaries die.

Spouse's Right to Property Regardless of Will: This listing provides the results of a spouse's right of election against the will. In all states, the surviving spouse has a right to a certain share of the deceased spouse's estate regardless of any provisions in the will of the deceased spouse that may give the surviving spouse less than this "statutory" or "community" property share.

Laws of Intestate Succession (Distribution If No Will): Under this listing the complex state provisions regarding intestate distribution of estates are outlined. This provides an overview of how your property would be distributed in the event that you die without a valid will. The laws in this area are extremely complex and differ widely from state to state. The outline of laws shown in this listing is intended to provide a simplified example of the particular state distribution scheme. If specific details of your state's distribution plan are needed, please consult the state statute directly.

A few definitions may be useful in deciphering the information listed in this section. The terms "per capita" and "per stirpes" are often used in these state plans. *Per capita* refers to a distribution to each member of a group equally. *Per stirpes* means distribution to a lower-level group based on "representation" in the upper level. For example, a parent has two children, each of whom have two grandchildren for a total of six descendents. However, one of the children died before the parent, leaving only five descendents. When the parent dies, a per capita distribution would divide the estate into five equal shares, with each descendent taking one-fifth. In a per stirpes distribution, the estate is divided into two equal halves; one for each original child's share. The living child takes one-half and the grandchildren who are children of the deceased child each take one-fourth. In effect, they share by "representation" their deceased parent's share of the estate. The grandchildren who are children of the living child would take nothing under a per stirpes distribution.

Another definition which may be useful is a "life estate." A *life estate* in real estate is provided to the surviving spouse in some states upon a spouse's death. A life estate means that the surviving spouse has the full use and enjoyment of any real estate for his or her entire life. However, upon his or her death, the property will pass automatically to the person who has the remaining share of the estate. Most often, this will be a child of the original, or first, deceased. The spouse who is given a life estate cannot leave such a property interest to anyone else.

Property Ownership: Whether the state follows the community property or common-law system of ownership of marital property is shown in this listing.

State Gift, Inheritance, or Estate Taxes: This listing shows the tax situation in each state as it relates to estates and wills. There are three basic taxes that apply: gift taxes, inheritance taxes, and estate taxes. Each individual state may impose any of these taxes and each tax rate may vary, depending on the state. Only one state, Nevada, does not impose any of these taxes.

Living Will Form: Under this listing, the exact location of a state's official living will form is provided.

Other Directives: The existence and location of additional official state directives relating to advance health care and powers of attorney are indicated in this listing. Examples of such forms are Durable Power of Attorney for Health Care, Durable Power of Attorney for Financial Affairs, Anatomical Gift Act forms (organ donation forms), Designation of Primary Physician, and other related forms.

Living Will Effective: This listing indicates the requirements of state law regarding when a living will becomes effective. Most states require that two physicians must diagnose and document that a patient either has a terminal illness with no hope of recovery or is in a permanent state of unconsciousness, or some similar diagnosis.

Living Will Witness Requirements: Under this listing are noted the specific state requirements for witnesses to the signing of a living will and any related advance health care directives. In general, most states require that there are two witnesses, and that the witnesses be over eighteen, not related by blood or marriage to the declarant, not entitled to any part of the declarant's estate, and not financially responsible for the declarant's health care costs. Note that a few states require that, if the declarant is a patient in a nursing home or hospital, one of the witnesses be a patient advocate or patient ombudsman. In some states, the patient advocate or ombudsman is required to be a third witness, in addition to the other two required witnesses.

Alabama

State Website: www.legislature.state.al.us/CodeofAlabama/1975/coatoc.htm

State Law Reference: Code of Alabama.

Court with Probate Jurisdiction: Probate Court. (Section 12-13-1).

Minimum Age for Disposing of Property by Will: 18. (Section 43-8-130).

Required Number of Witnesses: Two. (Section 43-8-131).

Can Witnesses Be Beneficiaries?: Yes. (Section 43-8-134).

Are There Provisions for Self-Proving Wills?: Yes. (Section 43-8-132).

Are Holographic Wills Permitted?: No provision.

How Does Divorce Affect the Will?: Revokes the will as to the divorced spouse unless expressly provided otherwise. (Sections 43-8-137 & 43-8-252).

How Does Marriage Affect the Will?: Revokes the will as to the spouse if he or she is not otherwise provided for. Spouse may still be entitled to his or her statutory share under the state intestate laws. (Section 43-8-90).

Who Must Be Mentioned in the Will?: Children, born or adopted; surviving spouse. (Sections 43-8-90 & 43-8-91).

Spouse's Right to Property Regardless of Will: The surviving spouse is entitled to either: (a) all of the deceased spouse's estate, reduced by the value of the surviving spouse's "augmented" estate; or (b) 1/3 of the "augmented" estate of the deceased spouse. In general, the "augmented" estate includes both the property that passes under the will and any other property that passes by other "non-will" transfers, such as under the terms of a living trust or a joint tenancy arrangement. (Section 43-8-70).

Laws of Intestate Succession (Distribution If No Will):

Spouse and children of spouse surviving: $50,000.00 and 1/2 of balance to spouse and 1/2 of balance to children.

Spouse and children not of spouse surviving: 1/2 to spouse and 1/2 to children.

Spouse, but no children or parent(s) surviving: All to spouse.

Spouse and parent(s), but no children surviving: $100,000.00 and 1/2 of balance to spouse and 1/2 of balance to parent(s).

Children, but no spouse surviving: All to children equally or to their children per stirpes.

Parent(s), but no spouse or children surviving: All to parents equally or to the surviving parent.

No spouse, children, or parent(s) surviving: All to brothers and sisters per stirpes; or if none, to grandparents or their children per stirpes; or if none, to deceased spouse's next-of-kin. (Sections 43-8-41 & 43-8-42).

Property Ownership: Common-law state. Tenancy-in-common is presumed if real estate is held jointly unless title creates joint tenancy with right of survivorship or similar words. No tenancy-by-the-entirety is recognized. Joint bank account deposits are payable to any survivor. (Section 35-4-7).

State Gift, Inheritance, or Estate Taxes: No gift tax; no inheritance tax; imposes state estate tax equal to federal credit for state death taxes. (Sections 40-15-1 to 40-15-19).

Living Will Form: Living Will (Section 22-8A-4).

Other Directives: Durable Power of Attorney Act (Section 26-1-2). Anatomical Gift Act (Section 22-19-40).

Living Will Effective: Two (2) physicians, one being the attending physician, must diagnose and document in the medical records that you either have a terminal illness or injury or are in a permanent state of unconsciousness.

Witness Requirements: Will must be signed in the presence of two (2) or more witnesses at least nineteen (19) years of age. Witnesses cannot be related by blood, adoption, or marriage, entitled to any part of your estate, or be directly financially responsible for your health care.

Alaska

State Website: www.legis.state.ak.us/folhome.htm

State Law Reference: Alaska Statutes.

Court with Probate Jurisdiction: Superior Court.

Minimum Age for Disposing of Property by Will: 18. (Section 13.12.501).

Required Number of Witnesses: Two. (Section 13.12.502).

Can Witnesses Be Beneficiaries?: Yes. (Section 13.12.505).

Are There Provisions for Self-Proving Wills?: Yes. (Section 13.12.504).

Are Holographic Wills Permitted?: Yes. (Section 13.12.502).

How Does Divorce Affect the Will?: Revokes the will as to the divorced spouse unless expressly provided otherwise. (Section 13.12.802).

How Does Marriage Affect the Will?: Revokes the will as to the spouse if he or she is not otherwise provided for. Spouse may still be entitled to his or her statutory share under the state intestate laws. (Section 13.12.301).

Who Must Be Mentioned in the Will?: Children, born or adopted; surviving spouse. (Sections 13.12.202 & 13.12.302).

Spouse's Right to Property Regardless of Will: The surviving spouse is entitled to 1/3 of the "augmented" estate of the deceased spouse. In general, the "augmented" estate includes both the property that passes under the will and any other property that passes by other "non-will" transfers, such as under the terms of a living trust or a joint tenancy arrangement. (Sections 13.12.202 & 13.12.203).

Laws of Intestate Succession (Distribution If No Will):

Spouse and children of spouse surviving: All to spouse.

Spouse and children not of spouse surviving: 1/2 to spouse and 1/2 to children or grandchildren per stirpes.

Spouse, but no children or parent(s) surviving: All to spouse.

Spouse and parent(s), but no children surviving: $200,000.00 and 3/4 of balance to spouse and 1/4 of balance to parent(s).

Children, but no spouse surviving: All to children equally or to their children per stirpes.

Parent(s), but no spouse or children surviving: All to parents equally or to the surviving parent.

No spouse, children, or parent(s) surviving: All to brothers and sisters per stirpes; or if none, 1/2 to paternal grandparents and their children per stirpes and 1/2 to maternal grandparents and their children per stirpes. (Sections 13.12.102 & 13.12.103).

Property Ownership: Common-law state. However, spouses may, by written agreement, declare that any or all of their property is community property. No joint tenancy in personal property. Persons with undivided interests in real estate are tenants-in-common. Spouses who acquire real estate hold it as tenants-by-the-entirety unless stated otherwise. Joint bank account deposits are payable to any survivor. (Sections 34.15.110, 34.15.730 & 34.77.030).

State Gift, Inheritance, or Estate Taxes: No gift tax; no inheritance tax; imposes state estate tax equal to federal credit for state death taxes. (Sections 43.31.011 to 43.31.430).

Living Will Form: Declaration Relating to Use of Life-Sustaining Procedures serves as Living Will (Section 18.12.010).

Other Directives: Durable Power of Attorney for Health Care (Section13.26.338 to 13.26.353). Anatomical Gift Act (Section 13.50.010 through 13.50.090). Durable Power of Attorney (Section 13.26.332).

Living Will Effective: Two (2) physicians determine that you are in a terminal condition and your death will result without using life-sustaining procedures. Your physician must then record your diagnosis and the contents of your Declaration in your medical records.

Witness Requirements: Sign your Declaration, or direct another to sign it, in the presence of two (2) adult witnesses or a notary public. Witnesses cannot be related by blood or marriage.

Arizona

State Website: www.azleg.state.az.us/

State Law Reference: Arizona Revised Statutes Annotated.

Court with Probate Jurisdiction: Superior Court.

Minimum Age for Disposing of Property by Will: 18. (Section 14-2501).

Required Number of Witnesses: Two. (Section 14-2502).

Can Witnesses Be Beneficiaries?: Yes. (Section 14-2505).

Are There Provisions for Self-Proving Wills?: Yes. (Section 14-2504).

Are Holographic Wills Permitted?: Yes. (Section 14-2503).

How Does Divorce Affect the Will?: Revokes the will as to the divorced spouse unless expressly provided otherwise. (Section 14-2802).

How Does Marriage Affect the Will?: Revokes the will as to the spouse if he or she is not otherwise provided for. Spouse may still be entitled to his or her statutory share under the state intestate laws. (Section 14-2301).

Who Must Be Mentioned in the Will?: Children, born or adopted; surviving spouse. (Sections 14-2301 & 14-2302).

Spouse's Right to Property Regardless of Will: Community property right to 1/2 of the deceased spouse's "community" property. In addition, the surviving spouse is entitled to a one-time allowance of $18,000.00. (Section 14-2402).

Laws of Intestate Succession (Distribution If No Will):

Spouse and children of spouse surviving: All of decedent's separate property and 1/2 of decedent's community property to spouse and 1/2 of decedent's community property to children.

Spouse and children not of spouse surviving: 1/2 of decedent's separate property to spouse and 1/2 of decedent's separate property and all of decedent's community property to children.

Spouse, but no children or parent(s) surviving: All to spouse.

Spouse and parent(s), but no children surviving: All to spouse.

Children, but no spouse surviving: All to children equally or to their children per stirpes.

Parent(s), but no spouse or children surviving: All to parents equally or to the surviving parent.

No spouse, children, or parent(s) surviving: All to brothers and sisters per stirpes; or if none, to the next-of-kin. (Sections 14-2102 & 14-2103).

Property Ownership: Community property state. Property acquired during marriage outside state before moving into state is quasi-community property. Joint tenancy between spouses if stated. Tenancy-by-the-entirety is not recognized. Joint bank account deposits are payable to any survivor unless clear evidence exists that deposit is payable only to specified survivor. (Section 25-211 and Section 33-431).

State Gift, Inheritance, or Estate Taxes: No gift tax; no inheritance tax; imposes state estate tax equal to federal credit for state death taxes. (Sections 42-4051 & 42-4052)

Living Will Form: Living Will (Sections 36-3261 and 36-3262).

Other Directives: Health Care Power of Attorney (Section 36-3224). Anatomical Gift Act (Sections 36-841 through 36-850). Durable Power of Attorney (Section 14-5501).

Living Will Effective: For the living will to become operative, a physician must certify that your condition is terminal, irreversible, or incurable.

Witness Requirements: Sign in the presence of two (2) or more witnesses or a notary public. Witnesses cannot be related by blood, adoption, or marriage, entitled to any part of your estate, or be directly financially responsible for your health care.

Arkansas

State Website: http://www.arkleg.state.ar.us/

State Law Reference: Arkansas Code.

Court with Probate Jurisdiction: Probate Court. (Section 28-1-104).

Minimum Age for Disposing of Property by Will: 18. (Section 28-25-101).

Required Number of Witnesses: Two. (Section 28-25-102).

Can Witnesses Be Beneficiaries?: Yes, but still must have 2 other disinterested witnesses. (Section 28-25-102).

Are There Provisions for Self-Proving Wills?: Yes. (Section 28-25-106).

Are Holographic Wills Permitted?: Yes. (Section 28-25-104).

How Does Divorce Affect the Will?: Revokes the will as to the divorced spouse. (Section 28-25-109).

How Does Marriage Affect the Will?: Does not revoke the will. (Section 28-25-109).

Who Must Be Mentioned in the Will?: Children, born or adopted; surviving spouse. (Sections 28-39-401 & 28-39-407).

Spouse's Right to Property Regardless of Will: Intestate share: 1/3 of personal property and 1/3 of real estate for life. (Section 28-39-401).

Laws of Intestate Succession (Distribution If No Will):

Spouse and children of spouse surviving: Real estate: 1/3 life estate to spouse and 2/3 to children equally or their children per stirpes. Personal property: 1/3 to spouse and 2/3 to children equally or their children per stirpes.

Spouse and children not of spouse surviving: Real estate: 1/3 life estate to spouse and 2/3 to children equally or their children per stirpes. Personal property: 1/3 to spouse and 2/3 to children equally or their children per stirpes.

Spouse, but no children or parent(s) surviving: All to spouse if married over 3 years. If married less than 3 years, 1/2 to spouse and 1/2 to brothers and sisters equally or their children per stirpes; or if no siblings or siblings' children, all to ancestors (up to great-grandparents); or if none, all to spouse.

Spouse and parent(s), but no children surviving: All to spouse if married over 3 years. If married less than 3 years, 1/2 to spouse and 1/2 to parent(s).

Children, but no spouse surviving: All to children equally or to their children per capita.

Parent(s), but no spouse or children surviving: All to parents equally or to the surviving parent.

No spouse, children, or parent(s) surviving: All to brothers and sisters per stirpes; or if none, to grandparents and their children per stirpes. (Sections 28-9-204, 28-9-205, & 28-9-206).

Property Ownership: Common-law state. Property acquired in a community property state is community property. Tenancy-in-common and joint tenancy are recognized. Tenancy-by-the-entirety is recognized when conveyance is to husband and wife. Joint bank account deposits are payable to any survivor. (Sections 18-12-106 & 18-12-603, & 23-47-204).

State Gift, Inheritance, or Estate Taxes: No gift tax; no inheritance tax; imposes state estate tax equal to federal credit for state death taxes. (Sections 26-59-101 to 26-59-122)

Living Will Form: Declaration serves as Living Will (Section 20-17-202).

Other Directives: Durable Power of Attorney for Health Care (Section 20-13-104). Anatomical Gift Act (Section 20-17-601). Durable Power of Attorney (Section 26-68-402).

Living Will Effective: Declaration applies when two (2) physicians diagnose you to have an incurable or irreversible condition that will cause death in a relatively short time.

Witness Requirements: Sign in the presence of two (2) witnesses. No other restrictions apply.

California

State Website: www.leginfo.ca.gov/

State Law Reference: California Law.

Court with Probate Jurisdiction: Superior Court.

Minimum Age for Disposing of Property by Will: 18. (Probate Code Section 6100).

Required Number of Witnesses: Two. (Probate Code Section 6110).

Can Witnesses Be Beneficiaries?: Yes. (Probate Code Section 6112).

Are There Provisions for Self-Proving Wills?: Yes. (Probate Code Section 8221).

Are Holographic Wills Permitted?: Yes. (Probate Code Section 6111).

How Does Divorce Affect the Will?: Revokes the will as to the divorced spouse unless expressly provided otherwise. (Probate Code Section 6122).

How Does Marriage Affect the Will?: Revokes the will as to the surviving spouse. However, spouse may still be entitled to statutory share. (Probate Code Section 21610).

Who Must Be Mentioned in the Will?: Children, born or adopted; grandchildren of deceased child; surviving spouse. (Probate Code Sections 21610 and 21620).

Spouse's Right to Property Regardless of Will: Community property right to 1/2 of the deceased spouse's "community" property. (Probate Code Section 100).

Laws of Intestate Succession (Distribution If No Will):

Spouse and children of spouse surviving: All of decedent's community property to spouse. If 1 child, 1/2 of decedent's separate property to spouse and 1/2 to child per stirpes. If more than 1 child, 1/3 of decedent's separate property to spouse and 2/3 to children per stirpes.

Spouse and children not of spouse surviving: 1/2 of community property, 1/3 life estate in separate real property, and 1/3 separate personal property to spouse; balance to children or grandchildren per stirpes.

Spouse, but no children or parent(s) surviving: All of decedent's community property to spouse. 1/2 of decedent's separate property to spouse and 1/2 of decedent's separate property to brothers and sisters equally or to their children per stirpes; or if none, all to spouse.

Spouse and parent(s), but no children surviving: All of decedent's community property to spouse. 1/2 of decedent's separate property to spouse and 1/2 of decedent's separate property to parents or surviving parent.

Children, but no spouse surviving: All to children equally or to their children per stirpes.

Parent(s), but no spouse or children surviving: All to parents equally or to the surviving parent.

No spouse, children, or parent(s) surviving: All to brothers and sisters per stirpes; or if none, to the next-of-kin. (Probate Code Sections 6401 and 6402).

Property Ownership. Community property state. Property in names of spouses as joint tenants is not community property unless stated. Joint tenancy must be stated. Tenancy-by-the-entirety is not recognized. Joint bank account deposits are payable to survivor if account had rights of survivorship stated. (Family Code Sections 750, 760, & 770 and Civil Code Section 683).

State Gift, Inheritance, or Estate Taxes: No gift tax; no inheritance tax; imposes state estate tax equal to federal credit for state death taxes. (Revenue and Taxation Code Sections 13301 and 13302).

Living Will Form: California Advanced Health Care Directive serves as Living Will (Probate Code Section 4701)

Other Directives: California Advanced Health Care Directive contains Power of Attorney for Health Care, Instructions for Health Care, Donation of Organs, and Appointment of Primary Physician (Probate Code Section 4701). Anatomical Gift Act (Health and Safety Code Sections 7150 - 7158). Durable Power of Attorney (Probate Code Sections 4120 - 4230).

Living Will Effective: This Directive becomes effective in the event that you have an incurable and irreversible condition that will result in death within a relatively short time, become unconscious and, to a reasonable degree of medical certainty, will not regain consciousness, or the likely risks and burdens of treatment would outweigh the expected benefits.

Witness Requirements: Sign in the presence of two (2) adult witnesses. A witness cannot be the person you appointed as your agent, your health care provider or an employee of your health care provider, or the operator or employee of a residential care facility for the elderly. Witnesses cannot be related to you by blood, marriage, or adoption, or be entitled to any part of your estate. A third witness, who must be a patient advocate or ombudsman, is required if the patient is in a skilled nursing facility (Probate Code Section 4701).

Colorado

State Website: www.leg.state.co.us/

State Law Reference: Colorado Revised Statutes.

Court with Probate Jurisdiction: District Court (Probate Court in Denver). (Section 13-9-103).

Minimum Age for Disposing of Property by Will: 18. (Section 15-11-501).

Required Number of Witnesses: Two. (Section 15-11-502(1)(c)).

Can Witnesses Be Beneficiaries?: Yes. (Section 15-11-505).

Are There Provisions for Self-Proving Wills?: Yes. (Section 15-11-504).

Are Holographic Wills Permitted?: Yes. (Section 15-11-502(2)).

How Does Divorce Affect the Will?: Revokes the will as to the divorced spouse. (Section 15-11-804).

How Does Marriage Affect the Will?: Revokes the will as to the spouse if he or she is not otherwise provided for. Spouse may still be entitled to his or her statutory share under the state intestate laws. (Section 15-11-301).

Who Must Be Mentioned in the Will?: Children, born or adopted; surviving spouse. (Sections 15-11-301 & 15-11-302).

Spouse's Right to Property Regardless of Will: The surviving spouse is entitled to 1/2 of the "augmented" estate of the deceased spouse. However, the amount is also dependent on the length of the marriage in years. In general, the "augmented" estate includes both the property that passes under the will and any other property that passes by other "non-will" transfers, such as under the terms of a living trust or a joint tenancy arrangement. (Section 15-11-201).

Laws of Intestate Succession (Distribution If No Will):

Spouse and children of spouse surviving: Spouse receives entire estate. (Section 15-11-102(1)(b)).

Spouse and children not of spouse surviving: $150,000.00 and 1/2 to spouse and 1/2 to children and grandchildren per stirpes. (Section 15-11-102(3)).

Spouse, but no children or parent(s) surviving: $200,000.00 and 3/4 of remainder to spouse, 1/4 to parent(s). (Section 15-11-102(1)(A)).

Spouse and parent(s), but no children surviving: All to spouse. (Section 15-11-102(2)).

Children, but no spouse surviving: All to children equally or to their children per capita at each generation. (Section 15-11-103(1)).

Parent(s), but no spouse or children surviving: All to parents equally or to the surviving parent. (Section 15-11-103(2)).

No spouse, children, or parent(s) surviving: All to brothers and sisters per capita at each generation; or if none, to grandparents and their children per capita at each generation; or if none, to nearest lineal ancestors and their children. (Section 15-11-102).

Property Ownership: Common-law state. Tenancy-in-common is presumed unless otherwise stated. Joint tenancy is recognized. Tenancy-by-the-entirety is not recognized. (Section 38-11-101).

State Gift, Inheritance, or Estate Taxes: No gift tax; no inheritance tax; imposes state estate tax equal to federal credit for state death taxes. (Sections 39-23.5+).

Living Will Form: Colorado Declaration as to Medical or Surgical Treatment serves as Living Will (Section 15-18-103).

Other Directives: Durable Power of Attorney for Health Care (Section 15-14-506). Anatomical Gift Act (Section 12-34-101). Durable Power of Attorney (Sections 15-1-1301 - 15-1-1320, 15-14-501 - 15-14-509 and 15-14-601 - 15-14-611).

Living Will Effective: Two (2) physicians must determine that you are in a terminal condition and your death will result without using life-sustaining procedures. Your physician must then record your diagnosis and the contents of your Declaration in your medical records.

Witness Requirements: Sign in the presence of two (2) adult witnesses. A witness cannot be a person who has claim against your estate upon your death, stands to inherit from your estate, or a physician, an employee of your attending physician or treating health care facility, or a patient of your treating health care facility.

Connecticut

State Website: www.cga.state.ct.us/2001/pub/Titles.htm

State Law Reference: Connecticut General Statutes Annotated.

Court with Probate Jurisdiction: Probate Court.

Minimum Age for Disposing of Property by Will: 18. (Section 45a-250).

Required Number of Witnesses: Two. (Section 45a-251).

Can Witnesses Be Beneficiaries?: Yes, but must still have 2 other disinterested witnesses. (Section 45a-258).

Are There Provisions for Self-Proving Wills?: No provision.

Are Holographic Wills Permitted?: No provision.

How Does Divorce Affect the Will?: Revokes the will completely. (Section 45a-257c).

How Does Marriage Affect the Will?: Revokes the will completely unless spouse was not a beneficiary under the will. (Section 45a-257a).

Who Must Be Mentioned in the Will?: Children, born or adopted; surviving spouse. (Section 45a-257).

Spouse's Right to Property Regardless of Will: The surviving spouse is entitled to 1/3 of the deceased spouse's real estate and personal property for the rest of his or her life. (Section 45a-436).

Laws of Intestate Succession (Distribution If No Will):

Spouse and children of spouse surviving: $100,000.00 and 1/2 of balance to spouse and 1/2 of balance to children or grandchildren per stirpes. (Section 45a-437(3)).

Spouse and children not of spouse surviving: 1/2 to spouse and 1/2 to children or grandchildren per stirpes. (Sections 45a-437(4) & 45a-438).

Spouse, but no children or parent(s) surviving: All to spouse. (Section 45a-437(1)).

Spouse and parent(s), but no children surviving: $100,000.00 and 3/4 of balance to spouse and 1/4 of balance to parents or surviving parent. (Section 45a-437(2)).

Children, but no spouse surviving: All to children equally or to their children per stirpes. (Section 45a-438).

Parent(s), but no spouse or children surviving: All to parents equally or to the surviving parent. (Section 45a-439(a)(1)).

No spouse, children, or parent(s) surviving: All to brothers and sisters per stirpes; or if none, to next-of-kin. (Section 45a-439(2)-(3)).

Property Ownership: Common-law state. Tenancy-in-common is presumed unless words "joint tenants" follow names. Joint tenancy automatically includes right of survivorship. Tenancy-by-the-entirety is recognized. (Section 47-14a).

State Gift, Inheritance, or Estate Taxes: No gift tax; no inheritance tax; imposes state estate tax equal to federal credit for state death taxes. (Sections 12-391 to 12-399).

Living Will Form: Connecticut Health Care Instructions serves as Living Will (Section 19a-575).

Other Directives: Connecticut Health Care Instructions also contain Appointment of Health Care Agent and Appointment of Attorney-In-Fact for Health Care Decisions. Anatomical Gift Act (Section 19a-270). Durable Power of Attorney (Section 45a-562).

Living Will Effective: When you have an incurable or irreversible medical condition which, without the use of life support, will result in death in a relatively short period of time, or you are in a permanent coma or a persistent vegetative state.

Witness Requirements: Sign in the presence of two (2) adult witnesses. Your appointed agent cannot be a witness. If you reside in a resident facility operated or licensed by the department of mental health or department of mental retardation, additional witness requirements must be met and you should consult an attorney.

Delaware

State Website: www.delcode.state.de.us/

State Law Reference: Delaware Code Annotated.

Court with Probate Jurisdiction: Chancery Court.

Minimum Age for Disposing of Property by Will: 18. (Section 12-201).

Required Number of Witnesses: Two. (Section 12-202).

Can Witnesses Be Beneficiaries?: Yes. (Section 12-203).

Are There Provisions for Self-Proving Wills?: Yes. (Section 12-1305).

Are Holographic Wills Permitted?: No.

Are Living Wills Recognized?: Yes. (Sections 16-2501 to 16-2518).

How Does Marriage Affect the Will?: Revokes the will as to the spouse if he or she is not otherwise provided for. The surviving spouse may still claim his or her statutory share of the decedent's estate. (Section 12-323).

Who Must Be Mentioned in the Will?: Children, born or adopted; surviving spouse. (Sections 12-301 to 12-321).

Spouse's Right to Property Regardless of Will: The surviving spouse is entitled to 1/3 of the deceased spouse's estate or $20,000.00, whichever is less. (Section 12-901(a)).

Laws of Intestate Succession (Distribution If No Will):

Spouse and children of spouse surviving: Real estate: life estate to spouse and all the rest to children or grandchildren per stirpes. Personal property: $50,000.00 and 1/2 of balance to spouse and 1/2 of balance to children or grandchildren per stirpes. (Section 12-502(3)).

Spouse and children not of spouse surviving: Real estate: life estate to spouse and all the rest to children or grandchildren per stirpes. Personal property: 1/2 to spouse and 1/2 to children or grandchildren per stirpes. (Section 12-502(4)).

Spouse, but no children or parent(s) surviving: All to spouse. (Section 12-502(1)).

Spouse and parent(s), but no children surviving: Real estate: life estate to spouse; remainder to parents or surviving parent. Personal property: $50,000.00 and 1/2 of balance to spouse and 1/2 of balance to parents or surviving parent. (Section 12-502).

Children, but no spouse surviving: All to children equally or to their children per stirpes. (Section 12-503(1)).

Parent(s), but no spouse or children surviving: All to parents equally or to the surviving parent. (Section 12-503(2)).

No spouse, children, or parent(s) surviving: All to brothers or sisters or their children per stirpes; or if none, to the next-of-kin per stirpes. (Section 12-503(3)(4)).

Property Ownership. Common-law state. Tenancy-in-common is presumed. If joint owners are married, tenancy-by-the-entirety is created. Joint tenancy created only if stated. Joint bank account deposits are payable to any survivor. (Sections 25-309, 25-311, & 25-701).

State Gift, Inheritance, or Estate Taxes: No inheritance tax; imposes state estate tax equal to federal credit for state death taxes. (Sections 30-1501+)

Living Will Form: Instructions for Health Care serves as Living Will (Section 16-2503).

Other Directives: Delaware Advance Directive contains Power of Attorney for Health Care and Instructions for Health Care (Section 16-2503). Anatomical Gift Act (Sections 16-2710 - 16-2719). Durable Power of Attorney (Section 12-4901 - 12-4905).

Living Will Effective: Two (2) physicians determine in writing that you have a terminal condition and/or are in a permanent state of unconsciousness.

Witness Requirements: Sign in the presence of two (2) adult witnesses. A witness cannot be a person who has claim against your estate upon your death, stands to inherit from your estate, be directly financially responsible for your health care, or be an owner, operator, or employee of a residential long-term health care institution in which you reside. If declarant is a patient in a nursing home, one of the witnesses must be a patient advocate or ombudsman.

District of Columbia (Washington D.C.)

State Website: http://dccode.westgroup.com/home/dccodes/default.wl

State Law Reference: District of Columbia Code Annotated.

Court with Probate Jurisdiction: Superior Court. (Section 16-3101).

Minimum Age for Disposing of Property by Will: 18. (Section 18-102).

Required Number of Witnesses: Two. (Section 18-103).

Can Witnesses Be Beneficiaries?: No, if they are eligible to take any portion of the estate under District intestacy law. (Section 18-104).

Are There Provisions for Self-Proving Wills?: No provision.

Are Holographic Wills Permitted?: No provision.

How Does Divorce Affect the Will?: Does not revoke the will. (Section 18-109).

How Does Marriage Affect the Will?: Does not revoke the will. (Section 18-109).

Who Must Be Mentioned in the Will?: Surviving spouse. (Sections 19-113).

Spouse's Right to Property Regardless of Will: The surviving spouse is entitled to 1/3 of the deceased spouse's estate. (Sections 19-113 & 19-302).

Laws of Intestate Succession (Distribution If No Will):

Spouse and children of spouse and decedent surviving: Real estate: 2/3 to spouse 1/3 to children.

Spouse and both children of spouse and children of spouse but not of decedent surviving: 1/2 to spouse, and 1/2 to children of spouse and decedent.

Spouse and any children of decedent who are not children of surviving spouse: 1/2 to spouse, and 1/2 to decedent's children.

Spouse, but no children, grandchildren, or parent(s) surviving: all to spouse.

Spouse and parent(s), but no children surviving: 3/4 to spouse, and 1/4 to parent(s).

Children but no spouse surviving: all to the children equally or to their children per stirpes.

Parent(s), but no spouse or children surviving: all to parent(s) equally, or to surviving parent.

No spouse, children, or parent(s) surviving: all to brothers and sisters or their children per stirpes, or if none, to collaterals; or if none, to grandparent(s). (Sections 301-302 & 305-312)

Property Ownership: Common-law state. Tenancy-in-common is presumed unless joint tenancy is stated. Joint ownership by husband and wife is presumed to be tenancy-by-the-entirety. Joint bank account deposits are payable to any survivor. (Section 42-576).

State Gift, Inheritance, or Estate Taxes: No gift tax; no inheritance tax; imposes state estate tax equal to federal credit for state death taxes. (Sections 47-3701 to 47-3723).

Living Will Form: District of Columbia Declaration serves as Living Will (Section 7-622).

Other Directives: Power of Attorney for Health Care (Section 21-2207). Anatomical Gift Act (Section 7-1521.04). Durable Power of Attorney (Section 21-2081).

Living Will Effective: Two (2) physicians determine that you are in a terminal condition and your death will result without using life-sustaining procedures. Your physician must then record your diagnosis and the contents of your Declaration in your medical records.

Witness Requirements: Sign in the presence of two (2) adult witnesses. A witness cannot be your appointed attorney-in-fact, health care provider, or an employee of your health care provider. Witnesses also cannot be related by blood, marriage, or adoption, stand to inherit from your estate, or be financially responsible for your health care.

Florida

State Website: http://www.flsenate.gov/statutes/index.cfm

State Law Reference: Florida Statutes Annotated.

Court with Probate Jurisdiction: Circuit Court.

Minimum Age for Disposing of Property by Will: 18. (Section 732.501).

Required Number of Witnesses: Two. (Section 732.502(1)(b)).

Can Witnesses Be Beneficiaries?: Yes. (Section 732.504).

Are There Provisions for Self-Proving Wills?: Yes. (Section 732.503).

Are Holographic Wills Permitted?: No. (Section 732.502).

How Does Divorce Affect the Will?: Revokes the will as to the divorced spouse. (Section 732.507(2)).

How Does Marriage Affect the Will?: Revokes the will as to the spouse if he or she is not otherwise provided for. Spouse will still be entitled to his or her statutory share under the state intestate laws regardless of prior will. (Section 732.301).

Who Must Be Mentioned in the Will?: Children, born or adopted; surviving spouse. (Sections 732.301 & 732.302).

Spouse's Right to Property Regardless of Will: The surviving spouse is entitled to 30 percent of the deceased spouse's estate. (Section 732.2065).

Laws of Intestate Succession (Distribution If No Will):

Spouse and children of spouse surviving: $60,000.00 and 1/2 of balance to spouse and 1/2 of balance to children and grandchildren per stirpes. (Sections 732.102) & 732.103).

Spouse and children not of spouse surviving: 1/2 to spouse and 1/2 to children and grandchildren per stirpes. (Section 732.102).

Spouse, but no children or parent(s) surviving: All to spouse. (Section 732.102).

Spouse and parent(s), but no children surviving: All to spouse. (Section 732.102).

Children, but no spouse surviving: All to children equally or to their children per stirpes. (Section 732.103).

Parent(s), but no spouse or children surviving: All to parents equally or to the surviving parent. (Section 732.103).

No spouse, children, or parent(s) surviving: All to brothers and sisters or their children per stirpes; or if none, 1/2 to maternal next-of-kin and 1/2 to paternal next-of-kin beginning with grandparents. (Section 732.103).

Property Ownership: Common-law state. Personal property or real estate owned by husband and wife is presumed to be a tenancy-by-the-entirety with survivorship. Joint tenancy includes survivorship only if stated. Joint bank account deposits are payable to any survivor. (Sections 689.11 & 689.15).

State Gift, Inheritance, or Estate Taxes: No gift tax; no inheritance tax; imposes state estate tax equal to federal credit for state death taxes. (Sections 198.01 to 198.44).

Living Will Form: Living Will (Section 765-303).

Other Directives: Designation of Health Care Surrogate (Section 765-203). Anatomical Gift Act (Sections 765.510 - 765.546). Durable Power of Attorney (Section 709.08).

Living Will Effective: Two (2) physicians determine in writing that you have a terminal condition, and/or are in a permanent state of unconsciousness and can no longer make your own health care decisions.

Witness Requirements: Sign in the presence of two (2) adult witnesses. At least one (1) of your witnesses must not be related to you by marriage or blood.

Georgia

State Website: www.legis.state.ga.us

State Law Reference: Code of Georgia Annotated.

Court with Probate Jurisdiction: Probate Court. (Section 15-9-30).

Minimum Age for Disposing of Property by Will: 14. (Section 53-4-10).

Required Number of Witnesses: Two. (Section 53-4-20).

Can Witnesses Be Beneficiaries?: Yes, but any gift to a witness who is a beneficiary is void unless there are also 2 other disinterested witnesses. (Section 53-4-23).

Are There Provisions for Self-Proving Wills?: Yes. (Section 53-4-24).

Are Holographic Wills Permitted?: No provision.

How Does Divorce Affect the Will?: Revokes the will completely unless expressly provided otherwise. (Section 53-4-49).

How Does Marriage Affect the Will?: Revokes the will completely unless expressly provided otherwise. (Section 53-4-48).

Who Must Be Mentioned in the Will?: Statute contains detailed provisions regarding this matter. Please refer directly to statute text or consult an attorney if this is a critical factor. (Section 53-4-48).

Spouse's Right to Property Regardless of Will: The surviving spouse is entitled to 1 year's support from the deceased spouse's estate. (Section 53-3-1).

Laws of Intestate Succession (Distribution If No Will):

Spouse and children of spouse surviving: Children or grandchildren and spouse all take equal shares with at least 1/4 to spouse. (Section 53-2-1).

Spouse and children not of spouse surviving: Children or grandchildren and spouse all take equal shares with at least 1/4 to spouse. (Section 53-2-1).

Spouse, but no children or parent(s) surviving: All to spouse. (Section 53-2-1).

Spouse and parent(s), but no children surviving: All to spouse. (Section 53-2-1).

Children, but no spouse surviving: All to children equally or to their children per stirpes. (Section 53-2-1).

Parent(s), but no spouse or children surviving: All to parents, brothers, and sisters equally or to their children per stirpes. (Section 53-2-1).

No spouse, children, or parent(s) surviving: All to brothers and sisters or their children per stirpes; or if none, to paternal and maternal next-of-kin. (Section 53-2-1).

Property Ownership: Common-law state. Tenancy-in-common is presumed unless "joint tenants" or similar language is stated specifically. Tenancy-by-the-entirety is not recognized. Joint bank account deposits are payable to any survivor unless clear evidence exists that deposit is payable only to specified survivor. (Section 44-6-120).

State Gift, Inheritance, or Estate Taxes: No gift tax; no inheritance tax; imposes state estate tax equal to federal credit for state death taxes. (Sections 48-12-1 to 48-12-6).

Living Will Form: Georgia Living Will (Section 31-32-3).

Other Directives: Durable Power of Attorney For Health Care (Section 31-36-1). Anatomical Gift Act Section 44-4-140). Durable Power of Attorney (Sections 10-6-140 through 10-6-142).

Living Will Effective: Two (2) physicians determine in writing that you have a terminal condition, and/or are in a permanent state of unconsciousness.

Witness Requirements: Sign in the presence of two (2) adult witnesses. A witness cannot be a person who has claim against your estate upon your death, stands to inherit from your estate, be directly financially responsible for your health care, or be an owner, operator, or employee of a health care institution in which you are a patient. Witnesses also cannot be related by blood or marriage.

Hawaii

State Website: http://www.capitol.hawaii.gov/

State Law Reference: Hawaii Revised Statutes.

Court with Probate Jurisdiction: Circuit Court. (Section 603-21.6).

Minimum Age for Disposing of Property by Will: 18. (Section 560:2-501).

Required Number of Witnesses: Two. (Section 560:2-502(3)).

Can Witnesses Be Beneficiaries?: Yes. (Section 560:2-505(b)).

Are There Provisions for Self-Proving Wills?: Yes. (Section 560:2-504).

Are Holographic Wills Permitted?: Yes. (Sections 560:2-502(b) & 560:2-503).

How Does Divorce Affect the Will?: Revokes the will as to the divorced spouse unless expressly provided otherwise. (Section 560:2-802).

How Does Marriage Affect the Will?: Revokes the will as to the spouse if he or she is not otherwise provided for. Spouse may still be entitled to his or her statutory share under the state intestate laws. (Section 560:2-301).

Who Must Be Mentioned in the Will?: Children, born or adopted; surviving spouse. (Sections 560:2-301 & 560:2-302).

Spouse's Right to Property Regardless of Will: The surviving spouse is entitled to 1/2 of the community property on the death of the other spouse. The surviving spouse's right to additional property regardless of provisions in the will depends on the length of the marriage. Please refer to the statute for details. (Section 510:10 and 560:2-202).

Laws of Intestate Succession (Distribution If No Will):

Spouse and children of spouse surviving: All to spouse. (Section 560:2-102(1)(A)).

Spouse and children not of spouse surviving: $150,000.00 and 1/2 of remaining estate to spouse and 1/2 to children equally or to the grandchildren. (Section 560:2-102(3)).

Spouse, but no children or parent(s) surviving: All to spouse. (Section 560:2-102(1)(A)).

Spouse and parent(s), but no children surviving: $200,000.00 and 3/4 of remaining estate to spouse and 1/4 to parents equally or surviving parent. (Section 560:2-102(2)).

Children, but no spouse surviving: All to children equally or to their children per stirpes. (Section 560:2-103(1)).

Parent(s), but no spouse or children surviving: All to parents equally or to the surviving parent. (Section 560:2-103(a)).

No spouse, children, or parent(s) surviving: All to brothers and sisters or their children per stirpes; or if none, to grandparents; or if none, to uncles and aunts equally. (Section 560:2-103(3)(4)).

Property Ownership: Community property state. Tenancy-in-common is presumed unless joint tenancy or tenancy-by-the-entirety is stated. Joint bank account deposits are payable to any survivor unless clear evidence exists that deposit is payable only to a specified survivor. (Sections 509-1, 509-2, & 510-22+).

State Gift, Inheritance, or Estate Taxes: No gift tax; no inheritance tax; imposes state estate tax equal to federal credit for state death taxes. (Section 236D-3).

Living Will Form: Instruction for Health Care serves as Living Will (Section 327E-3).

Other Directives: Hawaii Advanced Health Care Directive has Durable Power of Attorney for Health Care and Instructions for Health Care (Section 327E-3). Anatomical Gift Act (Section 327-1). Durable Power of Attorney (Sections 551D-1 through 551D-7).

Living Will Effective: In the event that you have an incurable and irreversible condition that will result in death within a relatively short time, become unconscious and, to a reasonable degree of medical certainty, will not regain consciousness, or the likely risks and burdens of treatment would outweigh the expected benefits.

Witness Requirements: Sign in the presence of two (2) adult witnesses. At least one (1) of your witnesses cannot be related to you by marriage or blood or entitled to any part of your estate. A witness cannot be the person you appoint as your agent, health care provider, or an employee of your health care provider.

Idaho

State Website: http://www3.state.id.us/

State Law Reference: Idaho Code.

Court with Probate Jurisdiction: District Court.

Minimum Age for Disposing of Property by Will: 18, or emancipated from parents. (Section 15-2-501).

Required Number of Witnesses: Two. (Section 15-2-502).

Can Witnesses Be Beneficiaries?: Yes. (Section 15-2-205).

Are There Provisions for Self-Proving Wills?: Yes. (Section 15-2-504).

Are Holographic Wills Permitted?: Yes. (Section 15-2-503).

How Does Divorce Affect the Will?: Revokes the will as to the divorced spouse unless expressly provided otherwise. (Section 15-2-802).

How Does Marriage Affect the Will?: Revokes the will as to the spouse if he or she is not otherwise provided for. Spouse may still be entitled to his or her statutory share under the state intestate laws. (Section 15-2-301).

Who Must Be Mentioned in the Will?: Children, born or adopted; surviving spouse. (Sections 15-2-301 & 15-2-302).

Spouse's Right to Property Regardless of Will: Community property right to 1/2 of the deceased spouse's "community" property. (Section 15-2-301).

Laws of Intestate Succession (Distribution If No Will):

Spouse and children of spouse surviving: All of decedent's community property to spouse; $50,000.00 and 1/2 of balance of decedent's separate property to spouse and 1/2 of balance to children or grandchildren per stirpes. (Sections 15-2-102(1)(3) & 15-2-103(a)).

Spouse and children not of spouse surviving: All of decedent's community property to spouse; 1/2 of decedent's separate property to spouse and 1/2 to children or grandchildren per stirpes. (Section 15-2-102(a)).

Spouse, but no children or parent(s) surviving: All to spouse. (Section 15-2-102(a)(1)).

Spouse and parent(s), but no children surviving: All of decedent's community property to spouse; $50,000.00 and 1/2 of balance of decedent's separate property to spouse and 1/2 of balance to parents or surviving parent. (Section 15-2-102(a)(2)).

Children, but no spouse surviving: All to children or to their children per stirpes. (Section 15-2-103(a)).

Parent(s), but no spouse or children surviving: All to parents equally or to the surviving parent. (Section 15-2-103(b)).

No spouse, children, or parent(s) surviving: All to brothers and sisters or their children, if surviving. If not, then 1/2 to living maternal grandparents or their children and 1/2 to paternal grandparents or their children. (Section 15-2-103(d)).

Property Ownership: Community property state. Tenancy-in-common is presumed unless joint tenancy is stated or property is acquired as partnership or as community property. Tenancy-by-the-entirety is not recognized. Joint bank account deposits are payable to any survivor unless clear evidence exists that deposit is payable only to specified survivor. (Sections 32-903 & 32-906, & Section 55-508).

State Gift, Inheritance, or Estate Taxes: No gift tax; imposes an inheritance tax of up to 30 percent; imposes state estate tax equal to federal credit for state death taxes less any amounts paid on state inheritance tax. Maximum total state inheritance and state estate tax is equal to the maximum allowable federal estate tax credit for state death taxes. (Sections 14-401 to 14-413).

Living Will Form: Idaho Living Will (Section 39-4504).

Other Directives: Durable Power of Attorney for Health Care (Section 39-4505). Anatomical Gift Act (Section 39-3413). Durable Power of Attorney (Section 15-5-503).

Living Will Effective: Two (2) physicians determine that you are in a terminal condition, your death will result without using life-sustaining procedures, or you are in a persistent vegetative state.

Witness Requirements: Sign in the presence of two (2) adult witnesses. No other restrictions apply.

Illinois

State Website: http://www.ilga.gov/

State Law Reference: Illinois Compiled Statutes.

Court with Probate Jurisdiction: Circuit Court.

Minimum Age for Disposing of Property by Will: 18. (Section 755-5/4-1).

Required Number of Witnesses: Two. (Section 755-5/4-3).

Can Witnesses Be Beneficiaries?: Yes, but any gift to a beneficiary who was a witness will be void unless there were also 2 other disinterested witnesses. However, a witness-beneficiary may still receive his or her intestate share. (Section 755-5/4-3).

Are There Provisions for Self-Proving Wills?: Not in statute. However, self-proving affidavits have been accepted in the courts. (Section 755-5/4-6).

Are Holographic Wills Permitted?: No provision.

How Does Divorce Affect the Will?: Revokes will as to the divorced spouse. (Section 755-5/4-7).

How Does Marriage Affect the Will?: Does not revoke the will. (Section 755-5/4-7).

Who Must Be Mentioned in the Will?: Children, born or adopted; surviving spouse. (Sections 755-5/4-10 & 755-5/15-1).

Spouse's Right to Property Regardless of Will: Generally, the surviving spouse is entitled to 1/2 of the deceased spouse's estate if there are no children and to only 1/3 if there are children. However, please refer directly to the statute as the provisions are detailed. (Section 755-5/2-8).

Laws of Intestate Succession (Distribution If No Will):

Spouse and children of spouse surviving: 1/2 to spouse and 1/2 to children equally or to the grandchildren per stirpes.

Spouse and children not of spouse surviving: 1/2 to spouse and 1/2 to children equally or to the grandchildren per stirpes.

Spouse, but no children or parent(s) surviving: All to spouse.

Spouse and parent(s), but no children surviving: All to spouse.

Children, but no spouse surviving: All to children equally or to their children per stirpes.

Parent(s), but no spouse or children surviving: All to parents, brothers, sisters, or children of brothers and sisters per stirpes. If only 1 surviving parent, he or she takes a double share.

No spouse, children, or parent(s) surviving: 1/2 to maternal grandparents and 1/2 to paternal grandparents equally or to surviving grandparent; or if none, to their children per stirpes; or if none, 1/2 to maternal great-grandparents and 1/2 to paternal great-grandparents equally or to surviving great-grandparent; or if none, to their children per stirpes; or if none of the above, all to the next-of-kin. (Section 755-5/2-1).

Property Ownership: Common-law state. Tenancy-in-common is presumed. Joint tenancy with right of survivorship created only by statement that property is held in joint tenancy and not tenancy-in-common. Tenancy-by-the-entirety is recognized. Joint bank account deposits are payable to any survivor. (Sections 205-105/4 to 105/8 & 765-1005/1 to 1005/4a).

State Gift, Inheritance, or Estate Taxes: No gift tax; no inheritance tax; imposes state estate tax equal to federal credit for state death taxes. (Sections 35-405/1 to 35-405/18).

Living Will Form: Illinois Declaration serves as Living Will (Section 755-35/1).

Other Directives: Durable Power of Attorney for Health Care (Section 755-45/4-1). Anatomical Gift Act (Section 755-50). Durable Power of Attorney (Section 755-45/2-1).

Living Will Effective: If death would occur without the use of death-delaying procedures. Your physician must personally examine you and certify in writing that you are terminally ill.

Witness Requirements: Sign in the presence of two (2) adult witnesses. Witnesses cannot be entitled to any part of your estate or financially responsible for your medical care.

Indiana

State Website: http://www.in.gov/legislative/ic/code/

State Law Reference: Indiana Code Annotated.

Court with Probate Jurisdiction: Circuit or Superior Court (Probate Court in St. Joseph and Vigo Counties).

Minimum Age for Disposing of Property by Will: 18, however, no minimum age if a member of Armed Forces or Merchant Marines. (Section 29-1-5-1).

Required Number of Witnesses: Two. (Section 29-1-5-3).

Can Witnesses Be Beneficiaries?: Yes, but any gift to a beneficiary who was a witness will be void. However, if the witness-beneficiary is entitled to receive an intestate share of the estate, he or she may receive the lesser of the intestate share or the property gifted to him or her under the will. (Section 29-1-5-2).

Are There Provisions for Self-Proving Wills?: Yes. (Section 29-1-5-3).

Are Holographic Wills Permitted?: No provision.

How Does Divorce Affect the Will?: Revokes the will as to the divorced spouse. (Section 29-1-5-8).

How Does Marriage Affect the Will?: Does not revoke the will. (Section 29-1-5-8).

Who Must Be Mentioned in the Will?: Children, born or adopted; surviving spouse. (Sections 29-1-3-1 & 29-1-3-8).

Spouse's Right to Property Regardless of Will: The surviving spouse is entitled to 1/2 of the deceased spouse's estate. If there are surviving children of a prior spouse, a second or subsequent spouse is entitled to 1/3 of the deceased's personal property and 1/3 of the deceased's real estate for the rest of his or her life. (Section 29-1-3-1).

Laws of Intestate Succession (Distribution If No Will):

Spouse and children of spouse surviving: 1/2 to spouse and 1/2 to children.

Spouse and children not of spouse surviving: Real estate: an amount equal to 1/4 of the fair market value of real estate to spouse and balance to children. Personal property: 1/2 to spouse and 1/2 to children.

Spouse, but no children or parent(s) surviving: All to spouse.

Spouse and parent(s), but no children surviving: 3/4 to spouse and 1/4 to parents or surviving parent.

Children, but no spouse surviving: All to children equally or their children per stirpes.

Parent(s), brothers, sisters, and children of brothers and sisters, but no spouse or children surviving: Surviving parents, brothers, sisters all share equally, but each surviving parent is entitled to at least 1/4 of estate.

No spouse, children, parent(s), or brothers or sisters surviving: All to brothers' and sisters' children per stirpes; or if none, to grandparents; or if none, to aunts and uncles per stirpes. (Section 29-1-2-1).

Property Ownership: Common-law state. Joint tenancy, tenancy-in-common, and tenancy-by-the-entirety are recognized. Tenancy-in-common is presumed unless joint tenancy stated. Joint ownership by husband and wife is presumed to be a tenancy-by-the-entirety. Joint bank account deposits are payable to any survivor. (Section 6-4.1-8-4 & 32-17-2-1, 32-17-3-1).

State Gift, Inheritance, or Estate Taxes: No gift tax; imposes an inheritance tax of up to 20 percent; imposes state estate tax equal to federal credit for state death taxes less any amounts paid on state inheritance tax. Maximum total state inheritance and state estate tax is equal to the maximum allowable federal estate tax credit for state death taxes. (Sections 6-4.1-5-1 & 6-4.1-11-2).

Living Will Form: Indiana Living Will Declaration (Section 16-36-4-10).

Other Directives: Durable Power of Attorney for Health Care Decisions and Appointment of Health Care Representative are contained within the Living Will document. Anatomical Gift Act (Section 29-2-16-1). Durable Power of Attorney (Section 29-3-5).

Living Will Effective: Your physician must certify in writing that you are in a terminal condition and your death would occur within a short period of time without the use of life-sustaining medical care.

Witness Requirements: Sign in the presence of two (2) adult witnesses. Witnesses cannot be entitled to any part of your estate, related to you by blood or marriage, financially responsible for your medical care, or be the person who signed the Declaration on your behalf.

Iowa

State Website: http://www.legis.state.ia.us/

State Law Reference: Iowa Code Annotated.

Court with Probate Jurisdiction: District Court. (Section 633.10).

Minimum Age for Disposing of Property by Will: 18 ("full age"). (Section 633.264).

Required Number of Witnesses: Two. (Section 633.279).

Can Witnesses Be Beneficiaries?: Yes, but any gift to a beneficiary who was a witness will be void unless there were also 2 other disinterested witnesses. However, a witness-beneficiary is still entitled to receive any intestate share. (Section 633.281).

Are There Provisions for Self-Proving Wills?: Yes. (Section 633.279).

Are Holographic Wills Permitted?: No provision.

Are Living Wills Recognized?: Yes, under the "Iowa Life Sustaining Procedures Act." (Sections 144A.1 to 144A.12).

How Does Divorce Affect the Will?: Revokes the will as to divorced spouse unless he or she remarries. (Section 633.271).

How Does Marriage Affect the Will?: Revokes the will as to the spouse if he or she is not otherwise provided for. Spouse may still be entitled to his or her statutory share under the state intestate laws. (Section 633.236).

Who Must Be Mentioned in the Will?: Children, born or adopted; surviving spouse. (Sections 633.236 & 633.267).

Spouse's Right to Property Regardless of Will: The surviving spouse is entitled to 1/3 of the deceased spouse's estate. (Section 633.238).

Laws of Intestate Succession (Distribution If No Will):

Spouse and children of spouse surviving: All to spouse.

Spouse and children not of spouse surviving: $50,000.00 and 1/2 of balance to spouse and 1/2 of balance to children.

Spouse, but no children or parent(s) surviving: All to spouse.

Spouse and parent(s), but no children surviving: All to spouse.

Children, but no spouse surviving: All to children equally or to their children per stirpes.

Parent(s), but no spouse or children surviving: All to parents equally or to the surviving parent.

No spouse, children, or parent(s) surviving: All to brothers and sisters or their children per stirpes; or if none, to ancestors and their children per stirpes; or if none, to spouse or heirs of spouse. (Sections 633.211, 633.212, & 633.219).

Property Ownership: Common-law state. Tenancy-in-common is presumed unless joint tenancy stated. Tenancy-by-the-entirety not recognized. Joint bank account deposits are payable to any survivor. (Sections 534.302 & 557.15).

State Gift, Inheritance, or Estate Taxes: No gift tax; imposes an inheritance tax of up to 15 percent; imposes state estate tax equal to federal credit for state death taxes less any amounts paid on state inheritance tax. Maximum total state inheritance and state estate tax is equal to the maximum allowable federal estate tax credit for state death taxes. (Sections 450.10 & 451.2).

Living Will Form: Iowa Declaration serves as Living Will (Section 144A.3).

Other Directives: Durable Power of Attorney for Health Care (Section 144B.2). Anatomical Gift Act (Section142C). Durable Power of Attorney (Section 633.705).

Living Will Effective: Two (2) physicians must certify in writing that you are in a terminal condition and your death would occur within a short period of time without the use of life-sustaining medical care.

Witness Requirements: Sign in the presence of two (2) witnesses eighteen (18) years or older or a notary public. A witness cannot be your health care provider or an employee of your health care provider.

Kansas

State Website: http://www.kslegislature.org/

State Law Reference: Kansas Statutes Annotated.

Court with Probate Jurisdiction: District Court.

Minimum Age for Disposing of Property by Will: 18, unless the testator is married, then the minimum age is 16. (Section 38-101 & 59-601).

Required Number of Witnesses: Two. (Section 59-606).

Can Witnesses Be Beneficiaries?: Yes, but a gift to a beneficiary who was a witness will be void unless there were also 2 other disinterested witnesses. If entitled to take under intestacy statutes, then witness takes lesser of intestate share or gift under the will. (Section 59-604).

Are There Provisions for Self-Proving Wills?: Yes. (Section 59-606).

Are Holographic Wills Permitted?: No provision.

How Does Divorce Affect the Will?: Revokes the will as to divorced spouse. (Section 59-610).

How Does Marriage Affect the Will?: Revokes the will if a child is later born to or adopted into the marriage. (Section 59-610).

Who Must Be Mentioned in the Will?: Surviving spouse. (Section 59-610).

Spouse's Right to Property Regardless of Will: The amount to which a surviving spouse is entitled to is dependent on the length of marriage. Please refer directly to the statute as the provisions are detailed. (Section 59-6a202).

Laws of Intestate Succession (Distribution If No Will):

Spouse and children of spouse surviving: 1/2 to spouse and 1/2 to children or grandchildren per stirpes.

Spouse and children not of spouse surviving: 1/2 to spouse and 1/2 to children or grandchildren per stirpes.

Spouse, but no children or parent(s) surviving: All to spouse.

Spouse and parent(s), but no children surviving: All to spouse.

Children, but no spouse surviving: All to children equally or to their children per stirpes.

Parent(s), but no spouse or children surviving: All to parents equally or to the surviving parent.

No spouse, children, or parent(s) surviving: All to brothers and sisters per stirpes. (Sections 59-504 to 59-508).

Property Ownership: Common-law state. Tenancy-in-common is presumed unless joint tenancy is stated. Tenancy-by-the-entirety not recognized. Joint bank account deposits are payable to any survivor. (Section 17-2213 & Section 58-501).

State Gift, Inheritance, or Estate Taxes: No gift tax; imposes an inheritance tax of up to 15 percent; imposes state estate tax equal to federal credit for state death taxes less any amounts paid on state inheritance tax. Maximum total state inheritance and state estate tax is equal to the maximum allowable federal estate tax credit for state death taxes. (Section 79-102 & Sections 79-15,100+).

Living Will Form: Kansas Declaration serves as Living Will (Section 65-28103).

Other Directives: Durable Power of Attorney for Health Care (Section 58-629). Anatomical Gift Act (Section 65-3209). Durable Power of Attorney (Section 58-629).

Living Will Effective: Two (2) physicians must certify in writing that you are in a terminal condition and your death would occur within a short period of time without the use of life-sustaining medical care.

Witness Requirements: Sign in the presence of two (2) witnesses eighteen (18) years or older or a notary public. Witnesses cannot be entitled to any part of your estate, be financially responsible for your medical care, be related to you by blood or marriage, or be the person who signed the Declaration on your behalf.

Kentucky

State Website: http://lrc.ky.gov/

State Law Reference: Kentucky Revised Statutes.

Court with Probate Jurisdiction: District Court.

Minimum Age for Disposing of Property by Will: 18. (Section 394.020).

Required Number of Witnesses: Two. (Section 394.040).

Can Witnesses Be Beneficiaries?: Yes, but interested witness may not take more than intestate share, if any. (Section 394.210).

Are There Provisions for Self-Proving Wills?: Yes. (Section 394.225).

Are Holographic Wills Permitted?: Yes. (Section 394.040).

How Does Divorce Affect the Will?: Revokes the will as to the divorced spouse unless expressly provided otherwise. (Section 394.092).

How Does Marriage Affect the Will?: Does not revoke the will. (Section 394.090).

Who Must Be Mentioned in the Will?: Children, born or adopted; surviving spouse. (Section 394.382).

Spouse's Right to Property Regardless of Will: The surviving spouse is entitled to 1/3 of the real estate acquired during the marriage and 1/2 of the deceased spouse's real estate and personal property. (Section 392.020).

Laws of Intestate Succession (Distribution If No Will):

Spouse and children of spouse surviving: Real estate: life estate of 1/3 of fee simple property acquired during marriage and 1/2 of other real estate to spouse; balance to children or grandchildren per stirpes. Personal property: 1/2 to spouse and 1/2 to children equally or to grandchildren per stirpes.

Spouse and children not of spouse surviving: Real estate: life estate of 1/3 of fee simple property acquired during marriage and 1/2 of other real estate to spouse; balance to children or grandchildren per stirpes. Personal property: 1/2 to spouse and 1/2 to children equally or to grandchildren per stirpes.

Spouse, but no children or parent(s) surviving: 1/2 to parents' children; or if none, all to spouse.

Spouse and parent(s), but no children surviving: 1/2 to spouse and 1/2 to parents or surviving parent.

Children, but no spouse surviving: All to children equally or to their children per stirpes.

Parent(s), but no spouse or children surviving: All to parents equally or surviving parent.

No spouse, children, or parent(s) surviving: All to brothers and sisters or their children per stirpes; or if none, 1/2 to maternal next-of-kin and 1/2 to paternal next-of-kin and their children per stirpes. (Sections 391.010 & 392.020).

Property Ownership: Common-law state. Tenancy-in-common is presumed between husband and wife unless joint tenancy stated. Tenancy-by-the-entirety is recognized. Joint bank account deposits are payable to any survivor. (Sections 381.130 & Section 391.315).

State Gift, Inheritance, or Estate Taxes: No gift tax; imposes an inheritance tax of up to 16 percent; imposes state estate tax equal to federal credit for state death taxes less any amounts paid on state inheritance tax. Maximum total state inheritance and state estate tax is equal to the maximum allowable federal estate tax credit for state death taxes. (Sections 140.070 & 140.130).

Living Will Form: Living Will Directive (Section 311.625).

Other Directives: Anatomical Gift Act (Sections 311.165 through 311.235). Durable Power of Attorney (Section 386.093).

Living Will Effective: When you become unable to make your own medical decisions.

Witness Requirements: Sign in the presence of two (2) witnesses eighteen (18) years or older or a notary public. Witnesses cannot be entitled to any part of your estate, financially responsible for your medical care, or related to you by blood or marriage.

Louisiana

State Website: http://www.legis.state.la.us/

State Law Reference: Louisiana Revised Statutes and Louisiana Civil Code Annotated.

Court with Probate Jurisdiction: District Court.

Minimum Age for Disposing of Property by Will: 16. (Civil Code, Section 1476).

Required Number of Witnesses: Three. (Civil Code, Section 1584).

Can Witnesses Be Beneficiaries?: No. (Civil Code, Section 1582 & 1582.1).

Are There Provisions for Self-Proving Wills?: No.

Are Holographic Wills Permitted?: Yes. (Civil Code, Section 1575).

How Does Divorce Affect the Will?: Revokes the will. (Civil Code, Section 1608).

How Does Marriage Affect the Will?: Does not revoke the will. (Civil Code, Section 1691).

Who Must Be Mentioned in the Will?: Children, born or adopted; surviving spouse. However, children may be disinherited for a just cause. (Civil Code, Section 1619-1624).

Spouse's Right to Property Regardless of Will: The Louisiana Civil Code provisions regarding this matter are detailed and should be consulted directly. (Civil Code, Sections 890+).

Laws of Intestate Succession (Distribution If No Will):

Spouse and children of spouse surviving: All community property to descendants per stirpes. However, the spouse has the right to use the property until remarried. All separate property to children equally or to grandchildren per stirpes.

Spouse and children not of spouse surviving: All community property to descendants per stirpes. However, the spouse has the right to use the property until remarried. All separate property to children equally or to grandchildren per stirpes.

Spouse, but no children or parent(s) surviving: All community property to spouse. All separate property to brothers and sisters or to their children per stirpes; or if none, to parent(s); or if none, all to spouse.

Spouse and parent(s), but no children surviving: All community property to spouse. All separate property to brothers and sisters or their children per stirpes; or if none, to parent(s); or if none, all to spouse.

Children, but no spouse surviving: All to children equally or to their children per stirpes.

Parent(s), but no spouse or children surviving: All to parents equally or to the surviving parent.

No spouse, children, or parent(s) surviving: To brothers and sisters equally or their children per stirpes; or if none, to next-of-kin. (Civil Code, Sections 880 to 991).

Property Ownership. Community property state. Joint ownership is presumed if 2 or more persons are listed as owners. No tenancy-by-the-entirety or tenancy-in-common. Joint bank account deposits are payable to any survivor. (Revised Statutes, Title 6, Section 1255 & Civil Code, Sections 2334 & 2335).

State Gift, Inheritance, or Estate Taxes: Imposes a state gift tax; imposes a minimal inheritance tax; imposes a state estate tax equal to federal credit for state death taxes less any amounts paid on state inheritance tax. Maximum total state inheritance and state estate tax is equal to the maximum allowable federal estate tax credit for state death taxes. (Revised Statutes, Title 47, Sections 2403 & 2432).

Living Will Form: Louisiana Declaration serves as Living Will (Title 40, Article 1299, Section 58-3).

Other Directives: Anatomical Gift Act (Section 17:2354).

Living Will Effective: Two (2) physicians must certify in writing that you are in a terminal condition and your death would occur within a short period of time without the use of life-sustaining medical care.

Witness Requirements: Sign in the presence of two (2) adult witnesses. Witnesses cannot be entitled to any part of your estate or related by blood or marriage.

Maine

State Website: http://janus.state.me.us/legis/statutes/

State Law Reference: Maine Revised Statutes Annotated.

Court with Probate Jurisdiction: Probate Court.

Minimum Age for Disposing of Property by Will: 18. (Section 18A-2-501).

Required Number of Witnesses: Two. (Section 18A-2-502).

Can Witnesses Be Beneficiaries?: Yes. (Section 18A-2-505).

Are There Provisions for Self-Proving Wills?: Yes. (Section 18A-2-504).

Are Holographic Wills Permitted?: Yes. (Section 18A-2-503).

How Does Divorce Affect the Will?: Revokes the will as to the divorced spouse unless expressly provided otherwise. (Section 18A-2-508).

How Does Marriage Affect the Will?: Revokes the will as to the spouse if he or she is not otherwise provided for. Spouse may still be entitled to his or her statutory share under the state intestate laws. (Section 18A-2-301).

Who Must Be Mentioned in the Will?: Children, born or adopted; grandchildren of deceased child; surviving spouse. (Sections 18A-2-301 & 18A-2-302).

Spouse's Right to Property Regardless of Will: The surviving spouse is entitled to 1/3 of the entire estate of the deceased spouse. (Section 18A-2-201).

Laws of Intestate Succession (Distribution If No Will):

Spouse and children of spouse surviving: $50,000.00 and 1/2 of balance to spouse and 1/2 of balance to children or grandchildren per capita at each generation. (Note: Surviving registered domestic partners are entitled to the same intestate share as a surviving spouse.)

Spouse and children not of spouse surviving: 1/2 to spouse and 1/2 to children or grandchildren per capita at each generation.

Spouse, but no children or parent(s) surviving: All to spouse.

Spouse and parent(s), but no children surviving: $50,000.00 and 1/2 of balance to spouse and 1/2 of balance to parents or surviving parent.

Children, but no spouse surviving: All to children equally or to their children per capita at each generation.

Parent(s), but no spouse or children surviving: All to parents equally or to the surviving parent.

No spouse, children, or parent(s) surviving: All to children of parents per capita; or if none, then 1/2 to paternal grandparents or their children per capita and 1/2 to maternal grandparents or their children per capita. (Sections 2-102 & 2-103).

Property Ownership: Common-law state. Ownership by 2 or more is presumed to be a tenancy-in-common unless joint tenancy is stated. Tenancy-by-the-entirety not recognized. Joint bank account deposits are payable to any survivor. (Sections 33-7-159 & 33-7-160).

State Gift, Inheritance, or Estate Taxes: No gift tax; no inheritance tax; imposes state estate tax equal to federal credit for state death taxes. (Section 18A-3-916).

Living Will Form: Instructions for Health Care serves as Living Will (Section 18A-5-8040).

Other Directives: Durable Power of Attorney for Health Care (Section 18-5-506). Anatomical Gift Act (Section 22-2-710). Durable Power of Attorney (Section 18A-5-502).

Living Will Effective: The Living Will becomes effective in the event that you have an incurable and irreversible condition that will result in death within a relatively short time, become unconscious and, to a reasonable degree of medical certainty, will not regain consciousness, or the likely risks and burdens of treatment would outweigh the expected benefits.

Witness Requirements: Sign in the presence of two (2) adult witnesses. No other restrictions apply.

Maryland

State Website: http://198.187.128.12/maryland/lpext.dll?f=templates&fn=fs-main.htm&2.0
State Law Reference: Maryland Code.
Court with Probate Jurisdiction: Orphan's Court (Circuit Court in Hartford and Montgomery Counties).
Minimum Age for Disposing of Property by Will: 18. (Estates & Trusts 4-101).
Required Number of Witnesses: Two. (Estates & Trusts 4-102).
Can Witnesses Be Beneficiaries?: Yes. (Estates & Trusts 4-102).
Are There Provisions for Self-Proving Wills?: Yes. (Estates & Trusts 4-102).
Are Holographic Wills Permitted?: Yes, if made outside U.S. by a member of the Armed Forces. Expires 1 year after testator's discharge from service if he or she is alive and has testamentary capacity. (Estates & Trusts 4-103).
How Does Divorce Affect the Will?: Revokes the will as to the divorced spouse. (Estates & Trusts 4-105).
How Does Marriage Affect the Will?: Revokes the will if a child is later born to or adopted into the marriage and survives the maker of the will. (Estates & Trusts 4-105).
Who Must Be Mentioned in the Will?: Children, born or adopted; grandchildren of deceased child; surviving spouse. (Estates & Trusts 4-105).
Spouse's Right to Property Regardless of Will: Generally, the surviving spouse is entitled to 1/2 of the deceased spouse's estate if there are no children, and only 1/3 if there are children. However, please refer directly to the statute for details. (Estates & Trusts 3-203).
Laws of Intestate Succession (Distribution If No Will):
Spouse and children of spouse surviving: If any surviving children are minors, 1/2 to spouse and 1/2 to children equally or grandchildren per stirpes; if no surviving children are minors, $15,000.00 and 1/2 of balance to spouse and 1/2 of balance to children equally or grandchildren per stirpes.
Spouse and children not of spouse surviving: If any surviving children are minors, 1/2 to spouse and 1/2 to children equally or grandchildren per stirpes; if no surviving children are minors, $15,000.00 and 1/2 of balance to spouse and 1/2 of balance to children equally or grandchildren per stirpes.
Spouse, but no children or parent(s) surviving: All to spouse.
Spouse and parent(s), but no children surviving: $15,000.00 to spouse and then 1/2 of balance to spouse and 1/2 of balance to parents or surviving parent.
Children, but no spouse surviving: All to children or to their children per stirpes.
Parent(s), but no spouse or children surviving: All to parents equally or to the surviving parent.
No spouse, children, or parent(s) surviving: 1/2 to paternal grandparents and 1/2 to maternal grandparents and their next-of-kin. (Title 3, Sections 3-102 to 3-104).
Property Ownership: Common-law state. Tenancy-in-common is recognized. Joint tenancy must be stated. Joint ownership by spouses is presumed to be a tenancy-by-the-entirety unless stated otherwise. Joint bank accounts are payable to any survivor. (Financial Institutions 1-204 & Real Property 2-117 & 4-108).
State Gift, Inheritance, or Estate Taxes: No gift tax; imposes an inheritance tax of 10 percent; imposes state estate tax equal to federal credit for state death taxes less any amounts paid on state inheritance tax. Maximum total state inheritance and state estate tax is equal to the maximum allowable federal estate tax credit for state death taxes. (Tax General 7-204 & 7-304).
Living Will Form: Advance Medical Directive Health Care Instructions serve as Living Will (Health General, Section 5-603).
Other Directives: Appointment of Health Care Agent (Health General, Section 5-603). Anatomical Gift Act (Health General 5-604.1). Durable Power of Attorney (Estates & Trusts 13-601).
Living Will Effective: Two (2) physicians must agree in writing that you are incapable of making an informed health care decision, but you are not unconscious or unable to communicate by any other means.
Witness Requirements: Sign in the presence of two (2) adult witnesses. The person you assign as your agent cannot be a witness. At least one (1) of your witnesses must be a person who is not entitled to any portion of your estate or financial benefit by reason of your death.

Massachusetts

State Website: http://www.mass.gov/legis/laws/mgl/

State Law Reference: Massachusetts General Laws.

Court with Probate Jurisdiction: Probate and Family Court.

Minimum Age for Disposing of Property by Will: 18. (Chapter 191, Section 1).

Required Number of Witnesses: Two. (Chapter 191, Section 1).

Can Witnesses Be Beneficiaries?: Yes, but any gift to a beneficiary who was a witness will be void unless there were also 2 other disinterested witnesses. (Chapter 191, Section 2).

Are There Provisions for Self-Proving Wills?: Yes. (Chapter 192, Section 2).

Are Holographic Wills Permitted?: No.

How Does Divorce Affect the Will?: Revokes the will as to the divorced spouse. (Chapter 191, Section 9).

How Does Marriage Affect the Will?: Revokes the will. (Chapter 191, Section 9).

Who Must Be Mentioned in the Will?: Children, born or adopted; grandchildren (if of deceased child); surviving spouse. (Chapter 191, Sections 15 & 20).

Spouse's Right to Property Regardless of Will: Generally, the surviving spouse is entitled to $25,000.00 and 1/2 of the deceased spouse's remaining estate if there are no children, and only 1/3 if there are children. However, please refer directly to the statute as the provisions are detailed. (Chapter 191, Section 15).

Laws of Intestate Succession (Distribution If No Will):

Spouse and children of spouse surviving: 1/2 to spouse and 1/2 to children equally or grandchildren per stirpes.

Spouse and children not of spouse surviving: 1/2 to spouse and 1/2 to children equally or grandchildren per stirpes.

Spouse, but no children or parent(s) surviving: $200,000.00 and 1/2 of balance to spouse and 1/2 of balance to brothers and sisters equally or their children per stirpes; or if none, to next-of-kin; or if none, all to spouse.

Spouse and parent(s), but no children surviving: $200,000.00 and 1/2 of balance to spouse and 1/2 of balance to parents equally or the surviving parent.

Children, but no spouse surviving: All to children equally or to their children per stirpes.

Parent(s), but no spouse or children surviving: All to parents equally or to the surviving parent.

No spouse, children, or parent(s) surviving: All to brothers and sisters equally or their children per stirpes; or if none, to the next-of-kin. (Chapter 190, Section 1).

Property Ownership: Common-law state. Tenancy-in-common, joint tenancy, and tenancy-by-the-entirety are recognized. Joint ownership by husband and wife creates a tenancy-in-common, unless otherwise stated. (Chapter 184, Section 7).

State Gift, Inheritance, or Estate Taxes: No gift tax; no inheritance tax; imposes state estate tax of up to 16 percent (not tied to federal estate tax credit). (Chapter 65C, Section 1).

Living Will Form: No state statute governing the use of Living Wills. However, you have a constitutional right to state your wishes about medical care. A form is provided in this book.

Other Directives: Massachusetts Health Care Proxy. (Chapter 201D, Sections 1-17)

Living Will Effective: In the event that you develop an irreversible condition that prevents you from making your own medical decisions.

Witness Requirements: Because Massachusetts does not have a statute governing the use of Living Wills, there are no specific requirements to make your Living Will legally binding. We suggest that you sign in the presence of two (2) witnesses eighteen (18) years or older or a notary public. A witness should not be your health care provider or an employee of your health care provider. Witnesses should not be entitled to any part of your estate, financially responsible for your medical care, or related to you by blood or marriage.

Michigan

State Website: http://www.michiganlegislature.org/

State Law Reference: Michigan Compiled Laws Annotated.

Court with Probate Jurisdiction: Probate Court. (Section 700.1302).

Minimum Age for Disposing of Property by Will: 18. (Section 700.1106(c)).

Required Number of Witnesses: Two. (Section 700.2502).

Can Witnesses Be Beneficiaries?: Yes, but any gift to a beneficiary who was a witness will be void beyond the amount that the witness-beneficiary would have received as an intestate share unless there were also 2 other disinterested witnesses. (Section 700.2505).

Are There Provisions for Self-Proving Wills?: Yes. (Section 700.2504).

Are Holographic Wills Permitted?: Yes. (Section 700.2502).

How Does Divorce Affect the Will?: Revokes the will as to the divorced spouse. (Section 700.2801).

How Does Marriage Affect the Will?: Revokes the will as to the spouse if he or she is not otherwise provided for. Spouse may still be entitled to his or her statutory share under the state intestate laws. (Section 700.2301).

Who Must Be Mentioned in the Will?: Children, born or adopted; surviving spouse. (Sections 700.2301 & 700.2302).

Spouse's Right to Property Regardless of Will: Generally, the surviving spouse is entitled to 1/2 of the deceased spouse's estate if there are no children, and only 1/4 if there are children. However, please refer directly to the statute as the provisions are detailed. (Sections 700.2201 to 700.2206).

Laws of Intestate Succession (Distribution If No Will):

Spouse and children of spouse surviving: $150,000.00 and 1/2 of balance to spouse and 1/2 of balance to children per stirpes. (Note: All amounts are adjusted for cost-of-living increases each year (Section 100.1210).

Spouse and children not of spouse surviving: First $100,000.00 to spouse and then 1/2 to spouse and 1/2 to children per stirpes.

Spouse, but no children or parent(s) surviving: All to spouse.

Spouse and parent(s), but no children surviving: $150,000.00 and 3/4 of balance to spouse and 1/4 of balance to parents or surviving parent.

Children, but no spouse surviving: All to children or to their children per stirpes.

Parent(s), but no spouse or children surviving: All to parents equally or to the surviving parent.

No spouse, children, or parent(s) surviving: All to brothers and sisters equally or to their children per stirpes; or if none, 1/2 to maternal grandparents or their children per stirpes and 1/2 to paternal grandparents or their children per stirpes. (Sections 700.2101 to 700.2114).

Property Ownership: Common-law state. Tenancy-in-common, joint tenancy and tenancy-by-the-entirety are recognized. Joint tenancy created only if stated. Joint tenancy by spouses and joint ownership of real estate by spouses is presumed to be a tenancy-by-the-entirety unless otherwise stated. Joint tenancy with right of survivorship must be in writing. Joint bank account deposits are payable to any survivor. (Chapter 554, Sections 554.44 & 554.45, & Chapter 557, Section 557.101).

State Gift, Inheritance, or Estate Taxes: No gift tax or inheritance tax; imposes state estate tax equal to federal credit for state death taxes. (Chapter 205, Section 205.202(a)).

Living Will Form: No state statute governing the use of Living Wills. However, you have a constitutional right to state your wishes about medical care. A form is provided in this book.

Other Directives: Michigan Designation of Patient Advocate for Health Care. (Section 700.5506).

Living Will Effective: In the event that you develop an irreversible condition that prevents you from making your own medical decisions.

Witness Requirements: Because Michigan does not have a statute governing the use of Living Wills, there are no specific requirements to make your Living Will legally binding. We suggest that you sign in the presence of two (2) witnesses eighteen (18) years or older or a notary public. A witness should not be your health care provider or an employee of your health care provider. Witnesses should not be entitled to any part of your estate, be financially responsible for your medical care, or be related to you by blood or marriage.

Minnesota

State Website: http://www.revisor.leg.state.mn.us/stats/

State Law Reference: Minnesota Statutes Annotated.

Court with Probate Jurisdiction: Probate Court.

Minimum Age for Disposing of Property by Will: 18. (Section 524.2-501).

Required Number of Witnesses: Two. (Section 524.2-502).

Can Witnesses Be Beneficiaries?: Yes. (Section 524.2-505).

Are There Provisions for Self-Proving Wills?: Yes. (Section 524.2-504).

Are Holographic Wills Permitted?: No.

How Does Divorce Affect the Will?: Revokes the will as to the divorced spouse. (Section 524.2-804).

How Does Marriage Affect the Will?: Revokes the will as to the spouse if he or she is not otherwise provided for. Spouse may still be entitled to his or her statutory share under the state intestate laws. (Section 524.2-301).

Who Must Be Mentioned in the Will?: Children, born or adopted; grandchildren (if of deceased child); surviving spouse. (Sections 524.2-202 & 524.2-302).

Spouse's Right to Property Regardless of Will: The elective share amount is dependent on length of marriage. (Sections 524.2-201 & 524.2-202).

Laws of Intestate Succession (Distribution If No Will):

Spouse and children of spouse surviving: All to spouse.

Spouse and children not of spouse surviving: $150,000.00 and 1/2 of balance of estate to spouse and 1/2 to children or grandchildren per stirpes.

Spouse, but no children or parent surviving: All to spouse.

Spouse and parent(s), but no children surviving: All to spouse.

Children, but no spouse surviving: All to children equally or to their children per stirpes.

Parent(s), but no spouse or children surviving: All to parents equally or to the surviving parent.

No spouse, children, or parent(s) surviving: All to brothers and sisters equally or their children per stirpes; or if none, to the next-of-kin. (Sections 524.2-102 & 524.2-103).

Property Ownership: Common-law state. Tenancy-in-common is presumed unless joint tenancy in writing. Tenancy-by-the-entirety not recognized. Joint bank account deposits are payable to any survivor unless clear evidence exists that deposit is payable only to specified survivor. (Sections 500.19 & 524.6-203).

State Gift, Inheritance, or Estate Taxes: No gift tax; no inheritance tax; imposes state estate tax equal to federal credit for state death taxes. (Section 291.03).

Living Will Form: Health Care Living Will (Chapter 145B, Section 04).

Other Directives: Appointment of Health Care Agent is included in Living Will (Section 145B-04). Anatomical Gift Act (Section 145B.07). Durable Power of Attorney (Section 523.01).

Living Will Effective: Living Will becomes effective in the event that you can no longer make your own medical decisions.

Witness Requirements: Sign in the presence of two (2) witnesses eighteen (18) years or older or a notary public. A witness cannot be the person whom you appointed as your agent. At least one (1) witness cannot be your health care provider or an employee of your health care provider.

Mississippi

State Website: http://www.mscode.com/

State Law Reference: Mississippi Code Annotated.

Court with Probate Jurisdiction: Chancery Court.

Minimum Age for Disposing of Property by Will: 18. (Section 91-5-1).

Required Number of Witnesses: Two. (Section 91-5-1).

Can Witnesses Be Beneficiaries?: No, however a witness-beneficiary is still entitled to receive a share of the estate not to exceed the amount he or she is entitled to as an intestate share. (Section 91-5-9).

Are There Provisions for Self-Proving Wills?: Yes. (Section 91-7-7).

Are Holographic Wills Permitted?: Yes. (Section 91-5-1).

How Does Divorce Affect the Will?: Does not revoke the will. (Section 91-5-27).

How Does Marriage Affect the Will?: Does not revoke the will. (Section 91-5-27).

Who Must Be Mentioned in the Will?: Children, born or adopted; surviving spouse. (Section 91-5-27).

Spouse's Right to Property Regardless of Will: Generally, the surviving spouse is entitled to 1/2 of the deceased spouse's estate if there are no children, and only 1/3 if there are children. However, please refer directly to the statute as the provisions are detailed. (Sections 91-5-25 & 91-5-27).

Laws of Intestate Succession (Distribution If No Will):

Spouse and children of spouse surviving: Spouse and any surviving children or grandchildren each take equal shares.

Spouse and children not of spouse surviving: Spouse and any surviving children or grandchildren each take equal shares.

Spouse, but no children or parent(s) surviving: All to spouse.

Spouse and parent(s), but no children surviving: All to spouse.

Children, but no spouse surviving: All to children equally or to their children per stirpes.

Parent(s), but no spouse or children surviving: All to parents, brothers, and sisters equally, or to children of brothers and sisters per stirpes. If no brothers or sisters or children of brothers or sisters, all to parents equally or the surviving parent.

No spouse, children, or parent(s) surviving: All to brothers and sisters equally, or to their children per stirpes; or if none, to grandparents, uncles, and aunts equally, or to their children per stirpes; or if none, to the next-of-kin. (Sections 91-1-3, 91-1-7, & 91-1-11).

Property Ownership: Common-law state. Tenancy-in-common, joint tenancy and tenancy-by-the-entirety are recognized. Ownership by 2 or more persons is presumed to be tenancy-in-common unless joint tenancy is stated. Joint bank account deposits are payable to any survivor. (Title 89, Chapter 1, Section 89-1-7).

State Gift, Inheritance, or Estate Taxes: No gift tax; no inheritance tax; imposes state estate tax of up to 16 percent. (State estate tax not tied to federal credit for state death taxes). (Title 27, Chapter 9, Sections 27-9-5).

Living Will Form: Instructions for Health Care serves as Living Will (Title 41, Chapter 41, Section 209).

Other Directives: Mississippi Advance Health Care Directive contains Power of Attorney for Health Care and Instructions for Health Care (Section 41-209). Anatomical Gift Act (Sections 41-39-31 through 41-39-51). Durable Power of Attorney (Section 87-3-1).

Living Will Effective: In the event that you have an incurable and irreversible condition that will result in death within a relatively short time, become unconscious and, to a reasonable degree of medical certainty, will not regain consciousness, or the likely risks and burdens of treatment would outweigh the expected benefits.

Witness Requirements: Sign in the presence of two (2) witnesses eighteen (18) years or older or a notary public. A witness cannot be the person whom you appointed as your agent, health care provider, or an employee of your health care provider. At least one (1) witness cannot be related to you by blood or marriage or entitled to your estate upon your death.

Missouri

State Website: http://www.moga.state.mo.us/STATUTES/STATUTES.HTM#T

State Law Reference: Missouri Annotated Statutes.

Court with Probate Jurisdiction: Circuit Court.

Minimum Age for Disposing of Property by Will: 18. (Section 474.310).

Required Number of Witnesses: Two. (Section 474.320).

Can Witnesses Be Beneficiaries?: Yes, but interested witness is limited to intestate share, if any, unless signed by 2 other disinterested witnesses. (Section 474.330).

Are There Provisions for Self-Proving Wills?: Yes. (Section 474.337).

Are Holographic Wills Permitted?: No provision.

How Does Divorce Affect the Will?: Revokes the will as to the divorced spouse. (Section 474.420).

How Does Marriage Affect the Will?: Spouse may still be entitled to his or her statutory share under the state intestate laws. (Section 474.420).

Who Must Be Mentioned in the Will?: Children, born or adopted; surviving spouse. (Sections 474.160 & 474.240).

Spouse's Right to Property Regardless of Will: Generally, the surviving spouse is entitled to 1/2 of the deceased spouse's estate if there are no children, and only 1/3 if there are children. However, please refer directly to the statute as the provisions are detailed. (Section 474.160).

Laws of Intestate Succession (Distribution If No Will):

Spouse and children of spouse surviving: $20,000.00 and 1/2 of balance to spouse and 1/2 of balance to children or grandchildren per stirpes.

Spouse and children not of spouse surviving: 1/2 to spouse and 1/2 to children or grandchildren per stirpes.

Spouse, but no children or parent(s) surviving: All to spouse.

Spouse and parent(s), but no children surviving: All to spouse.

Children, but no spouse surviving: All to children equally or to their children per stirpes.

Parent(s), but no spouse or children surviving: All to parents, brothers, and sisters equally, or to their children per stirpes; or if none, all to parents or to the surviving parent.

No spouse, children, or parent(s) surviving: All to brothers and sisters equally or to their children per stirpes; or if none, to grandparents, uncles, and aunts and their children per stirpes; or if none, to the nearest lineal ancestor and their children. (Section 474.010).

Property Ownership: Common-law state. Tenancy-in-common, joint tenancy and tenancy-by-the-entirety are recognized. Ownership by 2 or more persons is presumed to be a tenancy-in-common unless joint tenancy is stated. Joint bank account deposits are payable to any survivor. (Title 29, Sections 442.025, 442.030, & 442.035).

State Gift, Inheritance, or Estate Taxes: No gift tax; no inheritance tax; imposes state estate tax equal to federal credit for state death taxes. (Title 10, Section 145.011).

Living Will Form: Missouri Declaration serves as Living Will (Chapter 459, Section 015).

Other Directives: Power of Attorney for Health Care (Section 404-822). Anatomical Gift Act (Sections 194.210 through 194290). Durable Power of Attorney (Section 404.705).

Living Will Effective: The Declaration becomes effective in the event that you have an incurable or irreversible medical condition which, without the use of life support, will result in death in a relative short period of time, or you are in a permanent coma or persistent vegetative state.

Witness Requirements: Sign in the presence of two (2) adult witnesses. If you have someone sign the Declaration on your behalf, that person cannot serve as a witness.

Montana

State Website: http://data.opi.state.mt.us/bills/mca_toc/index.htm

State Law Reference: Montana Code Annotated.

Court with Probate Jurisdiction: District Court. (Chapter 3, Section 3-5-302).

Minimum Age for Disposing of Property by Will: 18. (Chapter 2, Section 72-2-521).

Required Number of Witnesses: Two. (Chapter 2, Section 72-2-522).

Can Witnesses Be Beneficiaries?: Yes. (Chapter 2, Section 72-2-525).

Are There Provisions for Self-Proving Wills?: Yes. (Chapter 2, Section 72-2-524).

Are Holographic Wills Permitted?: Yes. (Chapter 2, Section 72-2-522).

How Does Divorce Affect the Will?: Revokes the will as to the divorced spouse. (Chapter 2, Sections 72-2-528 & 72-2-814).

How Does Marriage Affect the Will?: Revokes the will as to the spouse if he or she is not otherwise provided for. Spouse will still be entitled to his or her statutory share under the state intestate laws. (Chapter 2, Section 72-2-331).

Who Must Be Mentioned in the Will?: Children, born or adopted; surviving spouse. (Chapter 2, Sections 72-2-221 & 72-2-332).

Spouse's Right to Property Regardless of Will: The surviving spouse is entitled to an elective share of the deceased spouse's "augmented" estate that ranges from a "supplemental amount" for spouses married for less than 1 year, 3 percent of the "augmented" estate for spouses married from 1-2 years, and up to 50 percent for spouses married over 15 years. Please consult the statute directly for complete details. In general, the "augmented" estate includes both the property that passes under the will and any other property that passes by other "non-will" transfers, such as under the terms of a living trust or a joint tenancy arrangement. (Chapter 2, Section 72-2-221).

Laws of Intestate Succession (Distribution If No Will):

Spouse and children of spouse surviving: All to spouse.

Spouse and children not of spouse surviving: If 1 child surviving, 1/2 to spouse and 1/2 to child; if more than 1 child surviving, 1/3 to spouse and 2/3 to children equally.

Spouse, but no children or parent(s) surviving: All to spouse.

Spouse and parent(s), but no children surviving: All to spouse.

Children, but no spouse surviving: All to children equally or to their children per stirpes.

Parent(s), but no spouse or children surviving: All to parents equally or to the surviving parent.

No spouse, children, or parent(s) surviving: All to brothers and sisters equally or their children per stirpes; or if none, 1/2 to paternal grandparents or their children and 1/2 to maternal grandparents or their children per stirpes. (Chapter 2, Sections 72-2-112 & 72-2-113).

Property Ownership: Common-law state. Tenancy-in-common and joint tenancy (called interests in common and joint interests) are recognized. No tenancy-by-the-entirety is recognized in personal property. Tenancy-in-common is presumed unless joint tenancy stated. Joint bank account deposits are payable to any survivor. (Title 40, Chapter 2, Section 40-2-105 & Title 70, Chapter 1, Section 70-1-310).

State Gift, Inheritance, or Estate Taxes: No gift tax or inheritance tax. Imposes state estate tax equal to federal credit for state death taxes. (Chapter 16, Section 72-16-904).

Living Will Form: Montana Declaration serves as Living Will (Title 50, Chapter 9, Section 103).

Other Directives: Appointment of Health Care Agent is included in Declaration (Section 50-9-103). Anatomical Gift Act (Section 72-17-101). Durable Power of Attorney (Section 72-5-501).

Living Will Effective: Becomes effective when you have an incurable or irreversible medical condition which, without the use of life support, will result in death in a relatively short period of time, or you are in a permanent coma or persistent vegetative state.

Witness Requirements: Sign in the presence of two (2) adult witnesses. No other restrictions apply. Do not use your appointed health care agent as one of your witnesses.

Nebraska

State Website: http://statutes.unicam.state.ne.us/

State Law Reference: Revised Statutes of Nebraska.

Court with Probate Jurisdiction: County Court.

Minimum Age for Disposing of Property by Will: 18, but no minimum age for married persons. (Section 30-2326).

Required Number of Witnesses: Two. (Section 30-2327).

Can Witnesses Be Beneficiaries?: Yes, however interested witness may be limited to receiving intestate share. (Section 30-2330).

Are There Provisions for Self-Proving Wills?: Yes. (Section 30-2329).

Are Holographic Wills Permitted?: Yes. (Section 30-2328).

How Does Divorce Affect the Will?: Revokes the will as to the divorced spouse. (Section 30-2333).

How Does Marriage Affect the Will?: Spouse will still be entitled to his or her statutory share under the state intestate laws. (Section 30-2320).

Who Must Be Mentioned in the Will?: Children, born or adopted; surviving spouse. (Sections 30-2313 & 30-2321).

Spouse's Right to Property Regardless of Will: The surviving spouse is entitled to 1/2 of the "augmented" estate of the deceased spouse. In general, the "augmented" estate includes both the property that passes under the will and any other property that passes by other "non-will" transfers, such as under the terms of a living trust or a joint tenancy arrangement. (Section 30-2313).

Laws of Intestate Succession (Distribution If No Will):

Spouse and children of spouse surviving: $50,000.00 and 1/2 of balance to spouse and 1/2 of balance to children.

Spouse and children not of spouse surviving: 1/2 to spouse and 1/2 to children.

Spouse, but no children or parent(s) surviving: All to spouse.

Spouse and parent(s), but no children surviving: $50,000.00 and 1/2 of balance to spouse and 1/2 of balance to parents or surviving parent.

Children, but no spouse surviving: All to children equally or to their children per stirpes.

Parent(s), but no spouse or children surviving: All to parents equally or to the surviving parent.

No spouse, children, or parent(s) surviving: All to brothers and sisters equally, or their children per stirpes; or if none, 1/2 to paternal grandparents or their children and 1/2 to maternal grandparents or their children per stirpes. (Sections 30-2302 & 30-2303).

State Property Ownership: Common-law state. Tenancy-in-common and joint tenancy are recognized. Tenancy-by-the-entirety is not recognized. Joint bank account deposits are payable to any survivor unless clear evidence exists that deposit is payable only to specified survivor. (Section 76-118).

State Gift, Inheritance, or Estate Taxes: No gift tax; imposes an inheritance tax of up to 16 percent; imposes state estate tax equal to federal credit for state death taxes less any amounts paid on state inheritance tax. Maximum total state inheritance and state estate tax is equal to the maximum allowable federal estate tax credit for state death taxes. (Sections 77-2001 to 77-2006 & 77-2101.01)

Living Will Form: Nebraska Declaration serves as Living Will (Chapter 20, Section 404).

Other Directives: Power of Attorney for Health Care (Section 30-3408). Anatomical Gift Act (Section 71-4804). Durable Power of Attorney (Section 30-2665).

Living Will Effective: Declaration becomes effective when your attending physician determines you to have an incurable or irreversible medical condition which, without the use of life support, will result in death in a relatively short period of time, or you are in a permanent coma or persistent vegetative state.

Witness Requirements: Sign in the presence of two (2) adult witnesses. Witnesses cannot be employees of your life or health insurance provider and at least one (1) witness must not be an administrator or employee of your treating health care provider.

Nevada

State Website: http://www.leg.state.nv.us/NRS/

State Law Reference: Nevada Revised Statutes Annotated.

Court with Probate Jurisdiction: District Court.

Minimum Age for Disposing of Property by Will: 18. (Section 133.020).

Required Number of Witnesses: Two. Electronic wills are also valid in Nevada. (Section 133.040 & 133.085).

Can Witnesses Be Beneficiaries?: No, unless there are 2 other competent witnesses. (Section 133.060).

Are There Provisions for Self-Proving Wills?: Yes. (Section 133.050).

Are Holographic Wills Permitted?: Yes. (Section 133.090).

How Does Divorce Affect the Will?: Revokes the will as to the divorced spouse, if will was signed prior to entry of divorce decree. (Section 133.115).

How Does Marriage Affect the Will?: Revokes the will as to the spouse if he or she is not otherwise provided for. Spouse may still be entitled to his or her statutory share under the state intestate laws. (Section 133.110).

Who Must Be Mentioned in the Will?: Statute contains detailed provisions regarding this. Please refer directly to statute or consult an attorney if this is a critical factor. (Sections 133.160 & 134.005).

Spouse's Right to Property Regardless of Will: Community property right to 1/2 of the deceased spouse's "community" property. (Section 123.250).

Laws of Intestate Succession (Distribution If No Will):

Spouse and children of spouse surviving: All of decedent's community property to spouse. If only 1 child is surviving, 1/2 of decedent's separate property to spouse and 1/2 to child or grandchildren per stirpes; if more than 1 child is surviving, 1/3 of separate property to spouse and 2/3 to the children or grandchildren per stirpes.

Spouse and children not of spouse surviving: All of decedent's community property to spouse. If only 1 child is surviving, 1/2 of decedent's separate property to spouse and 1/2 to child or grandchildren per stirpes; if more than 1 child is surviving, 1/3 of separate property to spouse and 2/3 to the children or grandchildren per stirpes.

Spouse, but no children or parent(s) surviving: All of decedent's community property to spouse. 1/2 of decedent's separate property to spouse and 1/2 to brothers and sisters equally or their children per stirpes; or if none, all to spouse.

Spouse and parent(s), but no children surviving: All of decedent's community property to spouse. 1/2 of decedent's separate property to spouse and 1/2 to parents equally or surviving parent.

Children, but no spouse surviving: All to children or their children per stirpes.

Parent(s), but no spouse or children surviving: All to parents equally or to the surviving parent.

No spouse, children, or parent(s) surviving: All to brothers and sisters equally, or their children per stirpes; or if none, to the next-of-kin. There are additional distribution possibilities listed in the statute. (Sections 134.040 to 134.160).

Property Ownership: Community property state. Tenancy-in-common, joint tenancy, and community property are recognized. Tenancy-by-the-entirety is not recognized. Joint bank account deposits are payable to any survivor. (Sections 111.060 & 111.065).

State Gift, Inheritance, or Estate Taxes: No gift tax; no inheritance tax; Imposes a state estate tax equal to the maximum allowable credit for federal estate taxes. (Section 375A.100).

Living Will Form: Nevada Declaration serves as Living Will (Section 449-610).

Other Directives: Power of Attorney for Health Care (Section 449-830). Anatomical Gift Act (Sections 451.500 through 451590).

Living Will Effective: Declaration becomes effective when your doctor determines that your death would occur without the use of life-sustaining medical care.

Witness Requirements: Sign in the presence of two (2) adult witnesses. No other restrictions apply.

New Hampshire

State Website: http://gencourt.state.nh.us/rsa/html/indexes/default.asp

State Law Reference: New Hampshire Revised Statutes.

Court with Probate Jurisdiction: Probate Court.

Minimum Age for Disposing of Property by Will: 18, but no minimum for married persons. (Chapter 551:1).

Required Number of Witnesses: Two. (Chapter 551:2).

Can Witnesses Be Beneficiaries?: Yes, but any gift to a beneficiary who was a witness will be void unless there were also 2 other disinterested witnesses. (Chapter 551:3).

Are There Provisions for Self-Proving Wills?: Yes. (Chapter 551:2a).

Are Holographic Wills Permitted?: No provision.

How Does Divorce Affect the Will?: Revokes the will as to the former spouse. (Chapter 551:13).

How Does Marriage Affect the Will?: Spouse may elect to receive statutory share. (Chapter 560:10).

Who Must Be Mentioned in the Will?: Children, born or adopted; grandchildren; surviving spouse. (Chapters 551:10 & 560:10).

Spouse's Right to Property Regardless of Will: Generally, the surviving spouse is entitled to 1/2 of the deceased spouse's estate if there are no children, and only 1/3 if there are children. However, please refer directly to the statute as the provisions are detailed. (Chapter 560:10).

Laws of Intestate Succession (Distribution If No Will):

Spouse and children of spouse surviving: $250,000.00 and 1/2 of balance to spouse and 1/2 of balance to children or grandchildren per stirpes. ($150,000.00 and 1/2 of the balance if surviving spouse also has children which are not decedents)

Spouse and children not of spouse surviving: 1/2 to spouse and 1/2 to children or grandchildren per stirpes.

Spouse, but no children or parent(s) surviving: All to spouse.

Spouse and parent(s), but no children surviving: $250,000.00 and 3/4 of balance to spouse and 1/4 of balance to parents or surviving parent.

Children, but no spouse surviving: All to children or to their children per stirpes.

Parent(s), but no spouse or children surviving: All to parents equally or to the surviving parent.

No spouse, children, or parent(s) surviving: All to brothers and sisters equally, or their children per stirpes; or if none, 1/2 to maternal grandparents or their children and 1/2 to paternal grandparents or their children per stirpes. (Chapter 561:1).

Property Ownership: Common-law state. Tenancy-in-common is presumed unless joint tenancy stated. Ownership by spouses creates joint tenancy. Tenancy-by-the-entirety is not recognized. Joint bank account deposits are payable to any survivor. (Title 47, Chapters 477:18 & 477:19).

State Gift, Inheritance, or Estate Taxes: No gift tax or inheritance tax. Imposes state estate tax equal to federal credit for state death taxes. (Title 87, Chapter 87:01).

Living Will Form: New Hampshire Declaration serves as Living Will (Chapter 137H, Section 3).

Other Directives: Power of Attorney for Health Care (Chapter 137-J:15). Anatomical Gift Act (Chapter 291-A).

Living Will Effective: Two (2) physicians must certify in writing that you are in a terminal condition and your death would occur within a short period of time without the use of life-sustaining medical care.

Witness Requirements: Sign in the presence of two (2) witnesses eighteen (18) years or older or a notary public. A witness cannot be a person who has a claim against your estate, stands to inherit from your estate, be your spouse, or be your doctor or a person acting under direction or control of your doctor. If you are a resident of a health care facility or a patient in a hospital, one of your witnesses may be your doctor or an employee of your doctor.

New Jersey

State Website: http:/www.njleg.state.nj.us

State Law Reference: New Jersey Revised Statutes.

Court with Probate Jurisdiction: Surrogate's Court.

Minimum Age for Disposing of Property by Will: 18. (Section 3B:3-1).

Required Number of Witnesses: Two. (Section 3B:3-2).

Can Witnesses Be Beneficiaries?: Yes. (Section 3B:3-8).

Are There Provisions for Self-Proving Wills?: Yes. (Section 3B:3-4).

Are Holographic Wills Permitted?: Yes. (Section 3B:3-3).

How Does Divorce Affect the Will?: Revokes the will as to the divorced spouse. (Section 3B:3-14).

How Does Marriage Affect the Will?: Spouse shall still be entitled to his or her statutory share under the state intestate laws. (Section 3B:5-15).

Who Must Be Mentioned in the Will?: Children born or adopted; grandchildren; surviving spouse. (Sections 3B:5-15 & 3B:5-16).

Spouse's Right to Property Regardless of Will: The surviving spouse is entitled to 1/3 of the "augmented" estate of the deceased spouse. In general, the "augmented" estate includes both the property that passes under the will and any other property that passes by other "non-will" transfers, such as under the terms of a living trust or a joint tenancy. (Section 3B:8-1).

Laws of Intestate Succession (Distribution If No Will):

Spouse and children of spouse surviving: 1/4 of estate (at least $50,000.00 but no more than 200,000.00) and 1/2 of balance to spouse and 1/2 of balance to children or grandchildren per stirpes.

Spouse and children not of spouse surviving: 1/2 to spouse and 1/2 to children or grandchildren per stirpes.

Spouse, but no children or parent(s) surviving: All to spouse.

Spouse and parent(s), but no children surviving: 1/4 of estate (at least $50,000.00 but no more than 200,000.00) and 1/2 of balance to spouse and 1/2 of balance to parents or surviving parent.

Children, but no spouse surviving: All to children or to their children per stirpes.

Parent(s), but no spouse or children surviving: All to parents equally or to the surviving parent.

No spouse, children, or parent(s) surviving: All to brothers and sisters equally, or their children per stirpes; or if none, 1/2 to maternal grandparents or their children and 1/2 to paternal grandparents or their children per stirpes. (Sections 3B:5-3 & 3B:5-4).

Property Ownership: Common-law state. Tenancy-in-common, joint tenancy and tenancy-by-the-entirety are recognized. Ownership by spouses is presumed to be a tenancy-by-the-entirety unless stated otherwise. Tenancy-in-common is presumed unless joint tenancy stated. Joint bank account deposits are payable to any survivor. (Title 46, Chapter 46-3, Sections 46:3-17, 46:3-17.1, & 46:3-17.2).

State Gift, Inheritance, or Estate Taxes: No gift tax; imposes an inheritance tax of up to 16 percent; imposes state estate tax equal to federal credit for state death taxes less any amounts paid on state inheritance tax. Maximum total state inheritance and state estate tax is equal to the maximum allowable federal estate tax credit for state death taxes. (Title 54, Chapters 54-34+, Sections 54:34-2 & 54:38-1)

Living Will Form: New Jersey Instruction Directive serves as Living Will (Section 26-2H-55).

Other Directives: Appointment of a Health Care Representative (Section 26-2H-58). Anatomical Gift Act (Section 26:6-65). Durable Power of Attorney (Section 3B:13a-10).

Living Will Effective: Your doctor or treating health care institution must receive this document. Your attending physician and one (1) other physician must confirm that you are unable to make health care decisions.

Witness Requirements: Sign in the presence of two (2) witnesses eighteen (18) years or older or a notary public. A witness cannot be the person whom you appointed as your agent.

New Mexico

State Website: http://www.legis.state.nm.us/

State Law Reference: New Mexico Statutes Annotated.

Court with Probate Jurisdiction: Probate or District Court.

Minimum Age for Disposing of Property by Will: 18. (Section 45-2-501).

Required Number of Witnesses: Two. (Section 45-2-502).

Can Witnesses Be Beneficiaries?: Yes. (Section 45-2-505).

Are There Provisions for Self-Proving Wills?: Yes. (Section 45-2-504).

Are Holographic Wills Permitted?: No.

How Does Divorce Affect the Will?: Revokes the will as to the divorced spouse. (Section 45-2-802).

How Does Marriage Affect the Will?: Spouse will still be entitled to his or her statutory share under the state intestate laws. (Section 45-2-301).

Who Must Be Mentioned in the Will?: Children, born or adopted; surviving spouse. (Sections 45-2-301 & 45-2-302).

Spouse's Right to Property Regardless of Will: Community property right to 1/2 of the deceased spouse's "community" property. (Section 45-2-805).

Laws of Intestate Succession (Distribution If No Will):

Spouse and children of spouse surviving: All of decedent's community property to spouse. 1/4 of decedent's separate property to spouse and 3/4 to children or grandchildren per stirpes.

Spouse and children not of spouse surviving: All of decedent's community property to spouse. 1/4 of decedent's separate property to spouse and 3/4 to children or grandchildren per stirpes.

Spouse, but no children or parent(s) surviving: All to spouse.

Spouse and parent(s), but no children surviving: All to spouse.

Children, but no spouse surviving: All to children equally or to their children per stirpes.

Parent(s), but no spouse or children surviving: All to parents equally or to the surviving parent.

No spouse, children, or parent(s) surviving: All to brothers and sisters equally, or their children per stirpes; or if none, 1/2 to maternal grandparents or their children and 1/2 to paternal grandparents or their children per stirpes. (Sections 45-2-102 & 45-2-103).

Property Ownership: Community property state. Tenancy-in-common, joint tenancy, and community property are recognized. Spouses may hold real estate as joint tenants. Tenancy-by-the-entirety is not recognized. Joint bank account deposits are payable to any survivor unless clear evidence exists that deposit is payable only to specified survivor. (Section 47-1-15).

State Gift, Inheritance, or Estate Taxes: No gift tax; no inheritance tax; imposes state estate tax equal to federal credit for state death taxes. (Sections 7-7-3 & 7-7-4).

Living Will Form: Optional Advance Health Care Directive (Section 24-7A-4).

Other Directives: Power of Attorney for Health Care (Section 24-7A-4). Anatomical Gift Act (Sections 24-6A-1 through 42-6A-15). Durable Power of Attorney (Sections 45-5-501 through 45-5-505).

Living Will Effective: This document becomes effective in the event that you have an incurable and irreversible condition that will result in death within a relatively short time, become unconscious and, to a reasonable degree of medical certainty, will not regain consciousness, or the likely risks and burdens of treatment would outweigh the expected benefits.

Witness Requirements: The law does not require that your advance directive be witnessed. To avoid future concerns, we recommend that you sign in the presence of two (2) witnesses eighteen (18) years or older or a notary public. A witness should not be the person whom you appointed as your agent.

New York

State Website: http://assembly.state.ny.us/leg/

State Law Reference: New York Consolidated Laws.

Court with Probate Jurisdiction: Probate Court.

Minimum Age for Disposing of Property by Will: 18. (Estates, Powers & Trusts, Section 3-1.1).

Required Number of Witnesses: Two. (Estates, Powers & Trusts, Section 3-2.1).

Can Witnesses Be Beneficiaries?: Yes, but any gift to a beneficiary who was a witness will be void unless there were also 2 other disinterested witnesses. (Estates, Powers & Trusts, Section 3-3.2).

Are There Provisions for Self-Proving Wills?: Yes. (SCPA, Section 1406).

Are Holographic Wills Permitted?: Yes, but restricted to members of the armed forces. (Estates, Powers & Trusts, Section 3-2.2).

How Does Divorce Affect the Will?: Revokes the will as to divorced spouse. (Estates, Powers & Trusts, Section 5-1.4).

How Does Marriage Affect the Will?: Does not revoke the will. Surviving spouse has right to take elective share of estate. (Estates, Powers & Trusts, Section 5-1.3).

Who Must Be Mentioned in the Will?: Children, born or adopted; surviving spouse. (Estates, Powers & Trusts, Sections 5-1.1-A & 5-3.2).

Spouse's Right to Property Regardless of Will: Generally, the surviving spouse is entitled to $50,000.00 or 1/3 of the deceased spouse's estate. However, please refer directly to the statute as the provisions are detailed. (Estates, Powers & Trusts, Section 5-1.1-A).

Laws of Intestate Succession (Distribution If No Will):

Spouse and children of spouse surviving: $50,000.00 and 1/2 of balance to spouse and 1/2 of balance to children or grandchildren per stirpes.

Spouse and children not of spouse surviving: $50,000.00 and 1/2 of balance to spouse and 1/2 of balance to children or grandchildren per stirpes.

Spouse, but no children or parent(s) surviving: All to spouse.

Spouse and parent(s), but no children surviving: All to spouse.

Children, but no spouse surviving: All to children equally or to their children per stirpes.

Parent(s), but no spouse or children surviving: All to parents equally or to the surviving parent.

No spouse, children, or parent(s) surviving: All to brothers and sisters equally, or their children per stirpes; or if none, to grandparents equally or their children per capita; or if none, to the next-of-kin. (Estates, Powers & Trusts, Section 4-1.1).

Property Ownership: Common-law state. Tenancy-in-common, joint tenancy and tenancy-by-the-entirety are recognized, however, tenancy-by-the-entirety in personal property is not recognized. Joint ownership by spouses is presumed to be a tenancy-by-the-entirety unless specified otherwise. Tenancy-in-common is presumed unless joint tenancy is stated. Joint bank account deposits are payable to any survivor. (Real Property, Section 240b).

State Gift, Inheritance, or Estate Taxes: Imposes a gift tax; no inheritance tax; imposes a state estate tax of up to 21 percent or not less than any federal credit for state death taxes. (Tax, Article 26, Sections 951 to 961).

Living Will Form: Order not to resuscitate acts as Living Will. (Health Care, Article 29-B, Sections 2960 -2979).

Other Directives: Health Care Proxy (Chapter 45, Article 29-C, Section 2980). Anatomical Gift Act (Sections 45-43-4300 through 45-43-4309). Durable Power of Attorney (Sections 24A-5-1501 through 24A-5-1506).

Living Will Effective: The Living Will becomes effective when you become terminally ill, permanently unconscious, or minimally conscious due to brain damage and will never regain the ability to make decisions.

Witness Requirements: Order not to resuscitate acts as Living Will in New York. You must sign in the presence of two (2) adult witnesses who do not benefit from your estate.

North Carolina

State Website: http://www.ncga.state.nc.us/

State Law Reference: North Carolina General Statutes.

Court with Probate Jurisdiction: Superior Court.

Minimum Age for Disposing of Property by Will: 18. (Section 31-1).

Required Number of Witnesses: Two. (Section 31-3.3).

Can Witnesses Be Beneficiaries?: Yes, but any gift to a beneficiary who was a witness will be void unless there were also 2 other disinterested witnesses. (Section 31-10).

Are There Provisions for Self-Proving Wills?: Yes. (Section 31-11.6).

Are Holographic Wills Permitted?: Yes. (Section 31-3.4).

How Does Divorce Affect the Will?: Revokes the will as to the divorced spouse. (Section 31-5.4).

How Does Marriage Affect the Will?: Does not revoke the will. (Section 31-5.3).

Who Must Be Mentioned in the Will?: Children, born or adopted; surviving spouse. (Chapter 29, Section 29-30 & Chapter 31, Section 31-5.5).

Spouse's Right to Property Regardless of Will: Generally, the surviving spouse has 2 choices if there is a will: (1) the surviving spouse is entitled to 1/2 of the deceased spouse's estate if there are 1 or no children of the spouses surviving, and only 1/3 of the estate if there are 2 or more children or grandchildren surviving; or (2) the surviving spouse may choose a life estate of 1/3 of all real estate that the decedent owned on his or her death. Please consult the statute directly as the terms are complex. (Chapter 29, Section 29-30 & Chapter 30, Section 30-3.1).

Laws of Intestate Succession (Distribution If No Will):

Spouse and children of spouse surviving: If only 1 child surviving, $30,000.00 (from personal property, if any) and 1/2 of balance to spouse and 1/2 of balance to children or grandchildren per stirpes. If more than 1 child surviving, $30,000.00 (from personal property, if any) and 1/3 of balance to spouse and 2/3 of balance to children or grandchildren per stirpes.

Spouse and children not of spouse surviving: If only 1 child surviving, $30,000.00 (from personal property, if any) and 1/2 of balance to spouse and 1/2 of balance to children or grandchildren per stirpes. If more than 1 child surviving, $30,000.00 (from personal property, if any) and 1/3 of balance to spouse and 2/3 of balance to children or grandchildren per stirpes.

Spouse, but no children or parent(s) surviving: All to spouse.

Spouse and parent(s), but no children surviving: $50,000.00 (from personal property, if any) and 1/2 of balance to spouse and 1/2 of balance to parents or surviving parent.

Children, but no spouse surviving: All to children equally or to their children per stirpes.

Parent(s), but no spouse or children surviving: All to parents equally or to the surviving parent.

No spouse, children, or parent(s) surviving: All to brothers and sisters equally, or their children per stirpes; or if none, 1/2 to maternal grandparents or their children and 1/2 to paternal grandparents or their children per stirpes. (Chapter 29, Sections 29-14 & 29-15).

Property Ownership: Common-law state. Tenancy-in-common, joint tenancy, and tenancy-by-the-entirety are recognized. However, a tenancy-by-the-entirety in personal property not recognized. Joint bank account deposits are payable to any survivor. (Chapter 39, Sections 39-7+).

State Gift, Inheritance, or Estate Taxes: Imposes a gift tax; does not impose an inheritance tax; imposes a state estate tax equal to federal credit for state death taxes.(Chapter 105, Section 105-32.2).

Living Will Form: Declaration of a Desire for a Natural Death serves as Living Will (Section 90-23-321).

Other Directives: Health Care Power of Attorney (Section 32A- 2- 25). Anatomical Gift Act (Section 130A-402). Durable Power of Attorney (Section 32A-8 through 32A-14).

Living Will Effective: Two (2) physicians must certify in writing that you are in a terminal condition and your death would occur within a short period of time without the use of life-sustaining medical care.

Witness Requirements: Sign in the presence of two (2) adult witnesses and a notary public. A witness cannot be a person who has claim against your estate upon your death, stands to inherit from your estate, be directly financially responsible for your health care, or be an owner, operator, or employee of a health care institution in which you are a patient. Witnesses also cannot be related by blood or marriage.

North Dakota

State Website: http://www.state.nd.us/lr/information/statutes/cent-code.html

State Law Reference: North Dakota Century Code.

Court with Probate Jurisdiction: County Court.

Minimum Age for Disposing of Property by Will: 18. (Section 30.1-08-01).

Required Number of Witnesses: Two. (Section 30.1-08-02).

Can Witnesses Be Beneficiaries?: Yes. (Section 30.1-08-05).

Are There Provisions for Self-Proving Wills?: Yes. (Section 30.1-08-04).

Are Holographic Wills Permitted?: No.

How Does Divorce Affect the Will?: Revokes the will as to the divorced spouse. (Section 30.1-10-02).

How Does Marriage Affect the Will?: Spouse will still be entitled to his or her statutory share under the state intestate laws. (Section 30.1-06-01).

Who Must Be Mentioned in the Will?: Children, born or adopted; surviving spouse. (Sections 30.1-06-01 & 30.1-06-02).

Spouse's Right to Property Regardless of Will: The surviving spouse is entitled to 1/3 of the "augmented" estate of the deceased spouse. In general, the "augmented" estate includes both the property that passes under the will and any other property that passes by other "non-will" transfers, such as under the terms of a living trust or a joint tenancy arrangement. (Section 30.1-05-01).

Laws of Intestate Succession (Distribution If No Will):

Spouse and children of spouse surviving: All to spouse.

Spouse and children not of spouse surviving: $150,000.00 and 1/2 of balance to spouse and 1/2 to children or grandchildren per stirpes.

Spouse, but no children or parent(s) surviving: All to spouse.

Spouse and parent(s), but no children surviving: $200,000.00 and 3/4 of balance to spouse and 1/4 of balance to parents or surviving parent.

Children, but no spouse surviving: All to children equally or to their children per stirpes.

Parent(s), but no spouse or children surviving: All to parents equally or to the surviving parent.

No spouse, children, or parent(s) surviving: All to brothers and sisters equally, or their children per stirpes; or if none, 1/2 to maternal next-of-kin and 1/2 to paternal next-of-kin. (Sections 30.1-04-02 & 30.1-04-03).

Property Ownership: Common-law state. Tenancy-in-common and joint tenancy are recognized. Tenancy-by-the-entirety is not recognized. Joint bank account deposits are payable to any survivor. (Chapter 47-1, Section 47-02-06).

State Gift, Inheritance, or Estate Taxes: No gift tax; no inheritance tax; imposes state estate tax equal to federal credit for state death taxes. (Chapter 57-37, Sections 57-37.1-02 & 1-04).

Living Will Form: Declaration serves as Living Will (Chapter 23, Section 6.4).

Other Directives: Power of Attorney for Health Care (Section 23-06.5). Anatomical Gift Act (Sections 23-06.2-01 through 23-06.2-12). Durable Power of Attorney (Section 30.1-30).

Living Will Effective: Two (2) physicians must certify in writing that you are in a terminal condition and your death would occur within a short period of time without the use of life-sustaining medical care.

Witness Requirements: Sign in the presence of two (2) adult witnesses and a notary public. A witness cannot be a person who has claim against your estate upon your death, stands to inherit from your estate, be directly financially responsible for your health care, or be your doctor. Witnesses also cannot be related by blood or marriage. If you are presently living in a nursing home or other long-term care facility, one (1) of your witnesses must be one (1) of the following: a member of the clergy, a lawyer licensed to practice in North Dakota, or a person designated by the Department of Human Services or the county court for the county in which the facility is located.

Ohio

State Website: http://onlinedocs.andersonpublishing.com/revisedcode/

State Law Reference: Ohio Revised Code Annotated.

Court with Probate Jurisdiction: Court of Common Pleas.

Minimum Age for Disposing of Property by Will: 18. (Section 2107.02).

Required Number of Witnesses: Two. (Section 2107.03).

Can Witnesses Be Beneficiaries?: Yes, but any gift to a beneficiary who was a witness will be void (beyond what that beneficiary would get as an intestate share) unless there were also 2 other disinterested witnesses. (Section 2107.15).

Are There Provisions for Self-Proving Wills?: No.

Are Holographic Wills Permitted?: No provision.

How Does Divorce Affect the Will?: Revokes the will as to the divorced spouse. (Section 2107.33).

How Does Marriage Affect the Will?: Does not revoke the will. (Section 2107.37).

Who Must Be Mentioned in the Will?: Children, born or adopted; surviving spouse. (Sections 2106.01 & 2107.34).

Spouse's Right to Property Regardless of Will: Generally, the surviving spouse is entitled to 1/2 of the deceased spouse's estate if there are one or fewer children, and only 1/3 if there are two or more children. However, please refer directly to the statute as the provisions are detailed. (Section 2106.01).

Laws of Intestate Succession (Distribution If No Will):

Spouse and children of spouse surviving: All to spouse.

Spouse and children not of spouse surviving: If only 1 child surviving, $20,000.00 and 1/2 of balance to spouse and 1/2 of balance to children or grandchildren per stirpes. If more than 1 child surviving, $20,000.00 and 1/3 of balance to spouse and 2/3 of balance to children or grandchildren per stirpes.

Spouse, but no children or parent(s) surviving: All to spouse.

Spouse and parent(s), but no children surviving: All to spouse.

Children, but no spouse surviving: All to children or to their children per stirpes.

Parent(s), but no spouse or children surviving: All to parents equally or to the surviving parent.

No spouse, children, or parent(s) surviving: All to brothers and sisters equally, or their children per stirpes; or if none, 1/2 to maternal grandparents or their children and 1/2 to paternal grandparents or their children per stirpes; or if none, to the next-of-kin. (Section 2105.06).

Property Ownership: Common-law state. Tenancy-in-common, joint tenancy, and tenancy-by-the-entirety are recognized. Joint tenancy must be stated. Joint bank account deposits are payable to any survivor. (Title 53, Sections 5302.19 & 5302.20).

State Gift, Inheritance, or Estate Taxes: No gift tax; no inheritance tax; imposes a state estate tax of up to 7 percent or not less than any federal credit for state death taxes. (Title 57, Section 5731.02).

Living Will Form: Living Will Declaration (Title 37, Chapter 2133, Section 04).

Other Directives: Power of Attorney for Health Care (Section 1337-12). Anatomical Gift Act (Section 2108.09). Durable Power of Attorney (Section 1337-01).

Living Will Effective: Two (2) physicians determine that you are in a terminal condition and your death will result without using life-sustaining procedures, including the determination that there is no reasonable possibility that you will regain the ability to make your own health care decisions.

Witness Requirements: Sign in front of two (2) witnesses eighteen (18) years or older or a notary public. Witnesses cannot be related to you by blood, marriage, or adoption, or be your doctor or the administrator of a nursing home in which you are receiving treatment.

Oklahoma

State Website: http://www.oscn.net/

State Law Reference: Oklahoma Statutes Annotated.

Court with Probate Jurisdiction: District Court.

Minimum Age for Disposing of Property by Will: 18. (84-41).

Required Number of Witnesses: Two. (84-55).

Can Witnesses Be Beneficiaries?: Yes, if witnessed by 2 other witnesses. However, any gift under the will to a witness-beneficiary is void if it exceeds the amount that he or she would receive as an intestate share of the estate. (Sections 84-143 & 84-144).

Are There Provisions for Self-Proving Wills?: Yes. (Section 84-55).

Are Holographic Wills Permitted?: Yes. (Section 84-54).

How Does Divorce Affect the Will?: Revokes the will as to the divorced spouse. (Section 84-114).

How Does Marriage Affect the Will?: Revokes the will if a child is later born into the marriage. (Section 84-131).

Who Must Be Mentioned in the Will?: Children, born or adopted; surviving spouse. (Section 84-131).

Spouse's Right to Property Regardless of Will: Generally, the surviving spouse is entitled to 1/2 of the deceased spouse's estate if there are no children, and only 1/3 if there are children. However, please refer to the statute for details. (Section 84-44).

Laws of Intestate Succession (Distribution If No Will):

Spouse and children of spouse surviving: If 1 child, then 1/2 to spouse and 1/2 to child or grandchildren. If deceased had more than 1 child, then 1/3 to spouse and 2/3 to children or grandchildren per stirpes.

Spouse and children not of spouse surviving: All of property acquired during the marriage by joint effort to spouse, and balance to children and spouse in equal shares.

Spouse, but no children or parent(s) surviving: 1/2 of other property to spouse and 1/3 to maternal grandparents or their children and 1/3 to paternal grandparents or their children per stirpes; or if none, to the next-of-kin.

Spouse and parent(s), but no children surviving: 1/2 of property to spouse and 1/2 to parents or surviving parent per stirpes.

Children, but no spouse surviving: All to children equally or grandchildren per stirpes.

Parent(s), but no spouse or children surviving: All to parents equally or to the surviving parent.

No spouse, children, or parent(s) surviving: All to brothers and sisters equally, or their children per stirpes; or if none, 1/2 to maternal grandparents or their children and 1/2 to paternal grandparents or their children per stirpes; or if none, to the next-of-kin. (Section 84-213).

Property Ownership: Common-law state. Tenancy-in-common, joint tenancy, and tenancy-by-the-entirety are recognized. Rights of survivorship must be stated. Joint bank account deposits are payable to any survivor. (Section 60-74).

State Gift, Inheritance, or Estate Taxes: No gift tax; no inheritance tax; imposes a state estate tax of up to 15 percent but not less than the federal credit for state death taxes. (Section 68-803).

Living Will Form: Is Part 1 of Advance Directive for Health Care (Title 63, Article 3101, Section 4).

Other Directives: Appointment of Health Care Proxy is Part 2 of Advance Directive for Health Care (Section 63-3101.4). Anatomical Gift Act (Sections 63-2201 through 63-2209). Durable Power of Attorney (Sections 15-1001 through 15-1020).

Living Will Effective: This Directive goes into effect once it is given to your doctor and you are unable to make your own medical decisions. In order to follow your instructions regarding life-sustaining treatment, your doctor must first consult another doctor to determine that you are persistently unconscious or suffering from a terminal condition.

Witness Requirements: Sign in the presence of two (2) adult witnesses. A witness cannot be any person who would inherit from you under any existing will or by operation of law.

Oregon

State Website: http://www.leg.state.or.us/ors/

State Law Reference: Oregon Revised Statutes.

Court with Probate Jurisdiction: Circuit or County Court.

Minimum Age for Disposing of Property by Will: 18, however, no minimum age for married persons. (Section 112.225).

Required Number of Witnesses: Two. (Section 112.235).

Can Witnesses Be Beneficiaries?: Yes. (Section 112.245).

Are There Provisions for Self-Proving Wills?: Yes. (Section 113.055).

Are Holographic Wills Permitted?: No provision.

How Does Divorce Affect the Will?: Revokes the will as to the divorced spouse. (Section 112.315).

How Does Marriage Affect the Will?: Revokes the will if the maker of the will is survived by a spouse. (Section 112.305).

Who Must Be Mentioned in the Will?: Statute contains detailed provisions regarding this matter. Please refer directly to statute text or consult an attorney if this is a critical factor. (Sections 112.405 & 114.105).

Spouse's Right to Property Regardless of Will: The surviving spouse is entitled to up to 1/4 of the deceased spouse's estate, including any property that was received under the deceased's will. Please refer directly to the statute for further details. (Section 114.105).

Laws of Intestate Succession (Distribution If No Will):

Spouse and children of spouse surviving: All to spouse.

Spouse and children not of spouse surviving: 1/2 to spouse and 1/2 to children or grandchildren per stirpes.

Spouse, but no children or parent(s) surviving: All to spouse.

Spouse and parent(s), but no children surviving: All to spouse.

Children, but no spouse surviving: All to children equally or to their children per stirpes.

Parent(s), but no spouse or children surviving: All to parents equally or to the surviving parent.

No spouse, children, or parent(s) surviving: All to brothers and sisters equally, or their children per stirpes; or if none, to the next-of-kin. (Sections 112.025 to 112.045).

Property Ownership: Common-law state. Tenancy-in-common and tenancy-by-the-entirety are recognized. Right of survivorship must be stated. Joint bank account deposits are payable to any survivor unless clear evidence exists that deposit is payable only to specified survivor. (Section 93.180).

State Gift, Inheritance, or Estate Taxes: No gift tax; imposes state estate (inheritance) tax equal to federal credit for state death taxes. (Section 118.010).

Living Will Form: Health Care Instructions serves as Living Will (Chapter 127, Section 531).

Other Directives: Appointment of Health Care Representative (Section 127-531). Anatomical Gift Act (Sections 97.950 through 97.964). Durable Power of Attorney (Section 127.005).

Living Will Effective: Two (2) physicians agree that you have an incurable and irreversible condition that will result in death within a relatively short time, will become unconscious and, to a reasonable degree of medical certainty, will not regain consciousness, or the likely risks and burdens of treatment would outweigh the expected benefits.

Witness Requirements: Sign in the presence of two (2) adult witnesses. If you have someone sign the Declaration on your behalf, that person cannot serve as a witness. Your attending physician cannot be a witness. At least one (1) of your witnesses cannot be related to you by blood, marriage, or adoption, entitled to any portion of your estate, or be an owner, operator, or employee of your treating health care facility.

Pennsylvania

State Website: http://members.aol.com/StatutesPA/Index.html

State Law Reference: Pennsylvania Code.

Court with Probate Jurisdiction: Court of Common Pleas.

Minimum Age for Disposing of Property by Will: 18. (Section 20-2501).

Required Number of Witnesses: Two. (Section 20-3132).

Can Witnesses Be Beneficiaries?: Yes. (Under Pennsylvania case law).

Are There Provisions for Self-Proving Wills?: Yes. (Section 20-3132.1).

Are Holographic Wills Permitted?: Yes. (Under Pennsylvania case law).

How Does Divorce Affect the Will?: Revokes the will as to divorced spouse. (Section 20-2507).

How Does Marriage Affect the Will?: Surviving spouse receives intestate share if marriage took place after will was signed, unless will gives greater share or will was expressly made in contemplation of marriage. Spouse may still be entitled to his or her statutory share under the state intestate laws. (Section 20-2507).

Who Must Be Mentioned in the Will?: Children, born or adopted; surviving spouse. (Sections 20-2203 & 20-2507).

Spouse's Right to Property Regardless of Will: The surviving spouse is entitled to 1/3 of the deceased spouse's estate. (Section 20-2203).

Laws of Intestate Succession (Distribution If No Will):

Spouse and children of spouse surviving: $30,000.00 and 1/2 of balance to spouse and 1/2 of balance to children or grandchildren per stirpes.

Spouse and children not of spouse surviving: 1/2 to spouse and 1/2 to children or grandchildren per stirpes.

Spouse, but no children or parent(s) surviving: All to spouse.

Spouse and parent(s), but no children surviving: $30,000.00 and 1/2 of balance to spouse and 1/2 of balance to parents or surviving parent.

Children, but no spouse surviving: All to children equally or their children per stirpes.

Parent(s), but no spouse or children surviving: All to parents equally or to the surviving parent.

No spouse, children, or parent(s) surviving: All to brothers and sisters equally, or their children per stirpes; or if none, 1/2 to maternal grandparents and 1/2 to paternal grandparents; or if none, all to aunts, uncles, or their children per stirpes. (Sections 20-2102 & 20-2103).

Property Ownership: Common-law state. Tenancy-in-common and tenancy-by-the-entirety are recognized. Joint tenancy with right of survivorship only if stated. Real estate jointly-owned by spouses is presumed to be a tenancy-by-the-entirety unless stated otherwise. Joint bank account deposits are payable to any survivor. (Section 68-110).

State Gift, Inheritance, or Estate Taxes: No gift tax; imposes an inheritance tax of up to 15 percent; imposes state estate tax equal to federal credit for state death taxes less any amounts paid on state inheritance tax. Maximum total state inheritance and state estate tax is equal to the maximum allowable federal estate tax credit for state death taxes. (Sections 72-2101+).

Living Will Form: Declaration serves as Living Will. (Section 20-5404).

Other Directives: Anatomical Gift Act (Section 20-8613).

Living Will Effective: The Declaration becomes effective when your physician receives a copy of it and determines that you are incompetent and in a terminal condition or a state of permanent unconsciousness.

Witness Requirements: Sign in the presence of two (2) adult witnesses. If you have someone sign the Declaration on your behalf, that person cannot serve as a witness.

Rhode Island

State Website: http://www.rilin.state.ri.us/Statutes/Statutes.html

State Law Reference: Rhode Island General Laws.

Court with Probate Jurisdiction: Probate Court.

Minimum Age for Disposing of Property by Will: 18. (Section 33-5-2).

Required Number of Witnesses: Two. (Section 33-5-5).

Can Witnesses Be Beneficiaries?: No. (Section 33-6-1).

Are There Provisions for Self-Proving Wills?: Yes. (Section 33-7-26).

Are Holographic Wills Permitted?: No provision.

How Does Divorce Affect the Will?: Revokes the will as to the former spouse. (Section 33-5-9.1).

How Does Marriage Affect the Will?: Revokes the will completely. (Section 33-5-9).

Who Must Be Mentioned in the Will?: Children, born or adopted; grandchildren (if of deceased child); surviving spouse. (Sections 33-6-23 & 33-25-2).

Spouse's Right to Property Regardless of Will: The surviving spouse is entitled to all of the deceased spouse's real estate for the rest of his or her life. (Section 33-25-2).

Laws of Intestate Succession (Distribution If No Will):

Spouse and children of spouse surviving: Real estate: life estate to spouse and balance to children equally or grandchildren per stirpes. Personal property: 1/2 to spouse and 1/2 to children or grandchildren per stirpes.

Spouse and children not of spouse surviving: Real estate: life estate to spouse and balance to children equally or grandchildren per stirpes. Personal property: 1/2 to spouse and 1/2 to children or grandchildren per stirpes.

Spouse, but no children or parent(s) surviving: Real estate: life estate and $75,000.00 to spouse (if court approves), balance to brothers and sisters equally; or if none, 1/2 to maternal grandparents and 1/2 to paternal grandparents; or if none, to aunts and uncles equally or their children per stirpes; or if none, to the next-of-kin; or if none, to the spouse. Personal property: $50,000.00 and 1/2 of balance to spouse and 1/2 of balance to brothers and sisters equally; or if none, 1/2 to maternal grandparents and 1/2 to paternal grandparents; or if none, to aunts and uncles equally or their children per stirpes; or if none, to the next-of-kin; or if none, to the spouse.

Spouse and parent(s), but no children surviving: Real estate: life estate and $75,000.00 to spouse (if court approves), balance to parents or surviving parent. Personal property: $50,000.00 and 1/2 of balance to spouse and 1/2 of balance to parents or surviving parent.

Children, but no spouse surviving: All to children or grandchildren per stirpes.

Parent(s), but no spouse or children surviving: All to parents equally or to parent.

No spouse, children, or parent(s) surviving: All to brothers and sisters equally, or their children per stirpes; or if none, 1/2 to maternal grandparents and 1/2 to paternal grandparents; or if none, to the next-of-kin. (Sections 33-1-5, 33-1-6, & 33-1-10).

Property Ownership: Common-law state. Tenancy-in-common is presumed unless stated otherwise. Tenancy-in-common, joint tenancy, and tenancy-by-the-entirety are recognized. Joint bank account deposits are payable to any survivor. (Title 34, Sections 34-3+).

State Gift, Inheritance, or Estate Taxes: No gift tax; no inheritance tax; imposes state estate tax equal to federal credit for state death taxes. (Title 44, Section 44-22-1.1).

Living Will Form: Declaration serves as Living Will (Chapter 23, Article 4, Section 11-3).

Other Directives: Power of Attorney for Health Care (Section 23-4.10). Anatomical Gift Act (Section 23-18.6). Durable Power of Attorney (Section 18-3-5).

Living Will Effective: Your doctor must determine that your death would occur without use of life-sustaining medical care.

Witness Requirements: Sign in the presence of two (2) adult witnesses. Witnesses cannot be related to you by blood, marriage, or adoption.

South Carolina

State Website: http://www.scstatehouse.net/code/statmast.htm/

State Law Reference: Code of Laws of South Carolina Annotated.

Court with Probate Jurisdiction: Probate Court.

Minimum Age for Disposing of Property by Will: 18, or if married. (Section 62-2-501).

Required Number of Witnesses: Two. (Section 62-2-502).

Can Witnesses Be Beneficiaries?: Yes, if there were also 2 additional competent witnesses, otherwise witness share not to exceed intestate share. (Section 62-2-504).

Are There Provisions for Self-Proving Wills?: Yes. (Section 62-2-503).

Are Holographic Wills Permitted?: No provision.

How Does Divorce Affect the Will?: Revokes the will as to the divorced spouse. (Section 62-2-507).

How Does Marriage Affect the Will?: Does not revoke the will and spouse may still receive intestate share. (Section 62-2-301).

Who Must Be Mentioned in the Will?: Children, born or adopted; surviving spouse. (Sections 62-2-201 & 62-2-302).

Spouse's Right to Property Regardless of Will: The surviving spouse is entitled to 1/3 of the deceased spouse's estate. (Section 62-2-201).

Laws of Intestate Succession (Distribution If No Will):

Spouse and children of spouse surviving: 1/2 to spouse and 1/2 to children or grandchildren per stirpes.

Spouse and children not of spouse surviving: 1/2 to spouse and 1/2 to children or grandchildren per stirpes.

Spouse, but no children or parent(s) surviving: All to spouse.

Spouse and parent(s), but no children surviving: All to spouse.

Children, but no spouse surviving: All to children equally or to their children per stirpes.

Parent(s), but no spouse or children surviving: All to parents equally or to the surviving parent if no brothers and sisters.

No spouse, children, or parent(s) surviving: All to brothers and sisters equally, or their children per stirpes; or if none, to lineal ancestors equally or to survivor; or if none, to aunts and uncles equally, or their children per stirpes; or if none, to the next-of-kin. (Sections 62-2-102 & 62-2-103).

Property Ownership: Common-law state. Tenancy-in-common and joint tenancy are recognized. Right of survivorship only if stated. Tenancy-by-the-entirety is not recognized. Joint bank account deposits are payable to any survivor. (Section 27-7-40).

State Gift, Inheritance, or Estate Taxes: Imposes a gift tax; no inheritance tax; imposes a state estate tax equal to the federal credit for state death taxes. (Section 12-16-510).

Living Will Form: Declaration of a Desire for a Natural Death serves as Living Will (Title 44, Chapter 77, Section 50).

Other Directives: Health Care Power of Attorney (Section 62-5-501). Anatomical Gift Act (Sections 44-43-10 through 44-43-50). Durable Power of Attorney (Section 62-5-501).

Living Will Effective: Two (2) physicians must determine you are in a terminal condition and your death will result without using life-sustaining procedures.

Witness Requirements: Sign in the presence of two (2) adult witnesses and a notary public. A witness cannot be a beneficiary of your life insurance policy, your health care provider, or an employee of your health care provider. Witnesses cannot be related to you by blood, marriage, or adoption, entitled to any part of your estate, or directly financially responsible for your health care. In addition, at least one (1) witness must not be an employee of a health facility in which you are a patient. If you are a resident in a hospital or nursing facility, one of the witnesses must also be an ombudsman designated by the State Ombudsman, Office of the Governor.

South Dakota

State Website: http://legis.state.sd.us/statutes/

State Law Reference: South Dakota Codified Laws Annotated.

Court with Probate Jurisdiction: Circuit Court.

Minimum Age for Disposing of Property by Will: 18. (Section 29A-2-501).

Required Number of Witnesses: Two. (Section 29A-2-502).

Can Witnesses Be Beneficiaries?: Yes. (Section 29A-2-505).

Are There Provisions for Self-Proving Wills?: Yes. (Section 29A-2-504).

Are Holographic Wills Permitted?: Yes. (Section 29A-2-502).

How Does Divorce Affect the Will?: Revokes the will as to the former spouse. (Section 29A-2-804).

How Does Marriage Affect the Will?: Does not revoke the will, but surviving spouse is entitled to intestate share. (Section 29A-2-301).

Who Must Be Mentioned in the Will?: Surviving spouse and children born or adopted. (Sections 29A-2-202 & 29A-2-302).

Spouse's Right to Property Regardless of Will: The surviving spouse is entitled to an elective share of the deceased spouse's "augmented" estate that ranges from a "supplemental amount" for spouses married for less than 1 year, 3 percent of the "augmented" estate for spouses married from 1-2 years, and up to 50 percent for spouses married over 15 years. Please consult the statute directly for complete details. (Section 29A-2-202).

Laws of Intestate Succession (Distribution If No Will):

Spouse and children of spouse surviving: All to spouse.

Spouse and children not of spouse surviving: $100,000.00 and 1/2 of balance to spouse, 1/2 to children or grandchildren per stirpes.

Spouse, but no children or parent(s) surviving: All to spouse.

Spouse and parent(s), but no children surviving: All to spouse.

Children, but no spouse surviving: All to children or to their children per stirpes.

Parent(s), but no spouse or children surviving: All to parents equally or to the surviving parent.

No spouse, children, or parent(s) surviving: All to brothers and sisters equally, or their children per stirpes; or if none, to the next-of-kin. (Sections 29A-2-101+).

Property Ownership: Common-law state. Tenancy-in-common and joint tenancy are recognized. Tenancy-by-the-entirety is not recognized. Joint bank account deposits are payable to any survivor. (Title 43, Sections 43-2-11 to 43-2-15).

State Gift, Inheritance, or Estate Taxes: No gift tax; imposes an inheritance tax of up to 30 percent; imposes state estate tax equal to federal credit for state death taxes less any amounts paid on state inheritance tax. Maximum total state inheritance and state estate tax is equal to the maximum allowable federal estate tax credit for state death taxes. (Title 10, Sections 10-40A-3 & 10-40-21).

Living Will Form: Living Will Declaration (Title 34, Chapter 12D, Section 3).

Other Directives: Power of Attorney for Health Care (Section 34-12C). Anatomical Gift Act (Sections 34-26-20 through 34-26-47). Durable Power of Attorney (Section 51A-11-4).

Living Will Effective: Declaration is effective when your death will result without using life-sustaining procedures, including the determination that there is no reasonable possibility that you will regain the ability to make your own health care decisions.

Witness Requirements: Sign in the presence of two (2) witnesses eighteen (18) years or older or a notary public. Although South Dakota does not have any restrictions on who can be a witness, we suggest that you not use your appointed attorney-in-fact or your health care provider.

Tennessee

State Website: http://www.michie.com

State Law Reference: Tennessee Code Annotated.

Court with Probate Jurisdiction: Probate Court.

Minimum Age for Disposing of Property by Will: 18. (Section 32-1-102).

Required Number of Witnesses: Two. (Section 32-1-104).

Can Witnesses Be Beneficiaries?: No, unless attested by 2 disinterested witnesses. (Section 32-1-103).

Are There Provisions for Self-Proving Wills?: Yes. (Section 32-2-110).

Are Holographic Wills Permitted?: Yes. (Section 32-1-105).

How Does Divorce Affect the Will?: Revokes the will as to the divorced spouse. (Section 31-1-102).

How Does Marriage Affect the Will?: Revokes the will if a child is later born to the marriage. (Section 32-1-201).

Who Must Be Mentioned in the Will?: Children, born or adopted; surviving spouse. (Sections 31-4-101 & 32-3-103).

Spouse's Right to Property Regardless of Will: A spouse's right to property regardless of provisions in the will is dependent on length of marriage. Please consult statute directly for provisions regarding this topic. (Section 31-4-101).

Laws of Intestate Succession (Distribution If No Will):

Spouse and children of spouse surviving: Family homestead and 1 year's support allowance and 1 child's share of estate (at least 1/3) to spouse, and balance to children equally or grandchildren per stirpes.

Spouse and children not of spouse surviving: Family homestead and 1 year's support allowance and 1 child's share of estate (at least 1/3) to spouse, and balance to children equally or grandchildren per stirpes.

Spouse, but no children or parent(s) surviving: All to spouse.

Spouse and parent(s), but no children surviving: All to spouse.

Children, but no spouse surviving: All to children equally or to their children per stirpes.

Parent(s), but no spouse or children surviving: All to parents equally or to the surviving parent.

No spouse, children, or parent(s) surviving: All to brothers and sisters equally, or their children per stirpes; or if none, 1/2 to maternal grandparents and 1/2 to paternal grandparents, or surviving grandparent; or if none, to the children of grandparents per stirpes. (Section 31-2-104).

Property Ownership: Common-law state. Tenancy-in-common and tenancy-by-the-entirety are recognized. Joint tenancy with right to survivorship has been abolished with regard to real estate. Joint bank account deposits are payable to any survivor. (Title 45, Section 45-2-703 & Title 66, Sections 66-1-107+).

State Gift, Inheritance, or Estate Taxes: Imposes a gift tax; imposes an inheritance tax of up to 16 percent; imposes state estate tax equal to federal credit for state death taxes less any amounts paid on state inheritance tax. Maximum total state inheritance and state estate tax is equal to the maximum allowable federal estate tax credit for state death taxes. (Sections 67-8-102, 67-8-204, & 67-8-314).

Living Will Form: Living Will (Section 32-22-105).

Other Directives: Power of Attorney for Health Care (Section 34-6-204). Anatomical Gift Act (Section 68-30-10). Durable Power of Attorney (Section 34-6-204).

Living Will Effective: The Living Will becomes effective when your death will result without using life-sustaining procedures.

Witness Requirements: Sign in the presence of two (2) adult witnesses and a notary public. A witness cannot be a person who has claim against your estate upon your death, stands to inherit from your estate, be your doctor or an employee of your doctor, or be an owner, operator, or employee of a health care institution in which you are a patient. Witnesses also cannot be related by blood or marriage.

Texas

State Website:www.capitol.state.tx.us

State Law Reference: Texas Statutes and Code Annotated.

Court with Probate Jurisdiction: County or Probate Court.

Minimum Age for Disposing of Property by Will: 18, however no minimum age for married persons or members of the Armed Forces. (Probate Code 4-57).

Required Number of Witnesses: Two. (Probate Code 4-59).

Can Witnesses Be Beneficiaries?: Yes, however the witness-beneficiary may not receive a bequest that exceeds the amount that he or she would have received as an intestate share of the estate. (Probate Code 4-61).

Are There Provisions for Self-Proving Wills?: Yes. (Probate Code 4-59).

Are Holographic Wills Permitted?: Yes. (Probate Code 4-59).

How Does Divorce Affect the Will?: Revokes the will as to the divorced spouse. (Probate Code 4-69).

How Does Marriage Affect the Will?: Does not revoke the will. (Probate Code 4-63).

Who Must Be Mentioned in the Will?: Children, born or adopted. (Probate Code 4-67).

Spouse's Right to Property Regardless of Will: Community property right to 1/2 of the deceased spouse's "community" property. (Probate Code 8-270).

Laws of Intestate Succession (Distribution If No Will):

Spouse and children of spouse surviving: 1/2 of community property, 1/3 life estate in separate real property, and 1/3 separate personal property to spouse; balance to children or grandchildren per stirpes.

Spouse and children not of spouse surviving: 1/2 of community property, 1/3 life estate in separate real property, and 1/3 separate personal property to spouse; balance to children or grandchildren per stirpes.

Spouse, but no children or parent(s) surviving: All community property, all separate personal property, and 1/2 separate real property to spouse; balance to brothers and sisters equally or their children per stirpes; or if none, to grandparents or their descendants; or if none, all to spouse.

Spouse and parent(s), but no children surviving: All community property, all separate personal property, and 1/2 separate real property to spouse; balance to parents (if both surviving); if only 1 parent surviving, 1/4 balance to parent and 1/4 to brothers and sisters equally, or their children per stirpes; or if none, entire 1/2 to parent.

Children, but no spouse surviving: All to children or to their children per stirpes.

Parent(s), but no spouse or children surviving: If both parents are surviving, all to parents equally; if only 1 parent surviving, 1/2 to parent and 1/2 to brothers and sisters equally, or their children per stirpes; or if none, all to parent.

No spouse, children, or parent(s) surviving: All to brothers and sisters equally, or their children per stirpes; or if none, 1/2 to maternal grandparents or their children and 1/2 to paternal grandparents or their children per stirpes. (Probate Code 2-38).

Property Ownership: Community property state. Tenancy-in-common is recognized. Tenancy-by-the-entirety is not recognized. Joint bank account deposits are payable to any survivor. (Family Code 3-3.002).

State Gift, Inheritance, or Estate Taxes: No gift tax; no inheritance tax; imposes state estate tax equal to federal credit for state death taxes. (Tax Code 211-051 through 056).

Living Will Form: Directive to Physicians and Family or Surrogate serves as Living Will (Health & Safety Code 166-033).

Other Directives: Medical Power of Attorney (Health & Safety Code 12-481). Anatomical Gift Act Texas (Health & Safety Code 166-152). Durable Power of Attorney (Probate Code 482).

Living Will Effective: This Directive becomes effective when your attending physician certifies in writing that you are in a terminal or irreversible condition.

Witness Requirements: At least one (1) witness cannot be related to you by blood, marriage, or adoption, designated to make treatment decisions for you, entitled to any part of your estate, or be your doctor or an employee of your doctor. A witness cannot be an employee of a health care facility in which you are a patient, an officer, director, partner, or a business office employee of the health care facility or any part of any parent organization of the health care facility, or have a claim against your estate after you die.

Utah

State Website: http://www.le.state.ut.us/

State Law Reference: Utah Code Annotated.

Court with Probate Jurisdiction: District Court.

Minimum Age for Disposing of Property by Will: 18. (Section 75-2-501).

Required Number of Witnesses: Two. (Section 75-2-502).

Can Witnesses Be Beneficiaries?: Yes. (Section 75-2-505).

Are There Provisions for Self-Proving Wills?: Yes. (Section 75-2-504).

Are Holographic Wills Permitted?: Yes. (Section 75-2-502 & 503).

How Does Divorce Affect the Will?: Revokes the will as to divorced spouse. (Section 75-2-804).

How Does Marriage Affect the Will?: Does not revoke the will and spouse is entitled to intestate share. (Section 75-2-301).

Who Must Be Mentioned in the Will?: Children, born or adopted; grandchildren (if of deceased child); surviving spouse. (Sections 75-2-202 & 75-2-302).

Spouse's Right to Property Regardless of Will: The surviving spouse is entitled to 1/3 of the deceased spouse's augmented estate. (Section 75-2-202).

Laws of Intestate Succession (Distribution If No Will):

Spouse and children of spouse surviving: All to spouse.

Spouse and children not of spouse surviving: $50,000.00 and 1/2 of balance to spouse and 1/2 to children or grandchildren per stirpes.

Spouse, but no children or parent(s) surviving: All to spouse.

Spouse and parent(s), but no children surviving: All to spouse.

Children, but no spouse surviving: All to children equally or to their children per stirpes.

Parent(s), but no spouse or children surviving: All to parents equally or to the surviving parent.

No spouse, children, or parent(s) surviving: All to brothers and sisters equally, or their children per stirpes; 1/2 to maternal grandparents or their descendants and 1/2 to paternal grandparents or their descendants per stirpes; or if none, to the next-of-kin. (Sections 75-2-102 & 75-2-103).

Property Ownership: Common-law state. Tenancy-in-common, and joint tenancy are recognized. Real estate is presumed to be tenancy-in-common, unless owned jointly by husband and wife; then ownership is presumed to be joint tenancy. Joint bank account deposits are payable to any survivor. (Section 57-1-5).

State Gift, Inheritance, or Estate Taxes: No gift tax; no inheritance tax; imposes state estate tax equal to federal credit for state death taxes. (Sections 59-11-103 & 59-11-104).

Living Will Form: Directive to Physicians and Providers of Medical Services serves as Living Will, (Section 75-2-1104).

Other Directives: Special Power of Attorney for Health Care (Section 75-2-1106). Anatomical Gift Act (Section 26-28-3). Durable Power of Attorney (Section 75-5-501).

Living Will Effective: Two (2) physicians must physically examine you and certify in writing you are in a terminal condition or persistent vegetative state.

Witness Requirements: Sign in the presence of two (2) witnesses eighteen (18) years or older. A witness cannot be entitled to any part of your estate, be financially responsible for your medical care, be related to you by blood or marriage, be the person who signed the Declaration on your behalf, or be an employee of your health care facility.

Vermont

State Website: http://www.leg.state.vt.us/statutes/statutes2.htm

State Law Reference: Vermont Statutes Annotated.

Court with Probate Jurisdiction: Probate Court.

Minimum Age for Disposing of Property by Will: 18. (Section 14-1-1).

Required Number of Witnesses: Three. (Section 14-1-5).

Can Witnesses Be Beneficiaries?: No, unless attested by 3 disinterested witnesses. (Section 14-1-10).

Are There Provisions for Self-Proving Wills?: No.

Are Holographic Wills Permitted?: No provision.

How Does Divorce Affect the Will?: Does not revoke the will. (Section 14-1-11).

How Does Marriage Affect the Will?: Does not revoke the will and spouse is entitled to intestate share of estate. (Section 14-1-11).

Who Must Be Mentioned in the Will?: Children, born or adopted; grandchildren (if of deceased child); surviving spouse. (Sections 14-45-555 & 556).

Spouse's Right to Property Regardless of Will: If there are no children or more than 1 child of the surviving spouse and the deceased, the surviving spouse is entitled to 1/3 of the deceased spouse's real estate. If there is only 1 child of the surviving spouse and the deceased, the surviving spouse is entitled to 1/2 of the deceased spouse's real estate. Please refer to the statute for instances when this effect may be barred. (Section 14-43-461).

Laws of Intestate Succession (Distribution If No Will):

Spouse and children of spouse surviving: If 1 child surviving: 1/2 of deceased's estate to spouse; balance to child or grandchildren per stirpes. If more than 1 child surviving: 1/3 to spouse and 2/3 to children or grandchildren per stirpes.

Spouse and children not of spouse surviving: If 1 child surviving: 1/3 of deceased's estate to spouse; balance to child or grandchildren per stirpes. If more than 1 child surviving: 1/3 to spouse and 2/3 to children or grandchildren per stirpes.

Spouse, but no children or parent(s) surviving: If spouse waives the statutory share and any will provisions, then $25,000.00 and 1/2 of balance to spouse and 1/2 of balance as if surviving spouse had not survived.

Spouse and parent(s), but no children surviving: $25,000.00 and 1/2 of balance to spouse and 1/2 of balance as if surviving spouse had not survived.

Children, but no spouse surviving: All to children equally or to their children per stirpes.

Parent(s), but no spouse or children surviving: All to parents equally or to the surviving parent.

No spouse, children, or parent(s) surviving: All to brothers and sisters equally, or their children per stirpes; or if none, to the next-of-kin. (Section 14-45-551).

Property Ownership: Common-law state. Tenancy-in-common, tenancy-by-the-entirety, and joint tenancy are recognized. Real estate is presumed to be held by tenancy-in-common unless it is ownership of husband and wife, in which case, joint tenancy is presumed. Joint bank account deposits are payable to any survivor. (Section 27-1-2).

State Gift, Inheritance, or Estate Taxes: No gift tax; no inheritance tax; imposes state estate tax equal to federal credit for state death taxes. (Section 32-190-7442a).

Living Will Form: Terminal Care Document serves as Living Will (Section 18-5253).

Other Directives: Power of Attorney for Health Care (Section 18-5276). Anatomical Gift Act (Section 18-109). Durable Power of Attorney (Section 14-3508).

Living Will Effective: Document becomes effective if death would occur regardless of the use of life-sustaining procedures.

Witness Requirements: Sign in the presence of two (2) witnesses eighteen (18) years or older. A witness cannot be entitled to any part of your estate, be your spouse, attending physician or any person acting under the direction or control of your attending physician, or any person who has a claim against your estate.

Virginia

State Website: http://leg1.state.va.us/

State Law Reference: Virginia Code Annotated.

Court with Probate Jurisdiction: Circuit Court.

Minimum Age for Disposing of Property by Will: 18. (Section 64.1-47).

Required Number of Witnesses: Two. (Section 64.1-49).

Can Witnesses Be Beneficiaries?: No. (Section 64.1-51).

Are There Provisions for Self-Proving Wills?: Yes. (Section 64.1-87.1).

Are Holographic Wills Permitted?: Yes. (Section 64.1-49).

How Does Divorce Affect the Will?: Revokes the will as to divorced spouse. (Section 64.1-59).

How Does Marriage Affect the Will?: Does not revoke the will and the spouse will be entitled to his or her elective share. (Section 64.1-13).

Who Must Be Mentioned in the Will?: Children, born or adopted; grandchildren (if of deceased child); surviving spouse. (Sections 64.1-16 & 64.1-71).

Spouse's Right to Property Regardless of Will: If there are no child(ren) of the deceased, the surviving spouse is entitled to 1/2 of the deceased spouse's augmented estate. If there are any surviving child(ren) of the deceased, the surviving spouse is entitled to 1/3 of the deceased spouse's augmented estate. (Section 64.1-16).

Laws of Intestate Succession (Distribution If No Will):

Spouse and children of spouse surviving: All to spouse.

Spouse and children not of spouse surviving: 1/3 to spouse and 2/3 to children or grandchildren per stirpes.

Spouse, but no children or parent(s) surviving: All to spouse.

Spouse and parent(s), but no children surviving: All to spouse.

Children, but no spouse surviving: All to children equally or to their children per stirpes.

Parent(s), but no spouse or children surviving: All to parents equally or to the surviving parent.

No spouse, children, or parent(s) surviving: All to brothers and sisters equally, or their children per stirpes; or if none, 1/2 to maternal grandparents or their children, or maternal next-of-kin (or if none, to paternal side) and 1/2 to paternal grandparents or their children, or paternal next-of-kin (or if none, to maternal side). (Section 64.1-1).

Property Ownership: Common-law state. Joint tenancy is recognized only if right of survivorship is stated. Tenancy-in-common and tenancy-by-the-entirety are recognized. Joint bank account deposits are payable to any survivor unless clear evidence exists that deposit is payable only to specified survivor. (Sections 55-20+).

State Gift, Inheritance, or Estate Taxes: No gift tax; no inheritance tax; imposes state estate tax equal to federal credit for state death taxes. (Sections 58.1-361 to 58.1-363).

Living Will Form: Advance Medical Directive serves as Living Will (Section 54.1-29-84).

Other Directives: Anatomical Gift Act (Section 32.1-8-290). Durable Power of Attorney (Sections 37.1-4-134.8 through 37.1-4-137.1).

Living Will Effective: This directive becomes effective in the event that you develop a terminal condition or are in a permanent vegetative state and can no longer make your own medical decisions.

Witness Requirements: Sign in the presence of two (2) witnesses eighteen (18) years or older. Witnesses cannot be related by blood or marriage.

Washington

State Website: http://www.leg.wa.gov/

State Law Reference: Washington Revised Code Annotated.

Court with Probate Jurisdiction: Superior Court.

Minimum Age for Disposing of Property by Will: 18. (Section 11.12.010).

Required Number of Witnesses: Two. (Section 11.12.020).

Can Witnesses Be Beneficiaries?: No, unless will is attested by 2 other disinterested witnesses. (Section 11.12.160).

Are There Provisions for Self-Proving Wills?: Yes. (Section 11.20.020).

Are Holographic Wills Permitted?: No provision.

How Does Divorce Affect the Will?: Revokes the will as to the divorced spouse. (Section 11.12.051).

How Does Marriage Affect the Will?: Revokes the will as to the surviving spouse. (Section 11.12.095).

Who Must Be Mentioned in the Will?: Statute contains detailed provisions regarding this matter. Please refer directly to statute text or consult an attorney if this is a critical factor. (Section 11.12.091).

Spouse's Right to Property Regardless of Will: Community property right to 1/2 of the deceased spouse's "community" property. (Under Washington case law).

Laws of Intestate Succession (Distribution If No Will):

Spouse and children of spouse surviving: All of decedent's community property and 1/2 of decedent's separate property to spouse; 1/2 of decedent's separate property to children or grandchildren per stirpes.

Spouse and children not of spouse surviving: All of decedent's community property and 1/2 of decedent's separate property to spouse; 1/2 of decedent's separate property to children or grandchildren per stirpes.

Spouse, but no children or parent(s) surviving: All to spouse.

Spouse and parent(s), but no children surviving: All of decedent's community property and 3/4 of decedent's separate property to spouse; 1/4 of decedent's separate property to parents or surviving parent or their children.

Children, but no spouse surviving: All to children equally or to their children per stirpes.

Parent(s), but no spouse or children surviving: All to parents equally or to the surviving parent.

No spouse, children, or parent(s) surviving: All to brothers and sisters equally, or their children per stirpes; or if none, to grandparents or their children. (Section 11.04.015).

Property Ownership: Community property state. Tenancy-in-common and joint tenancy are recognized. Joint tenancy with right of survivorship is created if specifically stated. No survivorship rights in tenancy-by-the-entirety. Joint bank account deposits are payable to any survivor unless evidence exists that deposit is payable only to specified survivor, and is subject to community property rights. (Sections 64-28+).

State Gift, Inheritance, or Estate Taxes: No gift tax; no inheritance tax; imposes state estate tax equal to federal credit for state death taxes. (Sections 83.100+).

Living Will Form: Health Care Directive serves as Living Will (Section 70.22.030).

Other Directives: Power of Attorney for Health Care (Section 11.94.010). Anatomical Gift Act (Section 68.50.540). Durable Power of Attorney (Sections 11.94.101 through 11.94.900).

Living Will Effective: Declaration applies when two (2) physicians diagnose you to have a incurable or irreversible condition that will cause death in a relatively short time and you can no longer make your own medical decisions.

Witness Requirements: Sign in the presence of two (2) witnesses eighteen (18) years or older. A witness cannot be entitled to any part of your estate, related by blood or marriage, be your attending physician or any person acting under the direction or control of your attending physician, or be any person who has a claim against your estate.

West Virginia

State Website: http://www.legis.state.wv.us/

State Law Reference: West Virginia Code Annotated.

Court with Probate Jurisdiction: County Court.

Minimum Age for Disposing of Property by Will: 18. (Section 41-1-2).

Required Number of Witnesses: Two. (Section 41-1-3).

Can Witnesses Be Beneficiaries?: Yes, but witness may lose bequest beyond intestate share, if any. (Section 41-2-1).

Are There Provisions for Self-Proving Wills?: Yes. (Section 41-5-15).

Are Holographic Wills Permitted?: Yes. (Section 41-1-3).

How Does Divorce Affect the Will?: Revokes the will as to former spouse. (Section 41-1-6).

How Does Marriage Affect the Will?: Revokes the will as to spouse. (Section 42-3-7).

Who Must Be Mentioned in the Will?: Children, born or adopted; grandchildren; and surviving spouse. (Sections 41-4-1, 41-4-2, & 42-3-1).

Spouse's Right to Property Regardless of Will: A surviving spouse's right to property regardless of provisions in a decedent spouse's will are dependent on length of marriage. Please consult the statute directly for provision regarding this topic. (Section 42-3-1).

Laws of Intestate Succession (Distribution If No Will):

Spouse and children of spouse surviving: All to spouse.

Spouse and children not of spouse surviving: 1/2 to spouse, 1/2 to deceased's children or grandchildren per stirpes.

Spouse, but no children or parent(s) surviving: All to spouse.

Spouse and parent(s), but no children surviving: All to spouse.

Children, but no spouse surviving: All to children equally or to their children per stirpes.

Parent(s), but no spouse or children surviving: All to parents equally or to the surviving parent.

No spouse, children, or parent(s) surviving: All to brothers and sisters equally, or their children per stirpes; or if none, 1/2 to maternal grandparents or their children, or to maternal uncles, aunts, or their children, or maternal next-of-kin (or if none, to paternal side) and 1/2 to paternal grandparents or their children, or paternal uncles, aunts, or their children, or paternal next-of-kin (or if none, to maternal side). (Sections 42-1-3 & 42-1-3a).

Property Ownership: Common-law state. Tenancy-in-common, joint tenancy, and tenancy-by-the-entirety are recognized. Right of survivorship is created if stated. Joint bank account deposits are payable to any survivor. (Section 36-1-19).

State Gift, Inheritance, or Estate Taxes: No gift tax; no inheritance tax; imposes state estate tax equal to federal credit for state death taxes. (Section 11-11-3).

Living Will Form: Living Will, (Section 16-30-4).

Other Directives: Medical Power of Attorney (Section 16-30-4). Anatomical Gift Act (Section 16-19-2). Durable Power of Attorney (Sections 39-4-1 through 39-4-7).

Living Will Effective: Your physician must certify in writing that you are in a terminal condition and your death would occur within a short period of time without the use of life-sustaining medical care.

Witness Requirements: Sign in the presence of two (2) adult witnesses and a notary public. A witness cannot be a person who stands to inherit from your estate, be directly financially responsible for your health care, be your attending physician, or be your health care representative or successor if you have a medical power of attorney. A witness cannot be related by blood or marriage or be the person who signed the document on your behalf.

Wisconsin

State Website: http://www.legis.state.wi.us/

State Law Reference: Wisconsin Statutes Annotated.

Court with Probate Jurisdiction: Circuit Court.

Minimum Age for Disposing of Property by Will: 18. (Section 853.01).

Required Number of Witnesses: Two. (Section 853.03).

Can Witnesses Be Beneficiaries?: Yes, but a witness-beneficiary's share under the will cannot exceed that person's intestate share, if any. (Section 853.07).

Are There Provisions for Self-Proving Wills?: Yes. (Section 853.04).

Are Holographic Wills Permitted?: No provision.

Are Living Wills Recognized?: Yes, under the "Wisconsin Natural Death Act." (Chapter 154, Sections 154.01 to 154.29).

How Does Divorce Affect the Will?: Revokes the will as to divorced spouse. (Section 853.11).

How Does Marriage Affect the Will?: Revokes the will as to the spouse if he or she is not otherwise provided for. Spouse may still be entitled to his or her statutory share under the state intestate laws. (Sections 853.11 & 853.25).

Who Must Be Mentioned in the Will?: Children, born or adopted; grandchildren (if of deceased child); surviving spouse. (Section 861.02).

Spouse's Right to Property Regardless of Will: Modified community property rights to 1/2 of the deceased spouse's "community" property. (Section 861.02).

Laws of Intestate Succession (Distribution If No Will):

Spouse and children of spouse surviving: All to spouse.

Spouse and children not of spouse surviving: 1/2 to spouse and 1/2 to children or grandchildren per stirpes.

Spouse, but no children or parent(s) surviving: All to spouse.

Spouse and parent(s), but no children surviving: All to spouse.

Children, but no spouse surviving: All to children or to their children per stirpes.

Parent(s), but no spouse or children surviving: All to parents equally or to the surviving parent.

No spouse, children, or parent(s) surviving: All to brothers and sisters equally, or their children per stirpes; or if none, to grandparents or surviving grandparent; or if none, to the next-of-kin. (Section 852.01).

Property Ownership: Community property state. The Wisconsin statute, however, uses unique terminology to describe this treatment of property. Tenancy-in-common and joint tenancy are recognized. Ownership by spouses is presumed to be joint tenancy unless stated otherwise. Tenancy-by-the-entirety is not recognized. Joint bank account deposits are payable to any survivor. (Sections 700.17, 700.19, & 700.20).

State Gift, Inheritance, or Estate Taxes: Imposes a gift tax; no inheritance tax; imposes state estate tax equal to federal credit for state death taxes. Maximum total state estate tax is equal to the maximum allowable federal estate tax credit for state death taxes. (Section 72.02).

Living Will Form: Declaration to Physicians serves as Living Will (Section 154-03).

Other Directives: Power of Attorney for Health Care (Section 155-05). Anatomical Gift Act (Section 157.06). Durable Power of Attorney (Section 243.07-1a).

Living Will Effective: This directive becomes effective in the event that your attending physician and one (1) other physician certifies you have developed a terminal condition or are in a permanent vegetative state and can no longer make your own medical decisions.

Witness Requirements: Sign in the presence of two (2) adult witnesses. A witness cannot be a person who stands to inherit from your estate, be directly financially responsible for your health care, be your attending physician, or be an employee of your health care provider or an inpatient health care facility in which you are a patient, unless the employee is a chaplain or social worker. A witness also cannot be related by blood or marriage.

Wyoming

State Website: http://legisweb.state.wy.us/

State Law Reference: Wyoming Statutes.

Court with Probate Jurisdiction: District Court.

Minimum Age for Disposing of Property by Will: 18. (Chapter 6, Section 2-6-101).

Required Number of Witnesses: Two. (Chapter 6, Section 2-6-112).

Can Witnesses Be Beneficiaries?: No, unless attested by 2 disinterested witnesses. (Chapter 6, Section 2-6-110).

Are There Provisions for Self-Proving Wills?: Yes. (Chapter 6, Section 2-6-114).

Are Holographic Wills Permitted?: Yes. (Chapter 6, Section 2-6-113).

Are Living Wills Recognized?: Yes, under the "Wyoming Living Will Act." (Title 35, Chapter 22, Sections 35-22-101 to 35-22-208).

How Does Divorce Affect the Will?: Revokes the will as to the divorced spouse. (Chapter 6, Section 2-6-118).

How Does Marriage Affect the Will?: Does not revoke the will. (Chapter 6, Section 2-6-118).

Who Must Be Mentioned in the Will?: Statute contains detailed provisions regarding this matter. Please refer directly to statute text or consult an attorney if this is a critical factor. (Chapter 5, Section 2-5-101).

Spouse's Right to Property Regardless of Will: Generally, the surviving spouse is entitled to 1/2 of the deceased spouse's estate if there are no children or if surviving spouse is parent of deceased's children; and only 1/4 if the surviving spouse is not the parent of any surviving children of the deceased. However, please refer directly to the statute as the provisions are detailed. (Chapter 5, Section 2-5-101).

Laws of Intestate Succession (Distribution If No Will):

Spouse and children of spouse surviving: 1/2 to spouse and 1/2 to children or grandchildren per stirpes.

Spouse and children not of spouse surviving: 1/2 to spouse and 1/2 to children or grandchildren per stirpes.

Spouse, but no children or parent(s) surviving: All to spouse.

Spouse and parent(s), but no children surviving: All to spouse.

Children, but no spouse surviving: All to children equally or to their children per stirpes.

Parent(s), but no spouse or children surviving: All to parents, brothers, and sisters equally, or to children of brothers and sisters per stirpes.

No spouse, children, or parent(s) surviving: All to grandparents, uncles, aunts, or their children, per stirpes. (Chapter 4, Section 2-4-101).

Property Ownership: Common-law state. Tenancy-in-common, joint tenancy, and tenancy-by-the-entirety are recognized. Right of survivorship created if stated. Joint bank account deposits are payable to any survivor. (Title 34, Chapter 1, Section 34-1-140).

State Gift, Inheritance, or Estate Taxes: No gift tax; no inheritance tax; imposes state estate tax equal to federal credit for state death taxes. (Title 39, Chapter 19, Sections 39-19-101+).

Living Will Form: Living Will Declaration (Section 35-22-102).

Other Directives: Power of Attorney for Health Care (Section 3-5-201). Anatomical Gift Act (Section 35-5-102). Durable Power of Attorney (Section 3-5-101).

Living Will Effective: This Declaration becomes effective when two (2) physicians agree that you have a terminal condition from which there can be no recovery and your death is imminent.

Witness Requirements: Sign in the presence of two (2) witnesses eighteen (18) years or older or a notary public. Witnesses cannot be entitled to any part of your estate or financially responsible for your medical care. A witness cannot be related to you by blood or marriage or be the person who signed the Declaration on your behalf.

Glossary of Legal Terms

Abatement: A reduction or complete extinguishment of a gift in a will where the estate does not have sufficient assets to make full payment.

Accounts Payable: Money owed to another and due to be paid.

Accounts Receivable: Money owed from another and due to be paid.

Acknowledgment: Formal declaration before a notary public.

Ademption: The withdrawal of a gift in a will by an act of the testator that shows an intent to revoke it. For example; by giving the willed property away as a gift during his or her life.

Administrator/Administratrix: One who is appointed to administer the estate of a deceased person who has died without a will or who has died with a will but has not named an executor. The distinction between the two titles (male and female) has largely been removed and *administrator* is proper usage for either male or female.

Advancement: A lifetime gift made to a child by a parent, with the intent that the gift be all or a portion of what the child will be entitled to upon the parent's death.

Affidavit: A person's signed and notarized statement.

Alternate Beneficiary: A person chosen to receive a gift under a will or trust should the originally chosen beneficiary not be available or surviving.

Amend: To change or alter.

Ancestor: One from whom a person is descended.

Annuity contract: A form of investment in which the purchaser is guaranteed a certain periodic payment for life or a certain term.

Appraisal: Valuation of a piece of property, generally by a person certified to conduct such a valuation.

Assets: Any property that you own. Your assets may consist of real estate or personal property. Your personal property may consist of cash, securities, or actual tangible property.

Attestation: To sign one's name as a witness to a will.

Augmented: An augmented estate is your estate left under a will plus the value of property transferred by other means, such as joint tenancies and living trusts. The augmented estate is used to calculate the value of a spousal share of an estate in those states that use this concept.

Bank Trust Account: A type of payable-on-death account under which the main account holder retains full and unilateral control of the account until death. Same as a *Totten Trust*.

Basic Will: A simple standardized type of will.

Beneficiary: One who is named in a will to receive property; one who receives a benefit or gift, as under the terms of a trust.

Bequest: Traditionally, a gift of personal property in a will. Synonymous with *legacy*. Now, *gift* is the appropriate usage for either a gift of real estate or personal property.

Blood Relative: A person who is directly related to another through birth descent.

Bond: A document by which a bonding company guarantees to pay an amount of money if the bonded person does not carry out his or her legal duties.

Bonds: A form of investment through which a company is indebted to the holder and, generally, pays interest to the holder.

Business Interest: Ownership of any form of business, such as a sole proprietorship, partnership, corporation, or limited liability company.

Buy-out Provisions: Contractual terms contained in a business ownership agreement (such as a partnership agreement) that specify the terms under which other owners may be required or have the option to purchase (buy-out) another owner's interest in the business, often upon the death of an owner.

Certificate of Deposit: A form of investment under which a bank issues a certificate indicating that it holds a deposit and will pay a certain rate of interest for a certain term.

Charitable Organization: A group that holds a Federal 501(c)3 "charitable organization" tax exemption status, and is able to receive tax-exempt donations.

Children's Trust: A form of trust under which gifts to children may be held in trust beyond the child's attainment of the legal age of majority.

Clause: A separate portion of a paragraph or sentence; an article or proviso in a legal document.

Close Corporation: A corporation operated by a small number of individuals, often family members. Is often exempt from certain state laws and may operate more informally. Also referred to as a "closely-held corporation."

Codicil: A formally-signed supplement to a will that is used to alter, amend or revoke provisions in the original will.

Coercion: The application to another of either physical or moral force.

Common Law: System of law that originated in England based on general legal principles rather than legislative acts.

Common-Law Property: Property held by spouse in a common-law state. Can be jointly-held or solely-owned property. The name(s) on the title document is/are the determining factor(s). See Appendix for those states where this system of marital property applies.

Community Property: The property acquired by either spouse during marriage, other than by gift or inheritance. Each spouse owns a half-interest in the community property. See Appendix for those states in which this system of marital property applies.

Conservator: Temporary court-appointed custodian of property.

Contest: Challenge the validity of a will.

Corporation: A company formed and authorized by law to act as a single person and provided with limited liability for any shareholders, and endowed by law with the capacity of succession.

Curtesy: In ancient common law, a husband's right to all of his wife's real estate for life upon her death. Now, generally abolished in most jurisdictions and replaced with a right to a certain statutory share of a spouse's property.

Death Benefits: Money, generally from either insurance policies or pension plans, that are payable to the beneficiaries of a decedent.

Deceased: No longer living; A dead person.

Decedent: One who has died.

Descend: To come from an ancestor or ancestry.

Descendant: One who is descended from another.

Descent: Inheritance by operation of law rather than by will.

Devise: Traditionally, a gift of real estate under a will. Now, *gift* is the appropriate usage for either a gift of real estate or personal property.

Disinherit: prevent deliberately (as by making a will) from inheriting

Disposition: A final settlement.

Domicile: A person's principal and permanent home.

Dower: In ancient common law, a wife's right to one-third of her husband's real estate for her life upon his death. Now, generally abolished in most jurisdictions and replaced with a right to a certain *statutory share* of a spouse's property.

Durable Power of Attorney: A form of power of attorney which is still in force despite the incapacity or disability of the maker.

Employee Benefits: Money or other benefits that are payable to an employee, such as health-care insurance, travel-expense compensation, etc.

Escheat: Reversion of property to the state, if no family member is found to inherit it.

Estate: All property owned by a person.

Estate Tax: A tax imposed on property that passes to another upon death.

Execution: The formal signing of a will.

Executor/Executrix: The person appointed in a will to carry out the testator's wishes and to administer the property.

Family Allowance: An amount that is allowed or granted to one family.

Federal Estate Tax: A percentage tax that is imposed upon the estate of a deceased person for the benefit of being able to pass the estate to others upon death. In 2002, the first $1 million dollars of a person's estate value are fully exempt from this tax, as is all estate property that passes from one spouse to another. The dollar value of the exemption is scheduled to rise to $3.5 million by 2009.

Fiduciary: A person with a duty of care to another. For example, a trustee has a duty of care to any beneficiary of a trust, and thus, is a *fiduciary*.

Forgery: The illegal production of something counterfeit.

Fraud: A deception deliberately practiced in order to secure unfair or unlawful gain.

Gift: A voluntary transfer of property to another without any compensation.

Grantor: The person who creates a trust. Also may be referred to as a *settlor*.

Guardian: A person with the legal power and duty to care for another person and/or a person's property.

Guardian "of the Person:" Guardian responsible for the actual care, custody, and upbringing of a minor child.

Guardian "of the Property:" Guardian who administers the property or money left to your child(ren).

Heirlooms: Treasured pieces of property that have been passed down from ancestors.

Heirs: Those persons who inherit from a person by operation of law if there is no will present.

Holographic: A will that is entirely handwritten by the testator and unwitnessed. No longer valid in most states.

Homestead Allowance: A monetary allowance given in some states to spouses and children to insure that they are not abruptly cut off from their support by any terms of a Living Trust. See *family allowance*.

Incapacitated: Being unable to care for one's self or handle one's own financial or other affairs.

Income Property: Real estate that is held for a commercial purpose; the generation of income.

Inheritance: The receipt of property from someone who has died.

Inheritance Tax: A tax on property received that is paid by the person who has actually inherited the property.

Intestate: To die without leaving a valid will.

Intestate Distribution: A state scheme that is used to determine the distribution of the property of any person who dies without leaving a valid will or another determination of how his or her property is to be distributed upon their death.

Invalid: Not legally or factually valid.

IRA: Individual Retirement Accounts under Internal Revenue Service regulations.

Irrevocable: Impossible to retract or revoke.

Joint Tenancy: Joint ownership of property under which the surviving owner automatically owns the deceased owner's share. This is called the *right of survivorship*. May be abbreviated as JTWROS or *joint tenancy with right of survivorship*.

Joint Tenancy with Right of Survivorship: See *joint tenancy*.

JTWROS: Joint tenancy with right of survivorship. See *joint tenancy*.

Jurisdiction: The right and power to interpret and apply the law. The territorial range of authority or control.

KEOGH: A form of retirement account.

Legacy: A gift of personal property in a will. Now, *gift* is the appropriate usage for either a gift of real estate or personal property. Synonymous with *bequest*.

Legal Age of Minority: The legal age above which a person may legally enter into contracts and otherwise act in the legal capacity of an adult.

Letters of Administration: The court order that officially appoints a person to administer the estate of another.

Letters Testamentary: The court order that officially appoints an executor named in a will as the person to administer the estate of the testator.

Liabilities: Something for which a person is liable, such as a debt.

Life Estate: Surviving spouse has the full use and enjoyment of any real estate for his or her entire life. Upon his or her death, property will pass automatically to person who has remaining share of estate. Recipient of a life estate cannot leave such property to anyone else.

Limited Liability Company: A type of business structure where the liability of a firm's owners are no more than what they have invested in the business.

Living Trust: A form of *revocable trust* which becomes irrevocable upon the death of the grantor.

Living Will: A document that can be used to state your desire that extraordinary life-support means not be used to artificially prolong your life in the event that you are stricken with a terminal illness or injury.

Loans Payable: Loans for which a person owes money to another.

Majority: The status of having reached full legal age, with attendant rights and responsibilities

Marital Property: Property which is considered owned by both spouses in a marriage, as opposed to property which is considered owned by each spouse separately. Also referred to as "community property" in those states which adhere to community property legal concepts.

Minor Child: A child who is under the legal age of majority (generally 18 or 21 years old).

Mortgage: A written statement of a debt owed for the purchase of real estate, under which the property is used as collateral.

Net Worth: A person's net value, determined by subtracting liabilities from assets.

Notarize: To have a notary public acknowledge the signing of a document.

Notary Acknowledgment: A formal declaration made to authenticate a witness's signature to ensure legal validity.

Notary Public: A person legally empowered to witness and certify the validity of documents and to take affidavits and depositions.

Notes Payable: Money owed to another based on a promissory note and that is due to be paid.

Notes Receivable: Money owed from another based on a promissory note and that is due to be paid.

Nuncupative: An oral will, usually made during a person's last illness and later reduced to writing by another. No longer valid in most states.

Obituary: A written statement regarding a person's death, usually in a newspaper.

Partnership: A contract between two or more competent persons for joining together their money, goods, labor, or skill, or any or all of them for the purpose of carrying on a legal trade, business, or adventure.

Pass Under: Distributed under the terms of a will or clause.

Payable-on-death Account: An account, generally a bank account, for which a beneficiary is chosen who will receive the proceeds of the account upon the death of the primary account holder. See *bank trust account* or *Totten trust*.

Pension Plan: Any plan under which an employee will receive any benefits after the end of his or her employment.

Per Capita: Equally; share and share alike. For example: if a gift is made to one's descendants, *per capita*, and one has two children and two grandchildren, and one of the children dies, then the gift is divided equally between the surviving child and the two grandchildren. This amounts to one-third to the child and one-third to each grandchild.

Per Stirpes: To share by representation. For example: if a gift is made to two children, *per stirpes*, and one should die but leave two grandchildren, the deceased child's share is given to the two grandchildren in equal shares. This amounts then to one-half to the surviving child and one-fourth to each of the grandchildren.

Personal Property: Movable property, as opposed to real estate property.

Personal Representative: A person who is appointed to administer a deceased's estate. Modern usage that replaces *Executor* and/or *Administrator*.

Posthumous Child: A child born after the father's death.

Pour-over Will: A will under which a trust is the main beneficiary.

Predeceased: Died before.

Pretermitted Child: A child who is left nothing in a parent's will and there is no intent shown to disinherit.

Probate: The court proceeding to determine the validity of a will and, in general, the administration of the property that passes under the will.

Promissory Note: A written promise to pay or repay a specified sum of money at a stated time or on demand.

Proprietorship: See *Sole Proprietorship*.

Proved: To have determined whether or not the document presented is actually the deceased's will.

Provision: A stipulation or qualification, especially a clause in a document or agreement.

Publication: For a will, the statement by the testator that the document that is being signed is his or her will.

Real Estate/Real Property: Land and that which is attached permanently to it, as opposed to personal property.

Relative: A person who is related by blood or marriage to another.

Residuary: The remainder of an estate after all debts, taxes, and gifts have been distributed.

Residuary Clause: A clause in a will or trust that designates a beneficiary of the residuary of an estate.

Residue: The remainder of a testator's estate after all claims, debts, and bequests are satisfied.

Revocable Trust: Another name for *Living Trust*. Upon death, a Living Trust becomes irrevocable and can no longer be changed or altered in any way. In general, however, any type of trust that can be revoked by the grantor.

Revocation: The annulment of a will, which renders it invalid. Accomplished either by complete destruction of the original will or by executing a later will that revokes the earlier one.

Revoke: To void or annul by withdrawing, or reversing. To entirely revoke a will, it must be physically destroyed or otherwise irrevocably damaged.

Right of Survivorship: The right of a joint owner of property to automatically obtain ownership over another deceased owner's share of the property. Generally true in a joint tenancy or a tenancy-by-the-entireties.

Self-Proving Affidavit: A document that may be completed by witnesses attesting to the signing of a will by which they affirm that they did indeed witness the signing. This affidavit may then be used later in a probate proceeding to prove the signing without the necessity of calling the witnesses to testify in person at the probate court.

Separate Property: The property of a spouse in a community property or common-law state that is considered the solely-owned property of that spouse, generally property that is solely owned prior to the marriage and any property that is obtained by gift or inheritance during the marriage.

Settlor: See *Grantor.*

Shared Property: The property of a spouse in a community property or common-law state that is considered property of both spouses jointly. In community property states, this would be all property that is not separate property. In common-law property states, this would be all property that is not separate property and which is actually held in some form of joint ownership, such as tenants-in-common or as a joint tenancy.

Sibling: A brother or sister.

Signature: One's name as written by oneself. The act of signing one's name.

Signing: To affix one's signature to.

Sole Proprietorship: A business that is owned by one owner and is not a corporation or limited liability company.

Sound Mind: A legal term that refers to the testator's ability to understand what gifts you are making and who your chosen beneficiaries are.

Spouse: A marriage partner; a husband or wife.

Spouse's Share: See *statutory share.*

Spouse's Right of Election: Surviving spouse has a right to a certain share of the deceased spouse's estate. This right is regardless of any provisions in the will of the deceased spouse that may give the surviving spouse less than this "statutory" or "community" property share. Occurs in all states.

Statutory Share: In common-law states, that portion of a person's property that a spouse is entitled to by law, regardless of any provisions in a will. In community property states, a surviving spouse receives half of all of the community property, regardless of any provisions in a will.

Successor Trustee: The person who is chosen to manage and distribute trust assets upon either the incapacitation or death of the original trustee of the trust.

Supplemental Will: Will used to supplement a living trust. Not a pour-over will.

Surviving: To outlive; to outlast; as, to survive a person or an event.

Survivorship Clause: A clause in a trust or will which provides that a beneficiary must outlive the decedent by a certain period of time in order to be considered a rightful beneficiary.

Tenancy-by-the-entirety: A form of joint tenancy that is only allowed for husbands and wives in certain states.

Tenancy-in-common: A form of joint ownership under which each owner owns a certain specific share of the property (perhaps one-half or another fraction). Upon the death of a co-owner, the deceased co-owner's share is passed to the heirs or beneficiaries of that co-owner, not to the other surviving co-owner(s). Compare to *joint tenancy*.

Testamentary: The expression of intent to dispose of property by will.

Testator/Testratrix: A male or female who makes a will.

Totten Trust: A type of payable-on-death account at a financial institution that allows a person to name a beneficiary. Similar to a joint account, but the joint co-owner has no rights until the death of the creator of the account. Also known as a *bank trust account*.

Transfer Documents: Any documents that may be necessary to formalize the change in ownership of property, such as a deed in the case of real estate, or a title in the case of a motor vehicle.

Trust: In general, an arrangement created by one party, the grantor, under which property is held by another party, the trustee, for the benefit of yet another party, the beneficiary. Under a Living Trust, one person may initially be all three of these parties.

Trust Estate: The assets that have been transferred into a trust by a grantor.

Trustee: A person appointed to administer a trust. In a Living Trust, the trustee and the grantor may be the same person.

Vacant Land: Real estate on which there are no buildings present.

Vacation House: Real estate that is owned for the purpose of being used for the owner's vacations.

Validity: The quality of having legal force or effectiveness.

Voiding: To make void or of no validity; invalidate.

Will: A formally-signed and witnessed document by which a person makes a disposition of his or her property to take effect upon his or her death.

Witness: A person who is present and sees another person sign a document.

Index

☆ Nova Publishing Company ☆
Small Business and Consumer Legal Books and Software

Law Made Simple Series

Basic Wills Simplified

ISBN 0-935755-90-X	Book only	$22.95
ISBN 0-935755-89-6	Book w/Forms-on-CD	$28.95

Divorce Agreements Simplified

ISBN 0-935755-87-X	Book only	$24.95
ISBN 0-935755-86-1	Book w/Forms-on-CD	$29.95

Living Trusts Simplified

ISBN 0-935755-53-5	Book only	$22.95
ISBN 0-935755-51-9	Book w/Forms-on-CD	$28.95

Living Wills Simplified

ISBN 0-935755-52-7	Book only	$22.95
ISBN 0-935755-50-0	Book w/Forms-on-CD	$28.95

Personal Bankruptcy Simplified (3rd Edition)

ISBN 1-892949-01-6	Book only	$22.95
ISBN 1-892949-02-4	Book w/Forms-on-CD	$28.95

Personal Legal Forms Simplified (3rd Edition)

ISBN 0-935755-97-7	Book w/Forms-on-CD	$28.95

Small Business Made Simple Series

Corporation: Small Business Start-up Kit (2nd Edition)

ISBN 1-892949-06-7	Book w/Forms-on-CD	$29.95

The Complete Book of Small Business Management Forms

ISBN 0-935755-56-X	Book w/Forms-on-CD	$24.95

Limited Liability Company: Small Business Start-up Kit (2nd Edition)

ISBN 1-892949-04-0	Book w/Forms-on-CD	$29.95

Partnership: Small Business Start-up Kit (2nd Edition)

ISBN 1-892949-07-5	Book w/Forms-on-CD	$29.95

S-Corporation: Small Business Start-up Kit (2nd Edition)

ISBN 1-892949-05-9	Book w/Forms-on-CD	$29.95

Small Business Accounting Simplified (3rd Edition)

ISBN 0-935755-91-8	Book only	$22.95

Small Business Bookkeeping Systems Simplified

ISBN 0-935755-74-8	Book only	$14.95

Small Business Legal Forms Simplified (4th Edition)

ISBN 0-935755-98-5	Book w/Forms-on-CD	$29.95

Small Business Payroll Systems Simplified

ISBN 0-935755-55-1	Book only	$14.95

Sole Proprietorship: Small Business Start-up Kit (2nd Edition)

ISBN 1-892949-08-3	Book w/Forms-on-CD	$29.95

Legal Self-Help Series

Divorce Yourself: The National No-Fault Divorce Kit (6th Edition)

ISBN 1-892949-11-3	Book only	$29.95
ISBN 1-892949-12-1	Book w/Forms-on-CD	$39.95
ISBN 1-892949-13-X	Forms-on-CD only	$12.95

Incorporate Now!: The National Corporation Kit (4th Edition)

ISBN 1-892949-00-8	Book w/Forms-on-CD	$29.95

Prepare Your Own Will: The National Will Kit (6th Edition)

ISBN 1-892949-14-8	Book only	$19.95
ISBN 1-892949-15-6	Book w/Forms-on-CD	$29.95

National Legal Kits

Simplified Bankruptcy Kit (2nd Edition)

ISBN 1-892949-19-9	Book only	$17.95

Simplified Divorce Kit (2nd Edition)

ISBN 1-892949-20-2	Book only	$19.95

Simplified Will Kit (2nd Edition)

ISBN 1-892949-21-0	Book only	$16.95

Simplified Family Legal Forms Kit

ISBN 1-892949-18-0	Book only	$18.95

☆ Ordering Information ☆

Distributed by:
National Book Network
4501 Forbes Blvd. Suite 200
Lanham MD 20706

Shipping: $4.50 for first & $.75 for each additional
Phone orders with Visa/MC: (800) 462-6420
Fax orders with Visa/MC: (800) 338-4550
Internet: www.novapublishing.com
Free shipping on all internet orders